P9-DCU-664

learn to garden

DK

LONDON, NEW YORK, MUNICH, MELBOURNE AND DELHI

Contributors

Guy Barter Alan Buckingham Philip Clayton Andi Clevely
Isabelle Van Groeningen Lia Leendertz Alan Toogood
Daphne Vince Prue Matthew Wilson

Senior editors	Katie Dock, Fiona Wild
Senior designer	Andrew Milne
Art editors	Alison Gardner, Alison Shackleton
Managing editor	Anna Kruger
Managing art editor	Alison Donovan
DTP designer	Louise Waller
Media resources	Lucy Claxton
Picture research	Jenny Baskaya
Production controller	Mandy Inness
Production editor	Sharon McGoldrick
U. S. Editor	Christine Heilman

First American Edition, 2008

Published in the United States by DK Publishing,
375 Hudson Street, New York, New York 10014

08 09 10 11 10 9 8 7 6 5 4 3

RD155—Feb. 08

Copyright © 2008 Dorling Kindersley Limited, London
Published in Great Britain by Dorling Kindersley Limited
in association with the Royal Horticultural Society

All rights reserved

Based on content first published in
Learn to Garden © Dorling Kindersley 2005

Without limiting the rights under copyright reserved above, no part
of this publication may be reproduced, stored in or introduced into a
retrieval system, or transmitted, in any form, or by any means (electronic,
mechanical, photocopying, recording, or otherwise), without the prior
written permission of both the copyright owner
and the above publisher of this book.

A catalog record for this book is available from the Library of Congress

ISBN 978-0-7566-3443-8

DK books are available at special discounts when purchased in bulk for
sales promotions, premiums, fund-raising, or educational use. For details,
contact: DK Publishing Special Markets, 375 Hudson Street, New York,
New York 10014 or SpecialSales@dk.com.

Color reproduction by MDP (Media Development Printing Ltd.)
Printed and bound in China by Sheck Wah Tong

Discover more at www.dk.com

learn to garden

CONTENTS

Introduction

If you are new to gardening, it may come as a surprise to learn that experienced hands envy you. You are about to embark on an enthralling and satisfying pursuit that may prove as rewarding to you as it is to those who have gardened for years. And the adventure lies before you.

Gardeners once learned their skills at their parents' knee, or perhaps from friends or neighbors. Today, a mass of books, magazines, television programs, and websites offer help and advice, but trying to piece together all this disparate information can be time-consuming and confusing.

In *Learn to Garden*, we bring together everything you need to know to begin gardening, and break the information down into straightforward, easy-to-follow steps. On every page, teams of experts share practical experience and offer sound advice to help with every problem and uncertainty. First there is a guide to the basics, so you can get to understand your soil and site, with advice on choosing good plants and caring for them properly, followed by a guide to propagation—how to make new plants for free. As your skills, experience, and knowledge increase, this book will remain a valued companion, always available to give a quick and to-the-point answer. In fact, you don't have to be a beginner to find it useful.

(left) **Simple drifts** and traditional borders are achievable, once you get to know your garden conditions and understand how to put plants together. Then experiment with the colors you most enjoy.

(right) **Restricting the color palette** can result in strikingly appealing effects. Here, roses and clematis of similar colors have been chosen for impact.

(far right) **However small your garden**, you can use a single, carefully chosen container plant to provide a focal point, or in this case, a woodland landscape in miniature.

Where to start?

Possibly you already have a vision of how you want the garden to look. Practical steps you can take to achieve it are outlined, starting perhaps with containers, or improving the lawn. Learning at your own pace, work up to flowerbeds and borders, trees, shrubs, and hedges. You won't find recipes for makeovers or grand designs; the aim is to help you make improvements now, and develop the know-how to create the garden of your dreams. Better to start small than risk lots of money in what may turn out to be a discouraging, costly disappointment.

Instead, take the time to look at your garden through the days and months; observation is at the heart of successful gardening, and this book will help you assess what you've got. Established trees, shrubs, or hedges can cast deep shade but might provide privacy, shelter, or beautiful features in other seasons with attractive bark, berries, or blossoms. You will learn how to renovate them if they need it, and to enhance them with flowering climbers, a scattering of bulbs, or a surrounding border.

Getting a plant's-eye view

Choosing plants that thrive in your garden, given its soil, site, and locality, is the key to gardening success. It follows that knowing a little bit about the plants themselves—how they work, what they need to survive, and how they have adapted to different amounts of sun, shade, heat, or drought—will help you match them to your own garden conditions. To this end, the book also includes a brief guide to how plants, soil, and climate work together—enough to help you fathom what is going on behind the scenes. It is equally important to learn to recognize plants and planting combinations that are never going to work in the way you want.

Just an inkling of these amazing, invisible processes can give you that bit of extra confidence so helpful in making the leap of faith involved in choosing plants, sowing seeds, or pruning a shrub. For example, knowing how plants respond to having stems removed will help you anticipate the consequences of when and where you make a pruning cut. Without this, you are really taking a stab in the dark.

(above) **A beautiful garden** is not necessarily a colorful one. Create year-round interest with a variety of foliage plants, mingling textures and shapes.

(far left) **Making new plants** can become an addictive hobby. You can gain a real sense of satisfaction from seeing your own cuttings thrive, and watching apparently lifeless seeds develop into healthy plants.

(left) **Watching the garden change** with the seasons helps you understand how it has evolved, and gives you the opportunity to assess the pros and cons of all its features.

Of course there will be setbacks. That (within reason) is part of the fascination. You may discover problems that are of your own making—and how to remedy them—but you can also take comfort from knowing that some things, like the weather, really are beyond your control.

Time spent gardening should be a pleasure. It is often best done in spurts; a relaxed, daily wander through the garden with pruners and a trowel allows you to deal with minor troubles before they get out of hand, and warns you when more robust remedies are needed. Get in the habit of keeping a notebook handy, however: you never know when inspiration will strike!

1. The Garden You Want

Whether you're faced with creating a new garden from scratch, taming an overgrown jungle, or making a few minor changes to an established yard, the very first thing to do is to think hard about what you want from the space. Try to visualize your dream garden. Does it include beds and borders packed with colorful plants? Do you need a play area for children? Somewhere to entertain family and friends? How much time do you want to spend gardening—a lot or a little? Do you want something traditional or a modern, contemporary design? Put all these factors into the mix and draw up a realistic plan before you head for the garden center and find yourself buying plants that simply catch your eye.

A low-maintenance garden like this, with paved areas instead of lawns and containers instead of mixed flower borders, is a good choice if your time for gardening is limited.

Family gardens

Most family gardens are multipurpose; they must satisfy a variety of different demands. Children need play areas—close to the house if they are young and you need to keep an eye on them, but farther away if they are older and don't want to be watched all the time. Grown-ups need areas to relax and unwind, if possible separated or screened from the hurly-burly of family life. And everyone benefits from outdoor seating areas for summer lunches and barbecues.

(above) **Seating and eating areas** are an important component of outdoor living, especially in the summer. Siting them on paved patios or decks close to the house helps promote a seamless flow between inside and outside spaces.

(right) **Children's play areas** are best kept to a separate area or corner of the yard if possible. Boisterous kids and their games do not mix with delicate flower borders. A screen, such as an arbor, trellis or hedge, can demarcate territory, and prevent stray balls from damaging your plants.

(left) **A lawn-free garden** may be the best solution for a large, active family. Paving and wooden decking is used for walkways and seating areas. A custom-built sandbox keeps younger children occupied, and bark chips make a safe surface beneath a swing. Wooden screens are used to divide the garden into discrete areas.

(right) **A multipurpose terrace** provides a quiet seating area, a place for cooking on the grill, and a safe playground for children. Paving in contrasting materials and colors, and varying levels connected by shallow steps, help to compartmentalize the space. The green foliage of a few trees and shrubs softens any hard edges.

(below) **A split-level yard** is one way of creating separate, self-contained areas. Here, an "upper deck" creates a space for outdoor seating, cooking, and eating, with containers providing touches of foliage, while a wooden staircase leads down to the garden at ground level.

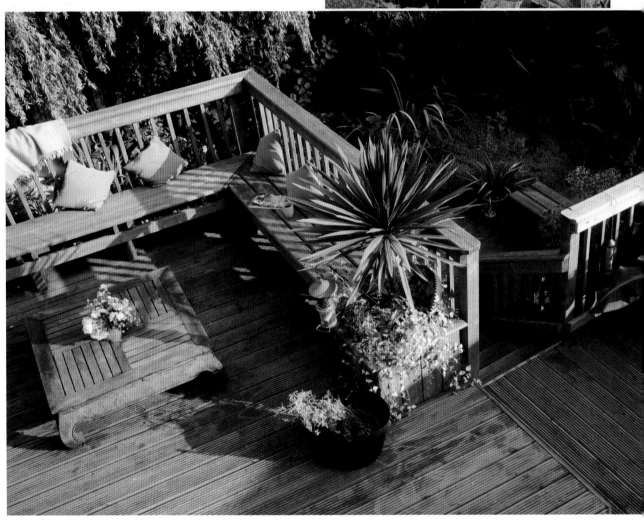

(right) **A private, sheltered corner** of the yard can act as an invaluable hideaway from the demands of hectic family life. Surrounding the space with shrubby plants to protect against chilly winds and to provide shade from the midday sun will only increase the welcome sense of seclusion and retreat.

(below right) **A vegetable garden,** however small, is a valuable addition to any family garden. Few things taste better—or are as good for you—as homegrown vegetables freshly picked from the garden and eaten soon after. At the very least, you should plant a few herbs or patio vegetables within easy reach of the kitchen door.

Small gardens

All small gardens present a challenge: how do you prevent them from feeling claustrophobic and create the illusion that they're larger than they really are? There are a number of tricks. Glass doors that open on to a deck or patio will link indoors and outdoors, increasing the sense of space in both. Uncluttered planting feels airy and spacious. And a cleverly positioned sculpture, container, or water feature can create a focal point that draws the eye in.

(below) **This tiny city garden** has been as carefully designed as any interior. White wisteria and a climbing rose soften the red brick walls, stone is used for both paving and a seating ledge, and a water feature is cleverly integrated.

(above) **An eclectic mix of styles** – mosaics, neatly trimmed boxwood, bamboos, vivid spikes of verbascum, and a curving wall topped with terra-cotta—provides plenty of visual interest for such a small space.

(left) **A Mediterranean courtyard**, almost empty save for one large pot planted with pelargoniums and another with a *Cordyline*, nevertheless manages to create a sense of cool calm.

(above) **Raised beds** introduce a sense of height and give climbing plants a head-start up on to a wall-mounted trellis. A restrained color scheme in shades of green, blue, and white is relaxing.

(below) **A sense of humor** takes the mind off just how small this garden is. Inset into the top of the table itself is a rectangle of sod, so that diners literally eat off the grass. It's the ultimate picnic table.

(left) **A raised wooden deck** leads straight out from the open French doors so that the dining area feels as if it is half indoors and half outdoors. Within just a year or two, the grape vine will grow right over the arbor to provide some welcome shade from the sun in the height of summer.

(right) **Mirrors** can be as useful outdoors as in. Setting one into this brightly painted wooden trellis not only creates intriguing reflections that make the yard seem larger than it is, but also conceals a sizable area of ugly brick wall.

(below) **Two curving granite paver paths** lead to a circular paved area where a wooden bench provides a simple seat. The layout draws the eye naturally through the garden and creates a slightly illusory sense of increased perspective.

Large gardens

A large garden is exciting. With plenty of space to play with, the possibilities are almost limitless. The best approach may be to think about compartmentalizing the space and creating mini-gardens-within-a-garden. Designate different areas for relaxing and entertaining, for laying out a kitchen garden, planting a few fruit trees, or installing a pond. And employ hedges or screens to form discrete garden rooms, perhaps with doorways or arches to lend a sense of secrecy or surprise.

(right) **When lack of space** is not an issue, you have to room to build. Summer houses, greenhouses, even workrooms all expand the practical uses of the garden and establish self-contained areas away from the main house for eating and entertaining, working, or cultivating plants that have special requirements.

(below) **A line of wooden posts** linked with chains and covered by climbing roses marks a boundary between the lawn and flower borders planted with spring bulbs. At the bottom of the garden, a beech hedge screens off a further, more heavily wooded area.

(above) **Clean, geometric lines** are the hallmark of this modernist design. Contrasting areas of wooden decking, stone paving, and raised squares of grass divide the space horizontally, while limestone walls, clipped hedges, and glass screens divide it vertically. Tall bamboos tower above everything.

(left) **Large gardens** need a certain amount of structure. Here, a framework is provided by flagstone paths edged with trimmed boxwood and spanned by arches over which fruit trees have been trained. They lead the eye naturally to focal points such as a central sundial and a distant gate in the hedge.

(right) **A dedicated kitchen garden** is the dream of many gardeners. If space permits, it can be laid out formally, in what is sometimes called a "potager" style, with neat brick paving and mixed plantings of vegetables, herbs, and flowers.

Cottage gardens

Most cottage gardens are small, almost by definition, and tend not to be highly structured, since geometric beds, formal hedging, and large areas of lawn or paving all take up a lot of valuable space. Traditionally, cottage gardeners would have worked their plots hard—to produce as large a harvest of flowers, vegetables, fruit, and herbs as possible. The overall effect is therefore one of profusion, with plants crowding one another and jostling for space.

(right) **A climbing rose** around the kitchen door may be a cliché, but it's one with perennial charm. Try to choose one of the scented, repeat-flowering varieties that produces blooms throughout the summer.

(below) **Mixed flower borders** are often a riot of unstructured color, combining annuals, biennials, and perennials such as these irises, verbascum, achillea, purple *Allium christophii*, and the poppy *Papaver orientale* 'Patty's Plum'.

(above) **A small stream** at the foot of this country garden provides a site for plants such as irises, astilbes, and primulas, all of which are happy to grow near water. Closer to the house are traditional cottage garden plants, such as a profusion of climbing roses and delphiniums.

(left) **A quiet corner** in a crowded cottage garden is the perfect place to escape and relax. Scented plants such as a fragrant honeysuckle complete the restorative experience.

(right) **Organized chaos** may be the overall effect here, yet there's some artful planning in the choice and siting of plants and antique gardening "props." Yellow giant scabious *Cephalaria gigantea*, the purple-red flowers of *Knautia macedonica*, sisyrinchium, and lupines all give height to the border, while alchemilla, salvia, and thyme spill out over the gravel at the front.

Meadow gardens

The most successful meadow gardens look completely natural, almost as if the countryside has spilled into the garden of its own accord. In fact, it takes planning and some maintenance to get the mix of grasses, wildflowers, and cultivated species just right and stop the site from degenerating into a mass of unwanted weeds. In large borders, perennials and ornamental grasses planted in drifts can create a wonderful, soft, naturalistic, meadowlike effect.

A wildflower corner may be an ideal solution for transforming a neglected area of the garden. Most wild flowers, including these marguerites or oxeye daisies, *Leucanthemum vulgare*, and field poppies, *Papaver rhoeas*, are quite happy in relatively infertile soil.

(right) **A mown grass path** is an inviting and practical route through a summer meadow left to self-seed with a carpet of wildflowers, including yellow buttercups and white oxeye daisies.

(below) **An old wooden gate leads into an orchard** where the grass has been allowed to grow tall during the summer. Many wild flowers, such as these foxgloves, will self-seed, but you can boost the proportion of flowers by sowing additional seeds yourself or by using plug plants.

Woodland gardens

Damp and shade are the predominant characteristics of most woodland gardens. While this rules out plants that need heat and light, there are still plenty of options for creating a wonderful, lush garden. Large-leaved foliage plants that like moisture will do best—hellebores, hostas, ferns, and rhododendrons, for example. Plenty of native woodland plants will flower profusely in spring before the leaf canopy of the trees begins to reduce the light.

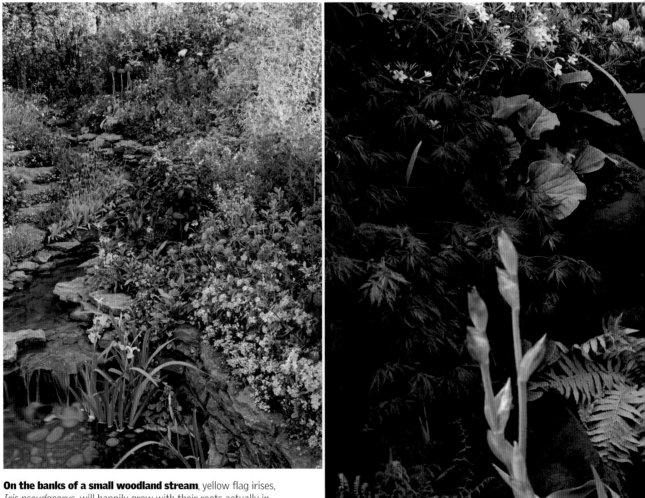

On the banks of a small woodland stream, yellow flag irises, *Iris pseudacorus*, will happily grow with their roots actually in water. The better-drained stream margins have been planted with alliums, primulas, violas, heliotropes, scabious, and phlox, among others.

(right) **A path through a woodland garden** is an invitation for a cool, relaxing stroll. In spring, the ground beneath the trees is likely to be carpeted with bluebells and lily-of-the-valley, and new, young foliage will be at its brightest, most vibrant green.

(below) **A shady rock garden** hosts a variety of plants that thrive in damp, cool conditions: ferns, hostas, acers, irises, primulas, and white-flowered *Houttuynia cordata*.

Water gardens

Water introduces a number of fresh elements into any garden. Pools create reflections and, depending on the weather and time of day, can play tricks with the changing light. Streams or rills bring movement, and waterfalls or fountains add relaxing sound. In addition, a pond or a bog garden creates a special environment for the kind of plants you might struggle to grow elsewhere. And, of course, most water features are a magnet for wildlife.

(above) **A courtyard water garden** provides a calm, contemplative space in which to relax. Colors are purposely restrained—white for the walls and a silvery wash for the wooden decking. Most of the plants are unusual exotics and are set in pebble-filled troughs and beds; they include palms, agaves, the tall, bronze-leaved *Canna* 'Assaut', and small pineapple flowers *Eucomis bicolor*.

(left) **A seat right by the water** offers an opportunity for quietly observing fish, frogs, toads, and other inhabitants of a garden pond, as well as visitors such as birds, butterflies, dragonflies, and other insects.

(right) **Traditional Japanese landscaping** is the inspiration for this highly stylized water garden. A miniature stream meanders through water meadows of dense, mat-forming mind-your-own-business (*Soleirolia soleirolii*), punctuated by artfully placed rocks and dwarf conifers.

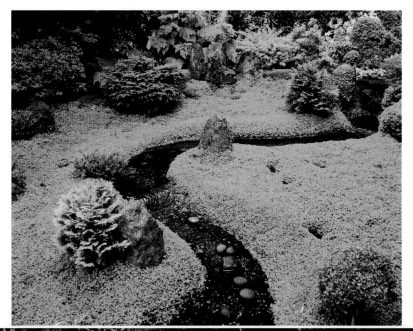

(below) **The geometric lines** of a modern garden pond are softened by densely planted flowerbeds that include perovskia, alchemilla, eremurus, euphorbia, and achillea. Tall, yellow flag irises *Iris pseudacorus* flank the eye-catching, mirrored sculpture in the water itself.

Wildlife gardens

Wildlife visitors not only make a garden more interesting, most are also positively beneficial. Bees are, of course, vital for pollination. The frogs and toads that a pond attracts devour slugs; ladybugs and hoverfly larvae eat aphids, and many birds feast on snails. To attract wildlife, choose plants whose fruits, seeds, and nectar provide food for small mammals, birds, and insects; hedges in which birds can shelter, and shrubs such as hebes, buddleja, lavender, and rosemary for butterflies and bees.

(above) **Bee boxes** are specially designed to provide safe and inviting nesting sites, in particular for mason bees often found in orchards. Site them in a sunny, south-facing position and you'll encourage bees to colonize them early in spring and get the whole process of pollination off to a good start.

(left) **Even in the smallest** of city gardens, there is room for a pond to attract wildlife. Plant large, shallow containers like this one with small waterlilies and the miniature cattail *Typha minima*.

(above) **Blue tits** prefer to eat from suspended bird feeders; they're rarely seen on the ground, where they feel vulnerable. If possible, hang your feeder close to trees or bushes in which the birds can take cover before approaching, and keep it filled with nuts and seeds so that they develop a routine of feeding from it.

(left) **A hand-woven wicker cage** surrounding a fat ball allows birds access to their food but prevents squirrels from stealing it. You're more likely to be successful in attracting birds if you employ a quiet, slightly overgrown, wild corner of the garden.

Formal gardens

Formal gardens appeal to our sense of order, and much of the pleasure we take from them comes from our love of structure and symmetry. Layouts are usually based on clean lines, shapes such as squares, rectangles and circles, and regular, repeating patterns. The garden's underlying structure is often clearly evident, underlined by hard landscaping, structured planting, lines of pleached trees, clipped hedges, and meticulously maintained, manicured flowerbeds and borders.

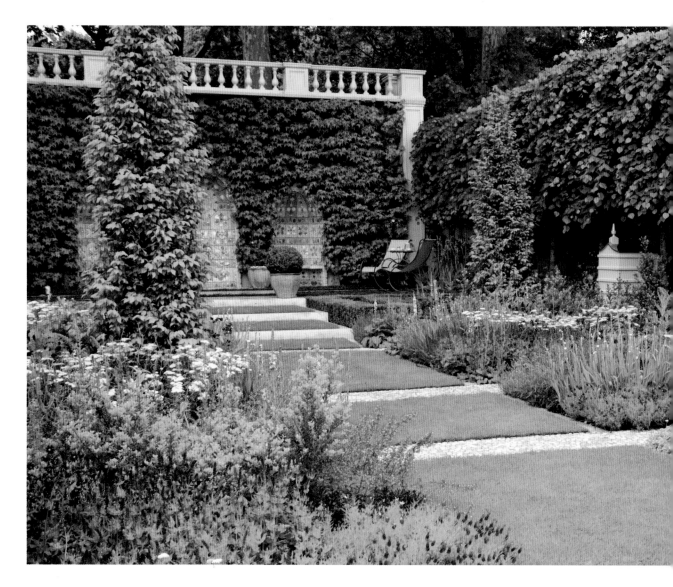

(right) **The perfect symmetry** of two rows of box-headed, pleached hornbeams creates a formal avenue leading to an outdoor seating area.

(below right) **Topiary** is a key component of the formal garden. The intricate design of this knot garden and the painstakingly precise forms of clipped boxwood demonstrate the gardener's complete mastery over the unruly forces of nature.

(below) **A formal layout** divides this garden into squares of lawn and flowerbeds marked out by perfect gravel paths. A row of pleached limes punctuated by Italianate beehives runs down one side, and even the liquidambar trees against the far wall have been trained and clipped to form three ornamental arches.

Contemporary gardens

Modern garden design is transforming not just the way our gardens look but the way we use and enjoy them, too. While the conventional yard, with its lawn and tended flowerbeds, is still with us, today you're as likely to see modern gardens that employ decking, paving, and glass to blur the distinction between inside and outside, and ones where modern materials such as concrete, metal, fiberglass, and plastic, often in bold colors, may be as striking as the plants.

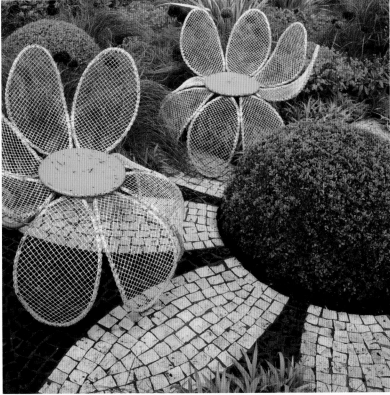

(above) **A screen of frosted plate glass** separates a dining area from the rest of the garden. A restricted planting plan features peonies in the foreground with clipped hedges and tall, arching bamboos elsewhere.

(right) **An irreverent sense of humor** permeates the design of this garden. Gigantic flowerheads are formed from mosaic paving blocks with clipped domes of boxwood (*Buxus sempervirens*) at their center. And retro daisy chairs feature padded yellow seats and wire-mesh petals.

(left) **Garden sculpture** is an increasingly common element in contemporary designs. This garden is completely enclosed by a high hornbeam hedge. At one end is an Italian red sandstone disk symbolizing the moon. Slightly in front of it, suspended over water, is an upright square slab from which a circle has been cut. Shapes and perspectives shift as you walk around the garden viewing the disk through the hole.

(left) **Hard landscaping materials** can be as attractive as plants. Here, walls are constructed from stuccoed concrete topped with reclaimed slate and freestanding sandstone blocks. The paving is granite pavers. A curved oak bench seems to float above the ferns and other woodland-floor foliage.

(below) **Spherical pods** are dotted around this stylized sci-fi garden to provide sheltered, secluded seating areas, relaxation zones, and outdoor workspaces. A field of densely planted lavender is punctuated by meadow flowers and clipped boxwood balls that echo the shape of the pods.

(above) **Modern construction materials** have enabled designers to rethink the hard landscaping that forms the backbone of any garden. Precast blocks or poured concrete can be treated with a limitless range of colors and textures, and even metals such as stainless steel and aluminum can be utilized for paving, screens, and containers.

(right) **An unusual cubic wooden arbor** is the centerpiece of this contemporary garden. Plain white concrete walls, split levels, and minimal planting contribute to the stark, modernist look and feel.

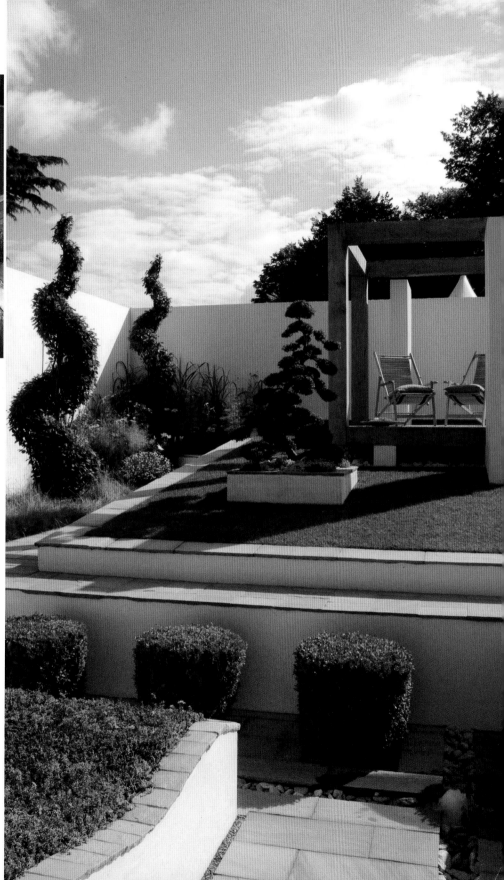

2. The Garden You've Got

The better you understand your garden, the better it will look and the happier your gardening experience will be. Not only will you be able to take full advantage of everything it has to offer, but you'll also avoid common pitfalls, which can be costly and disheartening. Understanding your garden will take time—there is no substitute for watching and learning as the seasons go by. The process never ends; what is a sunny spot today could become an area of dappled shade with the addition of a tree. And nature is always ready to change the rules just when everything is "just so"—especially in the longer term, as climate change is expected to have a major impact.

Digging in organic matter will boost the fertility of any soil and give hungry plants a little much-appreciated extra help.

How to assess your garden

Brand new gardens can be a bleak prospect, especially if the "topsoil" is little more than a token gesture to cover up construction rubble, plastic bags, and broken tools. An "inherited" garden can be a double-edged sword, depending on whether it is to your taste or not, and how enthusiastically the previous owners gardened. An old, neglected garden can be just as daunting as a new one—what should stay, and what should go?

The garden's purpose

There are a few crucial questions you must ask:

■ **Who will use it?** You may love spiky plants and ponds, but if you have a young family, then they will probably not be the best choice.

■ **What will the yard be used for?** Yards can be designed for entertaining, as a fun space for children, or simply to show off plants. You might want to encourage wildlife, such as birds or butterflies, into your garden; consider how to balance your needs with that of the wildlife you want to encourage.

■ **How much time can you spare?** Work out how much free time you have at the moment, and how much of it you are willing to give up. You don't want your yard to become a millstone rather than a pleasure. The free time you have will inform your plant choice, border sizes, even whether you have a lawn or not.

■ **What are your timescale and budget?** It may be better to tackle a small area each year rather than embark on a grand and costly plan. Start with the area you see the most, perhaps laying a patio or redoing a border. Any hard landscaping should be carried out in sections as you can afford them. If you might be moving on, buying fast-growing plants might be a better idea than investing in long-term projects.

Being able to entertain in the backyard is important for many people. A patio can easily be adapted into an outdoor eating area by adding a barbecue grill, a table, and some chairs.

What kind of garden do you have?

What you do with your garden will be affected by whether it is brand new, established, or neglected.

NEW GARDEN

■ **Your soil** If it is terrible, buy in good quality topsoil from a local source. Reject soil that is dusty, stony, weedy, wet, or "blue" (which is what happens when the air has been squeezed out). Before the soil is unloaded from the truck, check that the pH is close to your own garden's pH.

■ **Establish your priorities** Once the plan is complete, decide which elements to establish first. It may be more practical to install a patio, a garden shed, and a compost bin before a pond and fountain.

NEGLECTED GARDEN

■ **Think before you act** Beneath some neglected gardens are treasures waiting to be revealed.

■ **Weeding** On a small scale, you can hand-weed; if the problem is overwhelming, using chemical weedkillers may be the only option. For an organic approach, clear the area with a string trimmer, then cover it with light-excluding tarpaulin or old carpet (this can take a few months to work).

■ **A clean sweep** If progressive renovation is out of the question, perhaps the best option is to think of the garden as "new" and consider the steps above.

MATURE GARDEN

■ **Assess the style** Reconstructing an established garden can be hard, but putting your own personality on a place is part of the experience of developing and enjoying a garden.

■ **Choose what to keep** Some features may be there for a good reason. A mature tree might conceal a distant high-rise or screen your yard from the neighbors' windows, so consider the existing features with care.

■ **Assess the utilities and hard landscaping** Gardens must be practical as well as beautiful. Take time to make sure you are not removing something you need. Conversely, is the garden missing something you consider essential, like an outdoor faucet or space for a grill?

(from top) **New garden, neglected garden, mature garden**

The weather

The climatic conditions that affect plants most are rainfall, extremes of temperature, wind strength and direction, and light levels. Knowing the local climate is the first step in understanding which plants grow best in your garden. While most gardens can be manipulated in one way or another to overcome prevailing conditions, the predominant climate—the macroclimate—will always influence plant selection.

The effects of cold

The length and severity of winter often dictate what you can grow. You can water in dry spells, or boost drainage where excess moisture is a problem, but it is harder to keep temperatures above damaging levels. Hardiness is vitally important, and it is worth understanding the different ways cold can affect plants.

An air frost—when the air temperature drops to 32°F (0°C) while the ground remains unfrozen— is most common in early fall. A ground frost occurs when the soil temperature falls below freezing; it is more frequent in winter, and can occur while the air is above freezing.

Long winter freezes largely define which plants are hardy in your climate. Less severe frosts tend to happen under cloudless skies on still nights, and are caused by the ground losing warmth by radiating it out into the night sky. If conditions persist, the ground freezes solid. Harder frosts are caused by a moving mass of cold air, with icy winds driving frost deep into the soil.

In a valley, rivers draw weather systems toward them, and hills can affect rainfall so one side of a valley is often wetter than the other. Cold or freezing air will often settle and persist in valleys.

Coastal gardens suffer few frosts because of the proximity of the sea and the regular sea breezes, although the air is salt-laden and can damage plants.

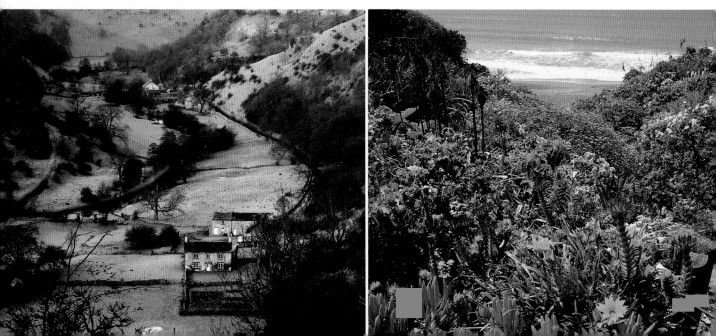

Evergreen plants keep losing moisture from their leaves in winter, especially in windy weather. With the soil frozen, they cannot take up more water; the foliage and green stems are scorched and killed, often leading to death.

Soil and moisture

Too much soil moisture in winter or too little in summer is a common theme of gardening life. Walls, fences, and hedges can affect soil moisture by casting "rain shadows." Dig down to check the depth of the dryness, as this will determine what you plant. Many plants actually prefer good drainage and will thrive in dry soil; incorporate plenty of moisture-retentive organic matter before planting.

It is much harder to improve damp soil. If your garden is soggy, create well-drained spots by building raised beds, or by planting on ridges and mounds. Otherwise, try to improve drainage as much as possible and choose plants that will tolerate wet conditions.

Gardens perched on top of hills are very exposed to the weather; the plants you choose need to be particularly resistant to drying winds and high light levels.

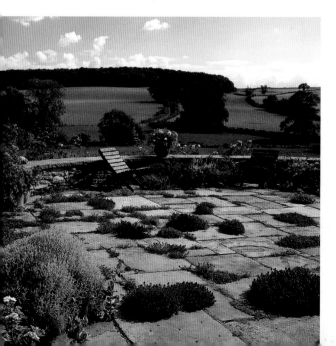

What is hardiness?

Hardiness is a plant's ability to withstand the local climate. In an area subject to frost, this means resistance to cold; elsewhere it means resistance to heat or drought. Knowing where a plant comes from does not automatically tell you if it will survive in your garden; lavender and rosemary, for example, grow naturally on well-drained land in a warm climate, but will thrive in moister conditions and cooler climates.

■ **Hardy plants** will survive the levels of frost we can usually expect. Most plants we call hardy make new growth when temperatures exceed 40–43°F (4–6°C); if temperatures stay around this point, there may be little growth.

■ **Half-hardy plants** might not make it through severe weather. In a cool climate, select spots with sheltered microclimates, mulching, providing good drainage and soil structure, and protecting with horticultural fleece and straw in winter.

■ **Tender plants** may not thrive at temperatures below 54°F (12°C). These plants have no real chance of surviving periods of severe weather, and need to be brought into shelter, such as a greenhouse, as soon as there is a threat of frost.

Hardiness zones

Large countries and continents are divided into hardiness zones based on average minimum winter temperatures. In the United States and southern Canada, the USDA Plant Hardiness Zone Map is widely used for determining which plants will grow in your area. To find your hardiness zone, use the online map at *www.usna.usda.gov/Hardzone/ushzmap.html*.

Sun, shade, and the seasons

Because some plants are adapted to a sunny place, and some to shade, finding out where the sun falls in your garden is crucial to success. The sun affects the amount of light and warmth, and therefore which plants you can grow. Take some time to observe the passage of the sun, not just through the course of the day, but throughout the seasons. This will allow you to build a picture of which areas are permanently shady, and which get the most sun. Once you are familiar with these areas, you can start to think about which plants will thrive in them, and plan your garden accordingly.

A sunny wall both stores and reflects heat. It can extend the growing season and help wood to ripen in late summer.

Exposure

First, find out which direction your yard faces—north, south, east, or west. This is known as its "exposure," and will help you to determine whether the back or the front yard receives the most sun. As a general rule, south- or west-facing gardens are warmer and sunnier than north- or east-facing plots.

Start by standing with your back to the house. The direction you are facing, whether it is north, east, south, or west, is the same as your yard. If you are unsure, remember that the sun rises in the east and sets in the west. East-facing gardens get the morning sun, while those facing west have sun during the afternoon. South-facing gardens are often bright for much of the day, but north-facing plots don't get much direct sun at all. East- and north-facing gardens can be unsuitable for tender plants, either because there is not enough warmth, or because the temperature rise after the nighttime cool is too rapid. Remember, though, that each wall or fence in the yard also has an exposure, and can create its own sun trap or shady area.

Where there is dappled shade from open trees, or where the shade from buildings lasts for less than half a day in summer, plants won't grow as much as in the open, but they will be more sheltered, which can make up for the lower light levels.

The effect of the seasons

The seasonal variation can be quite marked—the trajectory of the sun varies from summer, when it rises high in the sky, to winter, when it hugs the horizon. Clever use of plants can make the most of these changes: the low, watery sunlight of midwinter, for example, will illuminate colorful stems, such as those of coppiced dogwoods and willows, and bring interest to the winter garden.

If you live in a city and your garden is surrounded by buildings, the winter sun may barely peep over the rooftops and into the garden, although it will be sunny in summer when the sun moves through the sky directly above.

The look of the garden can change considerably through the seasons. The light quality and brightness change and patches of shade move. Deciduous trees and shrubs lose their leaves in winter, at the same time as most herbaceous plants die down. It takes care to make a garden look interesting and attractive year-round.

■ **In spring**, the bare branches of deciduous trees allow lots of light into the garden; spring bulbs and early-flowering perennials such as hellebores and lungworts can take advantage of this. Tree blossom provides a touch of color.

■ **In summer**, shade appears as deciduous trees come into full leaf. In darker areas, grow shade-tolerant plants such as heucheras or geraniums. Variegated shrubs, like the mock orange *Philadelphus coronarius* 'Variegatus', or white-flowered shrubs such as hydrangeas, can brighten up gloomy corners.

■ **In fall**, enjoy the colored leaves of deciduous trees before they drop. Light levels are similar to those of springtime as the sun sinks lower, but the quality of the light is often more subdued.

■ **In winter**, observe the garden critically—if the structure works now, it should work the rest of the year. Sculptural evergreens are constant, but don't be tempted to include too many or the effect will be spotty. Areas under trees have some protection from the worst effects of frost.

Your microclimate

Microclimates are local variations in the general climate—they can include soil type, exposure or shelter, and sun or shade. Understanding microclimates enables you to exploit them to your advantage. Even across a small area, there will be enough variation to grow a broader range of plants than you might first think. Microclimates can even be created; for example, when laying a patio, leave a few gaps between paving slabs and fill them with gritty soil to make planting pockets. In a sunny spot, drought-tolerant herbs like thyme or oregano will thrive in the additional reflected heat and light from the paving.

Wind turbulence

Wind is probably the most important factor in the garden environment. Gales and storms can cause substantial physical damage, but even normal breezes have an impact because they dry out leaves, and plants will need watering more often. Even in a small yard, some areas may be more exposed to wind than others. Wind turbulence is caused by solid walls, fences, and buildings as the wind tumbles over them, creating an eddying effect. You can reduce the problem by using barriers that let some air through. Try to identify the windier or more turbulent parts of your garden and reduce the problem by planting hedges

Wind damage caused by gusts and eddies swirling around solid barriers is nearly as bad as that of unchecked wind. Semipermeable barriers, such as trees and shrubs, hedges, trellis, or nonsolid walls and fences, provide more effective shelter. They may also cast less shade, and don't completely block your views.

or living screens. A barrier to wind can shelter an area of garden behind it equivalent in length to five times the barrier's height.

Wind disturbs the moist air layer on the surface of leaves, making them lose water more quickly than on a still day. As the plants begin to dry out, the leaves close their pores. This prevents carbon dioxide from getting into plants, and photosynthesis—and therefore growth—stops. This is why plants grow best in the shelter of hedges and fences.

Shelter belts slow wind speed over some distance, creating a niche for large, leafy plants that can be made ragged or lose too much water in a breeze.

Sun traps

Walls and greenhouses will absorb heat in the sun, then release it slowly later. Walls can also create frost shadows, so placing containers against them during winter will help to keep plants frost-free; a tender azara, for example, will exploit the conditions found in a very sheltered corner of the garden and help brighten up a dark spot. South-facing walls reflect heat and provide the perfect planting opportunity for less hardy plants. They are traditionally used for growing and ripening fruit like peaches and plums, and for ornamentals such as roses, which may flower earlier due to the extra warmth.

Frost pockets

Frost pockets form as chilly air sinks to the lowest point it can. Areas at risk include dips, valley bottoms, and places where cold air can collect behind a barrier. Slopes are generally dry because water runs to the lowest-lying areas in a garden. Lower areas may also be more prone to frost, because cold air sinks. The combination of frost and wet soil is especially damaging, and only fully hardy plants will tolerate such conditions.

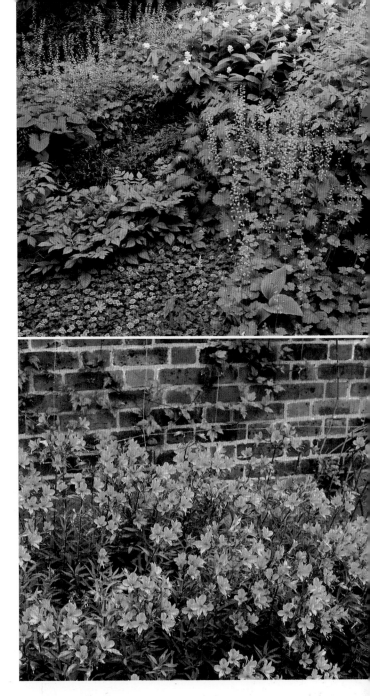

(top) **Deep, damp shade** is ideal for lush, leafy plants that dislike high temperatures. Damp shade can either be sheltered and relatively frost-free or, if a barrier such as a hedge or fence is creating a frost pocket, be cold and slow to thaw in winter.

(bottom) **The ground at the foot of a wall** will be sheltered from rain; sun-loving plants, such as these alstroemeria, will thrive there, although they'll need extra care while they establish.

Your soil

Far from being mere "dirt", soil is the raw material with amazing properties out of which you create your gardening dreams. Plant roots find moisture and food in the spaces between soil particles, and the soil's job is to hold enough moisture to sustain the garden in dry spells, but allow surplus water to drain away in wet weather. It also protects roots from heat and cold. Soil is just a thin skin on the planet's surface, but all life on land depends on it.

Adding grit to clay soil will open up its structure and improve drainage, thus reducing the tendency for it to become heavy, compacted, or waterlogged.

What kind of soil do I have?

Assessing your soil is essential for successful planting; while some plants tolerate a range of soil types, many have definite preferences. Dig an inspection pit; it will help you evaluate your soil in terms of the following factors:

■ **Texture** This can vary from sandy through to loam, to clay, and all types in between.

■ **Depth of topsoil** or uppermost, fertile layer—the deeper, the better.

■ **Type and depth of subsoil** Your garden might reveal surprising combinations, such as gravelly soil over clay, or even acidic loam over limestone. If your topsoil is shallow, the subsoil is more important, particularly for trees and larger shrubs that need deep roots for stability.

■ **Moisture content** Different soil types have different water-holding capacities; a little rain may drain through sand quickly, while the same amount can make a clay soil quite wet.

Clay soil or sandy soil?

The size of soil particles determines its texture and what grows best in it. Take a handful of moist topsoil, and shape it into a ball. Try to work it into a sausage shape, and rub it between your fingers. The "ideal" soil is loam, which will hold together in a ball and show finger impressions, without being sticky. Most soils, however, tend toward either clay or sand.

Clay soil feels smooth and sticky, will roll into a sausage and bend into a loop, and is shiny when rubbed. The tiny particles pack together so water does not easily drain, and air spaces are minute. It is slow to warm up in spring and sticky to work.

Sandy soil feels gritty and falls apart as you try to mold it into a ball. Sand grains are the largest soil particle, with big air spaces through which water can drain freely. Sandy soils warm up fast in spring but dry out quickly in droughts.

Acidic soil or alkaline soil?

Your soil's acidity or alkalinity affects what plants you can grow. Some, like rhododendrons, do not grow well in an alkaline soil, while others, such as clematis, thrive on alkaline, or "limy," sites. The term pH is a way of expressing how acidic or alkaline a substance is: the lower the pH number, the more acidic the soil. Acidity and alkalinity depend on how much calcium is in the soil. Acidic soil lacks calcium and alkaline soil has it in excess, while neutral soil (7 on the pH scale) has just enough calcium to mop up acidity.

■ **Alkaline soils** have a pH of over 7. You cannot make them acidic in the long-term, and acid-loving plants will certainly fail. However, limy soil is often well-drained and quick to warm up in spring. Incorporate plenty of organic matter and a wide range of plants will thrive, but don't overfertilize—this results in tall, floppy plants.

■ **Acidic soils** have a pH of 1–6. They are ideal for a wide range of plants, but acid-loving or "ericaceous" plants are almost impossible to grow elsewhere. If your soil is not acidic, you can grow them in containers filled with ericaceous compost. You can make acidic soil more alkaline by adding lime, but think carefully before using it. Most plants will put up with some acidity, and you can grow a wider range in mildly acidic soils. In theory, you can add acidic material to limy soils to lower the pH, but acidifying materials, such as sulfur dust, act slowly, are needed in very large amounts, and are expensive.

TESTING SOIL FOR PH LEVEL

You can get a good idea of your garden's pH with a test kit from a garden center or hardware store. Kits come with full instructions, are quick and simple to use, and are usually more reliable than the meters sold for home use.

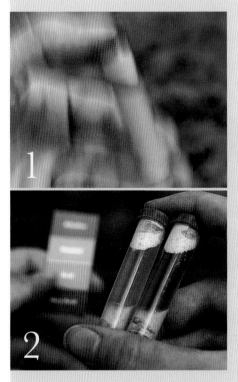

1 Take samples from different parts of the garden, as soil is seldom uniform. Make a note of where each sample comes from so that you can exploit any variations, such as an acidic patch, when you draw up your planting plan. Add the soil to the chemical solution in the test tube and shake to mix.

2 Match the colored solution against the pH chart to assess what kind of soil you have. Dark green indicates alkaline soil, bright green is neutral, and yellow or orange indicates acidic soil.

Top plants for acidic soils

1 *Acer palmatum* 'Sango-kaku'
Coral-bark Japanese maple
A beautiful acer that produces coral-pink shoots in winter. The leaves change color from yellow in spring, through green in summer, to orange-yellow in fall. H 20 ft (6 m); S 15 ft (5 m).

2 *Skimmia japonica* 'Bronze Knight'
Skimmia
Robust, evergreen shrub with attractive foliage and dark red buds in winter.
H 4 ft (1.2 m); S 4 ft (1.2 m).

3 *Rhododendron* 'Palestrina'
Azalea
Compact, evergreen azalea with masses of pure white flowers in late spring.
H 4 ft (1.2 m); S 4 ft (1.2 m).

4 *Fothergilla gardenii*
Witch alder
Small, dense, acidic-soil-loving shrub with white spring flowers and russet fall tones, good for a woodland garden.
H 3 ft (1 m); S 3 ft (1 m).

5 *Erica vagans* 'Birch Glow'
Cornish heath
A low-growing, spreading, heathland shrub with bright, rose-pink flowers.
H 12 in (30 cm); S 20 in (50 cm).

6 *Cornus kousa* 'China Girl'
Dogwood
A small garden tree that starts to flower when very young, with a mass of lime-green, petal-like bracts. H 22 ft (7 m); S 15 ft (5 m).

7 *Gaultheria tasmanica*
Pernettya
Spreading, matlike plant with white flowers in spring followed by berrylike fruits. H 3 in (8 cm); S to 10 in (25 cm).

8 *Camellia japonica* 'Guilio Nuccio'
Camellia
Large, elegant, evergreen shrub with semidouble, rose-red flowers from late winter to midsummer. H 28 ft (9 m); S 25 ft (8 m).

Top plants for alkaline soils

1 *Clematis* 'Huldine'
Clematis
Happy in most soils but especially when
the pH is high. Cup-shaped, white and
mauve flowers from late summer into
fall. H 10–15 ft (3–5 m); S 6 ft (2 m).

2 *Crocus tommasinianus* 'Ruby Giant'
Crocus
A reliable, easy-to-grow variety that
flowers early and may produce either
pale lilac or reddish-purple flowers.
H 3–4 in (8–10 cm); S 1 in (2.5 cm).

3 *Photinia davidiana*
Photinia
Tall evergreen usually grown for fall leaf
color and bright red, berrylike fruits.
H 25 ft (8 m); S 20 ft (6 m).

4 *Caryopteris* x *clandonensis*
'Worcester Gold'
Caryopteris
Mound-shaped shrub that thrives in
chalky soil. 'Worcester Gold' has small,
lavender-blue flowers and yellow-green
foliage. H 3 ft (1 m); S 5 ft (1.5 m).

5 *Malus* x *purpurea* 'Lemoinei'
Crab apple
A mid-sized garden tree with dark red-
purple leaves and wine-red blossoms in
spring. H 25 ft (8 m); S 25 ft (8 m).

6 *Hebe* 'Great Orme'
Hebe
Evergreen shrub with distinctive spikes
of deep pink flowers that gradually lose
their color and fade to white.
H 4 ft (1.2 m); S 4 ft (1.2 m).

7 *Campanula glomerata* 'Superba'
Campanula
Vigorous, spreading perennial with round
heads of bell-shaped, purple flowers.
H 24 in (60 cm); S 3 ft (1 m) or more.

8 *Forsythia suspensa*
Forsythia
A deciduous shrub valued for its early
spring display of bright yellow flowers.
H 10 ft (3 m); S 10 ft (3 m).

3. Flowerbeds and Borders

Strictly speaking, a border is a planting bed that runs along a boundary line, such as a fence, hedge, or wall, although traditionally, borders were often used to enclose formal parterres or lawns. Beds, on the other hand, are freestanding, and frequently used as focal points in the center of a lawn or gravel garden. Formal gardens, such as parterres, use geometric-shaped beds, often edged with low, evergreen hedging and set out in a symmetrical pattern. For many centuries, beds have been used for growing vegetables, herbs, and flowers, and still offer a practical solution for vegetable gardens, with plants on all sides receiving sun throughout the day.

Mixed borders depend for their success on careful planning. The effect may appear effortless, but layered planting such as this requires knowledge of when different plants come into flower and how large they will grow.

Designing beds and borders

The first step when planning your garden—whether you are faced with an overgrown jungle or a pretty yard that needs only minor adjustments—is to write down what you want from your space. Does your dream garden include beds and borders packed with colorful plants, an activity area for children, somewhere to entertain family and friends, or a combination of all three? You also need to consider practicalities: where will the compost bin go, do you need a bike rack, how much space is required for the dining table?

Garden style and structure

The style of garden you choose will affect the size, shape, and position of beds and borders, as well as the hard landscaping. Even if you don't want a neatly ordered garden, introduce a basic structure so that your yard looks interesting in the winter months. Consider planting a tree, and outline beds or borders with bricks, paving slabs, clay tiles, or a low hedge, to help define and structure the space. The harsh outlines will soon soften once the growing season starts and plants spill over the edges.

Take time to plan your planting and you will be rewarded with interest year-round. Evergreen trees and shrubs provide structure in winter; mix these with perennials that retain attractive seedheads in winter, such as sedums, achilleas, and echinops. Although their winter display is not colorful, they create interesting shapes and prevent borders from looking flat and lifeless. Perennials also provide a wonderful spectacle on frosty mornings, and draw birds into the garden to feast on the seeds and insects hibernating inside empty pods.

Grasses offer invaluable interest in fall and winter gardens. The dried flower spikes of some, such as *Stipa gigantea* and molinias, stand well into fall, while miscanthus and calamagrostis remain upright until spring.

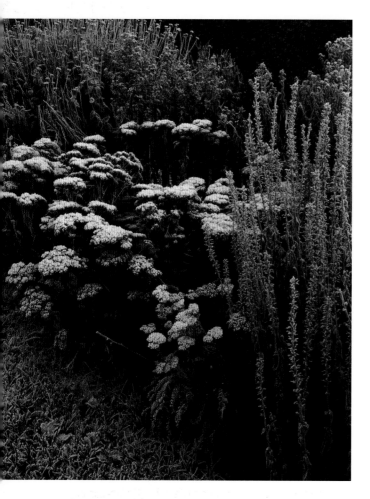

Over winter, leave herbaceous plants to stand, rather than cutting back the dead growth. Their dried seedheads and stems will take on a magical quality when dusted with frost or snow.

A formal garden will have lines of uniform planting. These boxwood trees have been pruned into neat balls, and the foliage of berberis and sage, rather than flowers, injects color.

In an informal garden, plants may billow freely over the path. Grasses and herbaceous perennials provide a colorful display all summer, and background shrubs and trees offer year-round structure.

Planting styles

Your choice of plants should reflect the overall style you want to achieve:

■ **Traditional herbaceous borders** consist only of herbaceous perennials, and will perform from early spring into fall. In the early 20th century, herbaceous borders were often only on show for six to eight weeks in summer, while themed areas, such as iris gardens, dahlia borders, and fall gardens, catered for the other seasons. Few small, modern yards can accommodate such themed garden rooms, and we need our borders to perform for as long as possible.

■ **Mixed beds and borders** consist of several different types of plants. Although perennials play a key role, they are assisted by shrubs and roses, and may also include annual flowers. If the border is backed by a wall or trellis, the height of the display can be increased with a backdrop of climbers. Alternatively, create height in a border by adding a tripod for climbers.

A mixed border offers both summer flowers and structure in the winter, but it has its drawbacks. Woody plants have spreading roots that take water and nutrients away from perennials, and

shrubs may shade out smaller plants; compensate by planting compact shrubs that have smaller root systems.

■ **Annual plantings** can be labor-intensive, but provide a great summer show. As many flower over a long period, the overall effect can be much more impressive than a herbaceous border, where plants come and go as the season progresses. When fall arrives, though, the bed or border will be empty for a few months. The ground will have to be dug and prepared each spring, before any seeds can be sown.

Styles of beds

Beds can be informal or formal, depending on their shape and design. Those that are part of a formal layout or parterre are usually geometric in shape and neatly edged, while informal beds have curved outlines and less defined edges.

■ **Formal beds** are typified by neatness and symmetry. Planting is kept in its allotted space with walls of close-cropped boxwood hedging, timbers, steel bands, clay tiles, or even glass bottle bottoms.

■ **Informal beds** have softer outlines and can be positioned to lead the eye to a focal point.

Size, shape, and layout

The planting of a border is like choreography: you need to choose and position the star plants as well as their supporting cast. You also need to take account of which plants flower when, and decide which colors should be brought together and which kept apart (*see pp.66–67*). Although this can take time, it is also fun. Even if you don't get it completely right the first time, you can take comfort in the fact that you could change it next year. When you are caught up in the excitement of planting—usually in spring or fall—it is easy to forget to include plants that may look uninspiring at the time but will provide a good show in another season. So plan ahead carefully, and ensure that your beds and borders perform well throughout the seasons.

Large swaths of colorful planting in broad, curved borders have a dynamic effect on designs. Find out when your chosen plants flower, and plan a succession of color all year.

Leafy plants, such as ornamental grasses and hostas, offer structure with their long season of interest, and help to disguise the unsightly dying foliage of earlier-flowering specimens.

Spacings and flowering times

Small flowering plants, such as aubretias and doronicums, perform the spring show in the garden. As the year progresses, larger flowering plants dominate. Many of the real giants, such as rudbeckias, do not come into their own until late summer. Although it is tempting to site all the small plants near the front and the tall ones at the back of a border, the result can be rather dull. It is also harder to get an even distribution of flowers through the season. To avoid this, bring a few tall, airy plants, such as grasses or the slender-stemmed *Verbena bonariensis*, closer to the front. They will make the overall shape of the display more interesting, while allowing you to see the plants behind.

When planning, allow enough space for each perennial plant to grow to its full height and spread. This may leave gaps between plants in the first year, but it is better than planting too closely and creating an overcrowded bed or border. Try covering the bare soil with hardy annuals in the first year; this should stop it from drying out and becoming overcome with weeds.

The style in which you plant borders and beds will be influenced by the type of plants you prefer. If you opt for mixed planting, consider planting shrubs or small trees for year-round structure. Use stakes or a broom to mark their intended positions, to get an impression of how they affect the rest of the garden.

Giving shape to beds

If you grow perennials in an open bed rather than against a wall or hedge, they won't need to compete for moisture or light, and rarely need staking. Informal island beds have little architectural presence, so create structure through planting. Use bold, architectural feature plants, such as New Zealand flax or *Euphorbia characias*.

Although most borders are formal rectangles that cling to the boundaries, the front edges can be curved to create an informal look. If you have a pair of facing borders, you could weave a path down the middle, and allow the borders to fill the spaces on either side. To allow easy access in summer when planting flows over the edges, make sure the path is at least 5 ft (1.5 m) wide. An S-shaped pathway also creates planting spaces of varying depths. In smaller gardens, this provides a few wide areas for trees, large shrubs, and swaths of perennials.

Whatever your garden style, borders under 3 ft (1 m) wide can be very limiting; any less than this, and you will be continually battling against plants breaking their boundaries and shading out lawns or covering pathways.

Choosing your plants

Flowering plants are traditionally classified according to their life cycle. Some live and die during the course of a single year, flowering and producing seeds that, with luck, will germinate the following year. Some have a two-year life cycle. And others are able—in theory, at least—to live indefinitely, year after year. This is where the terms "annual," "biennial," and "perennial" come from.

Plant types and characteristics

■ **Annuals** germinate, produce leaves, stems, and flowers, set seed, and die—all within a year. If the plant can withstand frost (a hardy annual), its seed may sprout almost immediately and grow into a young plant before winter. Other seeds lie dormant, ready to germinate in the following spring.

■ **Biennials** germinate and grow into good-sized plants in the first year (some, such as foxgloves, or *Digitalis*, produce rosettes of leaves). It is not until the second year that a biennial goes on to produce flowers and set seed. After this, the entire plant dies down and its life cycle is complete.

■ **Perennials** regrow year after year from an underground rootstock. They produce leaves, flowers, and seeds before dying down at the end of the season, usually after the first fall frost. In the following spring, new shoots appear and the cycle begins again.

■ **Bulbs** are also perennials, but their fleshy roots and sometimes their growth habits are different from those of garden perennials. With bulbs are included corms, rhizomes, and tubers (*see pp.116–127*).

■ **Shrubs** are woody-stemmed plants. They may be evergreen or deciduous and are often grown for their foliage rather than flowers (*see p.130*). Most shrubs are bushlike and grow from a number of different stems at their base.

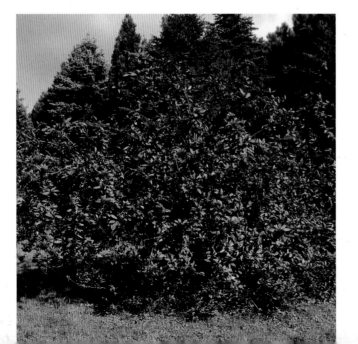

(opposite, clockwise from top left)
Pot marigolds (annual), **foxgloves** (biennial), **daffodils** (bulb), **sea holly** (perennial)

(left) **Cotoneaster** (shrub)

Easy-care plants, such as the rudbeckias and daylilies shown here, have sturdy stems that don't need staking. Daylilies' strappy leaves also provide lush cover when early-summer-flowering plants are dying back.

Spring bulbs such as daffodils and alliums (*below*) bloom for many years before you will need to lift and divide them. Alliums have sturdy stems that don't need staking and handsome, long-lasting seedheads.

Bedding plants or annuals?

Traditionally, bedding plants are used in geometric, formal display beds, and are stripped out and replaced at the start of each season. Therefore for winter and spring you could grow winter-flowering pansies, followed by bellis daisies, forget-me-nots, wallflowers, and spring bulbs, such as grape hyacinths and tulips. For the summer, try any of the many tender bedding plants, such as busy Lizzies, heliotropes, lobelias, marigolds, pelargoniums, and *Salvia splendens*.

Although this system provides a great color show for many months of the year, as well as allowing you to experiment with different planting plans, it is labor-intensive. Twice a year, the bed has to be cleared, dug, and replanted. You also need to buy a large number of plants each time at considerable expense, or raise some of them in advance in a frost-free greenhouse.

Easier and cheaper are hardy annuals. You can grow these from seed, which you can scatter straight onto the spot where you want them to flower (*see pp.110–113*). The main drawback is that you may have to wait 10–16 weeks for the flowers to bloom. Success rates can also be unpredictable—numerous factors influence germination, such as age of the seed, soil moisture, and temperature. Seedlings are also vulnerable to weather damage, and some pests and diseases.

Low-maintenance plants

If you choose your plants wisely, you can make life easier and reduce the time you need to spend maintaining them. Stick to sturdy herbaceous perennials and grasses, and avoid using annuals or bedding plants. Supplement the perennials with some small evergreens and ground-cover shrubs, such as euonymus, heathers, or tiny-leaved creeping cotoneasters, in mixed beds and borders to provide year-round greenery.

Don't grow plants such as delphiniums and double peonies that need staking. Instead, look for easy-care alternatives. For example, monkshoods, like delphiniums, are great for punctuating a border with their tall flower spikes in shades of blue and purple. But unlike delphiniums, they are not eaten by slugs, and stay upright without staking.

Every garden has sites with different growing conditions, or microclimates (*see pp.50–51*), so finding plants that perform well may involve some trial and error. Don't be afraid to move a plant if it fails in one spot; it may thrive elsewhere. Once you have planted a bed or border, keep it free of weeds by mulching it regularly (*see pp.280–281*).

You can even design your garden with low-maintenance plants and still enjoy color and interest throughout the year (*see below*).

Summer is the highlight of the flower-garden year. For a low-maintenance display, fill the borders with showy plants that reach for the skies. *Nepeta sibirica* has masses of flowers on self-supporting, tall stems (*below*).

Fall flowers include Michaelmas daisies and chrysanthemums. Also keep an eye out for colorful berries or seedheads, such as these Chinese lanterns (*Physalis alkekengi*) with their fiery orange seed capsules.

Winter blooms are precious commodities, since few flowering plants brave the cold. Violas (*below*) are among the most reliable, and perform best in a warm spot, such as on a patio. Hellebores also bloom in winter.

Creating color schemes

Flowers and plants offer an exceptional color palette that would make any artist envious. The subtlety in shades and hues, further enhanced by the different textures of the leaves and petals, creates a vast range of colors to play with. Remember that plants are not the only source of color in a garden, and it is also important to consider fences, walls, paving, and containers, all of which add to the final effect.

For some, the huge choice of color in the garden offers an exciting design opportunity, but for others, choosing color schemes can be nothing short of daunting. Many different color theories are used by garden designers, but if you are nervous that your yard may end up a frenzy of clashing hues, or a poor palette of dull shades, the color wheel offers a helpful guide (*see panel, right*).

Opposing colors

The color wheel is made up of primary colors (red, yellow, and blue), and secondary colors (orange, green, and purple); the latter are formed when the two primary colors on either side are mixed together.

These primary and secondary colors provide the foundation for successful color schemes. You will see that each primary color sits opposite a secondary color. These "opposing colors" are complementary and work extremely well when used together in a garden context. Thus, red goes well with green, yellow with purple, and blue with orange.

Bearing in mind that most foliage is green, and that—on a good day, at least—the sky is blue, it is difficult to be strict about this theory, because the majority of colors in the garden go well with blue and green. However, it is undeniable that blue and orange do combine very well, and that yellow and purple create a pleasing match.

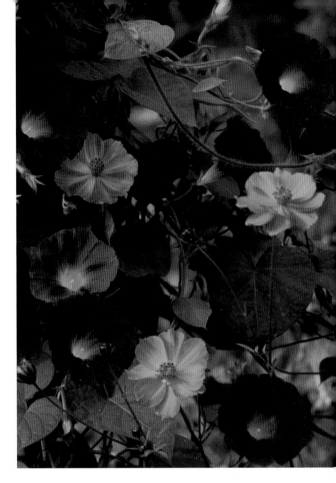

Using opposing colors guarantees an eye-catching display. This simple but effective combination of fiery orange cosmos and purple-blue morning glories works especially well.

Adjoining colors

Opposing colors create visual excitement, but can be overbearing. Adjoining colors, which sit side-by-side on the color wheel, create more subtle combinations. These were favored by Gertrude Jekyll, who created many amazing gardens in the early 20th century. She divided the colors into two categories: cool colors, consisting of blues, purples, lilacs, and pinks, and hot colors, which include yellows, oranges, and reds. Jekyll saw that it was important to use the in-between shades to create subtle blends. Rather than planting only yellows and reds, fuse the two with shades of orange and some plants with yellow and red in their foliage to carry the color theme throughout the year.

Monochrome planting

If you are disciplined enough, restrict your palette to just one color. Try creating a sunny yellow border, or a cool silvery-white one. It may seem straightforward to plant a monochrome garden using plants of the same color, but it is important to try to create variation and contrast within a plan, as without that, it will appear bland and monotonous.

For example, when using white, do not restrict yourself to pure white flowers, but also allow cream, lime green, and pinkish and mauve-tinted whites. Likewise, choose the foliage of the plants carefully, and include pale to dark greens, gray, silver, and blue-tinted leaves. When opting for yellows or reds, go for the full tonal spectrum within those colors, and mirror your color choice in the accompanying foliage.

Green

This is the most dominant and important color in the garden, and there are myriad shades of green to choose from. For color that will outlast a flowering display, mix foliage in various shades of lime, apple, and blue-green.

THE COLOR WHEEL

A color wheel is an at-a-glance guide to which colors work well together. It is very easy to use and takes the guesswork out of creating successful color combinations within the garden.

Monochromatic plans can be monotonous unless you include interesting foliage colors. Here, cream and white flowers are mirrored by silver and yellow variegated hostas and grasses.

Choosing plants for year-round color

Certain plants will inject color into the garden all year. They provide structure and a sense of permanence as everything else changes day by day. Some are suitable for containers as focal points, while others will enhance a colorful display in a border.

White
- ■ *Artemisia stelleriana* 'Boughton Silver'
- ■ *Euonymus fortunei* 'Silver Queen'
- ■ *Hebe pinguifolia* 'Pagei'
- ■ *Betula utilis* 'Silver Shadow'

Purple
- ■ *Ophiopogon planiscapus* 'Nigrescens'
- ■ *Salvia officinalis* 'Purpurascens'
- ■ *Ajuga reptans* 'Atropurpurea'
- ■ *Phormium tenax* Purpureum Group

Blue
- ■ *Festuca glauca* 'Elijah Blue'
- ■ *Leymus arenarius*
- ■ *Juniperus squamata* 'Blue Star'
- ■ *Ruta graveolens* 'Jackman's Blue'

Green
- ■ *Fatsia japonica*
- ■ *Hedera hibernica*
- ■ *Pittosporum tobira*
- ■ *Stipa gigantea*

Yellow
- ■ *Choisya ternata* Sundance
- ■ *Ilex aquifolium* 'Golden Milkboy'
- ■ *Carex oshimensis* 'Evergold'
- ■ *Hebe ochracea* 'James Stirling'

Color through the seasons

One of the most effective ways to use color is to allow the seasons to dictate the palette. When spring arrives, nature seems so relieved that the dreary weather is over that it responds with a burst of sunny colors and every imaginable shade of green. As the season progresses into early summer, the color palette calms down a little, concentrating on clean, fresh colors, such as the blues of delphiniums and geraniums, and white and pink roses and peonies.

As summer heats up, so do the colors: warm yellows, burnt oranges, and velvety reds signal hot, sunny days. The fading light that heralds fall is reflected in the subdued tones of asters. Winter's colors, while more subtle, are just as effective—white snowdrops never fail to cut through the gloom.

(opposite, clockwise from top left)
Spring sees an abundance of sunshine yellows and vibrant golds typified by narcissi.

Late summer flower colors heat up before fall with amber heleniums and golden crocosmias.

Fall color is provided by bright berries and fruits, and the rich reds, oranges, yellows, and browns of dying leaves.

Winter needn't be dreary with ice-white snowdrops and cheery pink cyclamen to look forward to.

Making a planting plan

Be generous when marking out the area for your bed or border. If you can afford the space, allow at least 10 ft (3 m) to provide a good planting width. You can then build up several layers of plants, one behind the other, and use shrubs and climbers to create height toward the back. If the choice is between two narrow borders and one deep one, you'll find the larger more rewarding, however intimidating it may seem at first.

Key plants, such as tall wispy grasses, add focal points to borders and beds. Structural foliage plants are useful inclusions as their impact is more enduring than transient flowers.

Choosing the key plants

Working from an accurate base plan makes designing a new bed or border easier, and helps you decide how many plants you need to fill it. When selecting plants, think of your border as a stage performance, and pick out the leading cast. This should include plants that have an important presence because of their handsome shape, decorative leaves, or long flowering season. Good candidates include colorful foliage shrubs, such as berberis and cotinus, and many of the grasses, sedums, and euphorbias. Repeating these every few yards brings rhythm into a plan.

Think of where you would like to see your stars: sedums flower in fall and are good front-of-the-border plants, while taller grasses, such as molinia or calamagrostis, are better placed in the middle or background. Mark the plants on your plan with a circle representing their final spread. Most of the larger perennials will spread to 18 in (45 cm), while smaller ones will reach 12 in (30 cm); check plant labels for the spreads of shrubs, and note that their size can be affected by your soil and garden conditions.

Planning in color

Once the key plants are on your plan, choose supporting players that offer more subtle effects. Keep a note of their flowering times and colors, and, if in doubt, make an overlay with tracing paper, onto which you can mark the color of each plant using different pen types or symbols. Do a few overlays for the different seasons to show when your chosen cast is in flower, where the gaps are, and at what time of year they need to be filled.

Contrasting flower shapes

Think of the contrasts in flower shape as well as color, height, and season. Plants with spiky flowers, such as veronicas, delphiniums, foxgloves, and verbascums, or upright, linear foliage, such as irises or daylilies, will introduce a vertical accent. Those with round, disklike flowerheads, such as sedums, yarrows, fennel, and all the cow-parsley relatives, create a horizontal plane. Mixing these two types of flowers paints an exciting picture. Distinctive spherical shapes, such as alliums and *Echinops ritro*, add to the structure.

(right, from top) **Combine different flower shapes**—such as foxgloves, yarrow, and echinops—in beds and borders to create an architectural feast for the eye.

Sunny sites

Sun-lovers tend to be among the most free-flowering of all garden plants. If you are lucky enough to have a sunny yard with reliably moist soil—from a natural watercourse, perhaps—you will be able to grow a huge range of plants. But more often, sun combines with little rain and you find that the soil dries out in summer. On a dry site, the trick is to select those plants that can cope with a lack of moisture and don't need constant watering, which is both time-consuming for you and costly to the environment.

A dry garden has been created at Hyde Hall, a Royal Horticultural Society garden. It is a large hillside garden that evokes a rocky, Mediterranean slope by using silvery, spiky-leaved plants that weave in and out of large boulders. Despite its size, it contains plenty of inspiration for domestic gardeners.

Recognizing sun-loving plants

The best plants to use in a sunny garden are those that would naturally be found in exposed positions with high light levels, low rainfall, and poor, fast-draining soil. Plants that can cope in such locations have evolved by developing certain characteristics. A sunny garden planted with suitable plants will be much easier to establish and maintain than one with poorly chosen plants.

(clockwise from top left)

■ **Silver or gray leaves** reflect heat and sunlight. Many silvery plants, particularly artemisias such as the *Artemisia alba* 'Canescens' shown here, are superb foliage plants.

■ **A low-growing** habit helps reduce the drying and damaging effects of wind in exposed places. This rose root (*Rhodiola rosea*) also conserves water with its fleshy leaves, silvery green foliage, and a thick, water-storing root.

■ **Small leaves**, such as those of this rock rose, *Helianthemum nummularium*, reduce the surface area through which moisture can be lost. Some shrubs, such as Spanish broom (*Genista hispanica*), go so far as to barely have leaves at all.

■ **Waxy leaves**, like those on the pretty, white-flowered *Cistus salviifolius*, are coated with a thick waterproof layer to slow down moisture loss and reduce leaf scorch in very hot weather.

Drought-tolerant plants

In addition to sun, plants that can survive without much water require the following:

■ **Good drainage:** few drought-tolerant plants will put up with a waterlogged soil in winter. As a general rule, it is cold combined with wet that kills these plants, not cold alone.

■ **Low nutrient levels:** overfertilizing encourages fast growth of soft, sappy foliage, which wilts in hot weather. Plants grown in poor soil also flower more profusely and for longer.

■ **Good air circulation:** this helps reduce fungal diseases and rotting at the plant's "neck" (the point at which the plant emerges from the soil).

Often, a garden may have the right climatic conditions for these plants but unsuitably wet, heavy soil. In this case it is essential to improve the drainage so that plants are able to survive the winter months. Incorporate plenty of sandy grit in the topsoil—down to a depth of 10 in (25 cm) or so—or make raised beds using stone, brick, or timbers. Build retaining walls at least 16 in (40 cm) high, add a 4-in (10-cm) layer of 1-inch (25-mm) gravel in the bottom, and fill to planting level with gritty topsoil. Individual plants can be planted in raised mounds up to 12 in (30 cm) high and 3 ft (1 m) across. This is especially effective for trees and shrubs.

Drought-tolerant, sun-loving plants are ideal for a variety of planting styles, including sunny beds and borders, and they will often thrive in containers on a patio. While classic Mediterranean plants, including herbs like lavender and rosemary, are often used in formal knot gardens and parterres, they are probably at their best in informal, naturalistic styles. Use gravel paths to draw the eye through the garden, as they wind among mounds of bright flowers and silvery foliage that are interspersed with aromatic herbs and shrubs.

Top plants for sunny sites

1 *Berberis thunbergii* 'Helmond Pillar'
Barberry
Will grow happily in partial shade but fall leaf and berry color is stronger in full sun. H 5 ft (1.5 m); S 24 in (60 cm).

2 *Eryngium* x *tripartitum*
Sea holly
Thistlelike flowers, midsummer to early fall. Use in a sunny gravel garden. H 24–36 in (60–90 cm); S 20 in (50 cm).

3 *Crocosmia masoniorum*
Montbretia
Long, arching stems produce vivid, bright red-orange flowers in midsummer. H 4 ft (1.2 m); S 3 in (8 cm).

4 *Stipa arundinacea*
Pheasant's tail grass
An evergreen whose new-season dark green leaves become streaked with orange from summer through to winter. H 3 ft (1 m); S 4 ft (1.2 m).

5 *Santolina chamaecyparissus*
Cotton lavender
Scented, gray-green foliage and bright yellow flowerheads. Grow on dry soils in full sun. H 20 in (50 cm); S 3 ft (1 m).

6 *Pelargonium* 'Apple Blossom Rosebud'
Pelargonium
Rounded clusters of bicolored pink and white flowers. Will grow in partial shade, but prefers full sun. H 12–16 in (30–40 cm); S 8–10 in (20–25 cm).

7 *Phlomis cashmeriana*
Phlomis
Evergreen shrub with sagelike leaves and hooded, lilac-purple flowers. H to 36 in (90 cm); S 24 in (60 cm).

8 *Papaver rhoeas* Mother of Pearl Group
Field poppy
Sun-loving annuals that self-seed freely. A wide-range of colors. H to 36 in (90 cm); S to 12 in (30 cm).

9 *Aster frikartii* 'Wunder von Stäfa'
Aster
A sun-lover with violet-blue, daisylike flowers in late summer and early fall. H 28 in (70 cm); S 18 in (45 cm).

10 *Hibiscus syriacus* 'Lady Stanley'
Hibiscus
Deciduous shrub with exotic, pink and white flowers, plentiful in hot, sunny summers. H 10 ft (3 m); S 6 ft (2 m).

11 *Anthemis punctata* subsp. *cupaniana*
Anthemis
Low-growing, spreading perennial with white, daisylike flowers, ideal for rock gardens. H 12 in (30 cm); S 36 in (90 cm).

12 *Tulipa* 'Ancilla'
Tulip
Small tulip with pink blooms flushed red at the petal base. Flowers in mid-spring. A good rock-garden plant. H 6 in (15 cm).

13 *Salvia patens*
Salvia
A perennial with hooded flowers from midsummer to mid-fall. H 18–24 in (45–60 cm); S 18 in (45 cm).

14 *Yucca filamentosa* 'Bright Edge'
Yucca
Clump of sharp leaves with yellow edges and tall spires of white flowers. Needs full sun. H 30 in (75 cm); S 5 ft (1.5 m).

15 *Cytisus* x *praecox* 'Allgold'
Broom
Pale yellow-flowering shrub that will tolerate poor soil but requires full sun. Good for dry borders and rock gardens. H 4 ft (1.2 m); S 5 ft (1.5 m).

16 *Cordyline australis* 'Albertii'
New Zealand cabbage palm
A palmlike, evergreen shrub that can grow to the size of a small tree. In frost-prone areas, grow in a container and provide shelter in winter. H 10–30 ft (3–10 m); S 3–12 ft (1–4 m).

Shady sites

You may see a shady area as having less potential than a sunny one, but there are plenty of plants that thrive in shade. Shade is seldom at a constant level throughout the day and across the seasons, so observation is essential. In a north-facing garden, the shade might be deep and constant close to the house, but less so farther away from it. Perhaps your yard is actually quite sunny, but a group of trees have created areas of shade. As always, plants that are adapted to the conditions will be the most successful, and are easily spotted (*see panel*). Reliably moist soil in shade will open up opportunities for species that would naturally grow at the edges of streams and ponds, while very dry shade will require a different, more limited, range of plants.

Moist shade is enjoyed by many plants. They will do even better if you improve the soil, and perhaps thin out some tree branches so the shade is less dense.

Improving the soil

The main problem in a shady garden tends to be the soil conditions. Trees growing in and around your garden require tremendous amounts of water and nutrients, and can leave the surrounding soil dry and barren. That said, if you are lucky enough to garden on the edge of old woodland, your soil will be enriched by leaf litter. Shade cast by a building, depending on the exposure, can result in soil that is either dry and thin or dank and structureless.

Soil pH (*see p.53*) can be affected by trees. A large pine tree, for example, can sometimes acidify the soil around it as its needles fall and rot down; this will affect the plants you can grow there. Nevertheless, all of these soil problems can be overcome with a little know-how and effort.

As most shade-tolerant plants originate from woodland environments, it makes sense to try to recreate similar conditions in your own garden by incorporating as much organic matter—composted bark, homemade leafmold and garden compost (*see p.286*)—into the soil as possible. This can take time, especially under trees where roots prevent digging in compost to any depth. Here it is best to lay the compost on the surface as a mulch, and keep applying it every spring and fall so it breaks down slowly into the soil, or is drawn down by earthworms.

Letting in more light

Reducing very dense shade vastly increases the number of plants you can grow. You can improve light levels in a number of simple ways.

Shade from buildings can be reduced by whitewashing the walls in order to reflect extra light into the garden.

Shade from dense tree canopies can be dealt with in the following ways:

■ **Thinning**, which removes alternate branches.

■ **Pollarding**, which involves regularly cutting back the main branches to the trunk or stem.

■ **Coppicing**, which means the tree is cut down to ground level to promote multiple vigorous and decorative new shoots.

■ **Crown lifting**, in which the lowest branches are removed to raise the height of the canopy.

Recognizing shade-loving plants

As with sun-loving plants, shade-tolerant species have adapted over millennia to the conditions in which they grow. You can recognize shade-lovers by looking for the following traits:

Flowering in spring or fall makes the most of the relatively high light and high rainfall when deciduous trees are leafless. Many bulbs use this strategy; they make the most of the short window of opportunity, flowering and replenishing their food stores, then spending the rest of the year dormant beneath ground.

Dark pigmentation in leaves allows plants to photosynthesize more effectively when they are subjected to low light conditions. Many ericaceous (acid-loving) woodland plants, including camellias, have very dark green, glossy leaves.

Large leaves help to maximize the surface area through which light is absorbed. The leaves of this evergreen bergenia are also thick and leathery, helping to reduce water loss.

Densely packed leaves increase the light-collecting surface area. Some ferns, such as *Polystichum setiferum*, are also covered in hairs to trap moisture, so they can establish and survive in comparatively dry soil.

Top plants for shady sites

1 *Hyacinthoides non-scripta*
Bluebell
The classic English bluebell is ideal for growing in shady borders. H 8–16 in (20–40 cm); S 3 in (8 cm).

2 *Epimedium x perralchicum*
Barrenwort or bishop's miter
Evergreen perennial flowering in spring. Will grow in shade beneath trees. H 16 in (40 cm); S 24 in (60 cm).

3 *Hedera helix* 'Glymii'
Ivy
Most green-leaved ivies grow in shade, if the soil is kept moist. Variegated ivies tend to need more light. H 6 ft (2 m).

4 *Pulmonaria saccharata*
Jerusalem sage
Spreading, ground-cover plant with white-flecked, green leaves and red-violet, violet, or white flowers in spring. H 12 in (30 cm); S 24 in (60 cm).

5 *Hosta* 'Buckshaw Blue'
Hosta
Slow-growing variety with deep blue-green leaves. Hostas thrive in damp shade—though watch out for slugs and snails. H 14 in (35 cm); S 24 in (60 cm).

6 *Trillium grandiflorum*
Trillium
Vigorous perennial bearing pure white flowers in spring and summer. H to 16 in (40 cm); S 12 in (30 cm).

7 *Hydrangea paniculata* 'Praecox'
Hydrangea
Large, deciduous shrub with clusters of open, white flowers from midsummer. H 10–22 ft (3–7 m); S 8 ft (2.5 m).

8 *Convallaria majalis* 'Albostriata'
Lily-of-the-valley
Beautifully scented shade-lover ideal for growing with ferns in a cool spot. H 9 in (23 cm); S 12 in (30 cm).

3

4

7

8

11

12

15

16

9 *Tiarella cordifolia*
Foam flower
The tiny flowers are borne over a long period from spring to summer. Spreads freely. H to 10 ft (3 m); S to 6 ft (2 m).

10 *Helleborus orientalis*
Lenten rose
Winter-flowering, in shades of purple, pink, and greeny white. Will tolerate a damp, shady woodland garden. H 18 in (45 cm); S 18 in (45 cm).

11 *Lamium maculatum* 'Album'
Dead nettle
Low-growing, spreading, nettlelike plant that thrives in shade. Good ground cover among shrubs or in woodland areas. H 6 in (15 cm); S 24 in (60 cm).

12 *Fuchsia* 'Mrs. Popple'
Fuchsia
A bushy, fast-growing fuchsia that should be as happy in light shade as in full sun. H 3 ft (1 m); S 3 ft (1 m).

13 *Viburnum tinus* 'Eve Price'
Viburnum
A dense, evergreen shrub with clusters of white flowers followed by blue-black fruits. H 10 ft (3 m); S 10 ft (3 m).

14 *Luzula nivea*
Woodrush
A tufted, grasslike perennial, found in the wild in moorland, bogs and woodland. Useful for damp shade. H 6 ft (2 m); S 8 ft (2.5 m).

15 *Dicentra spectabilis*
Bleeding heart
A perennial with dangling, heart-shaped flowers. Grows well in partial shade and sun. H to 4 ft (1.2 m); S 18 in (45 cm).

16 *Geranium phaeum*
Cranesbill
A good plant for damp shade. Late spring and early summer flowers, deep purple-black, maroon or white. H 32 in (80 cm); S 18 in (45 cm).

Wet, sticky soil

Wet, sticky, clay soil can be among the hardest to work with: it is all too easy to destroy its structure and leave behind a gooey, unworkable mess. However, there is no need to be downhearted over this, because clay can be the most rewarding of all soils if prepared well and planted with things that appreciate its moist, fertile nature.

Cultivating wet, sticky soil

Working wet soil is best attempted when the soil is at its driest, assuming it dries to some degree at some point in the year. This can mean cultivating at unusual times of the year, such as midsummer, and planting in early rather than late fall when the soil is still warm and comparatively dry. It may even result in summer cultivation followed by spring planting.

There are advantages to this approach, as it makes sure that, rather than sitting in wet soil through the winter, young plants can start actively growing and producing new roots as soon as they are put in the ground. How much cultivation is needed depends on how wet the soil is, and to what depth—this is easily determined by digging inspection pits at varying times of the year and in different

Soil that is always moist can support many specialized plants that would be impossible to grow otherwise. If you have a large, wet area, then you could take your cue from nature and create a water meadow garden. This will not only make life easier, but it is also a good way to attract wildlife.

A raised bed is a good option where conditions alternate between wet and dry, making cultivation difficult. It needs to be at least 16 in (40 cm) high and can be built from timbers, brick, or stone. Fill it with topsoil that has been improved with organic matter (or grit for clay soil) to improve the drainage.

locations. Armed with this knowledge, you can then decide whether it is worth working with the prevailing conditions, or trying to manipulate them.

Damp and drought

Soil that fluctuates from wet in the winter to dry in the summer can be improved by incorporating materials to improve drainage into about the top 12 in (30 cm) of soil. This helps water move through the soil and also creates air spaces so roots can penetrate more easily. Grit, sand, and gravel are excellent long-term drainage improvers. Add lots of organic matter as well, to help the soil hold water through dry spells so your moisture-loving plants don't suffer. Individual plants, especially trees and shrubs, can be planted on mounds of soil. This is an old technique to prevent water from naturally settling where the soil has been disturbed—which often results in a newly planted specimen immediately drowning in a water-filled pit.

Reliably moist soil

If you are lucky enough to have a soil that always remains moist, the opportunity to grow huge, lush bog plants is just too good to miss. Incorporating a little grit or light potting soil may aid structure to some degree, and the application of thick, dry mulch, such as chipped bark, is certainly worthwhile as it will help to retain the moisture but also allow you to walk on the soil when you need to weed or replant— useful when it comes to weeding or replanting. In very damp gardens, consider constructing decks and raised boardwalks to provide seating areas and paths. You can then enjoy your garden all through the year without getting muddy feet or compacted soil.

How plants tolerate wet soil

Moisture-loving and marginal plants are suitable for reliably wet soil because they have adapted in various ways so they don't drown in wet, anaerobic (airless) conditions. Moisture-loving plants thrive in the kind of moist soil found by ponds, streams, and rivers. Marginal plants are similar, but prefer to grow in shallow water, or reliably wet soil that is regularly submerged.

Air channels that run from shoot to root allow oxygen to circulate around bog plants like arum lilies, whose roots would otherwise be starved of oxygen.

Shallow roots are typical because there is no need to search for water—bog buttercups, for example, spread across the soil surface.

Huge leaves are characteristic of wetland plants such as rodgersias. Due to the fact that there is no shortage of water, it doesn't matter if they lose it rapidly.

Special equipment is used by the swamp cypress; it can live in water because it develops breathing apparatus on its roots. They push up through the water surface and take in oxygen so the submerged roots can breathe.

Top plants for wet, sticky soil

1 *Ajuga reptans* 'Burgundy Glow'
Bugle
Justly renowned for tolerating poor, damp soil and full shade. H 6 in (15 cm); S 24–36 in (60–90 cm).

2 *Aconitum* 'Bressingham Spire'
Aconite or Monkshood
A tall perennial with deep violet flowers that likes cool, moist soil and partial shade. H 3 ft (1 m); S 12 in (30 cm).

3 *Rosa* L'Aimant
Rose
A reliable, easy-to-grow rose with scented flowers and a tolerance for clay soils. H 3 ft (1 m); S 30 in (75 cm).

4 *Astilbe* x *arendsii* 'Fanal'
Astilbe
Perennial with feathery, plumelike dark crimson flowers that will grow in fertile clay soil as long as it stays moist in summer. H 24 in (60 cm); S 18 in (45 cm).

5 *Lysimachia ciliata* 'Purpurea'
Loosestrife
A perennial whose natural habitat is damp grassland or woodland, often near water. H 4 ft (1.2 m); S 24 in (60 cm).

6 *Galanthus nivalis* Sandersii Group
Snowdrop
Common snowdrops like heavy soil, as long as it doesn't dry out, and partial shade. H 4 in (10 cm); S 1–3 ft (30 cm–1 m).

7 *Eupatorium purpureum*
Joe Pye weed
Pink, pinkish purple, or creamy white flowers are borne from summer to early autumn. H 5 ft (1.5 m); S 12 in (30 cm).

8 *Carex pendula*
Sedge
Most sedges are found naturally in bog, moorland, or damp woodland, and should thrive in moist, clay soil. H to 5 ft (1.5 m); S to 5 ft (1.5 m).

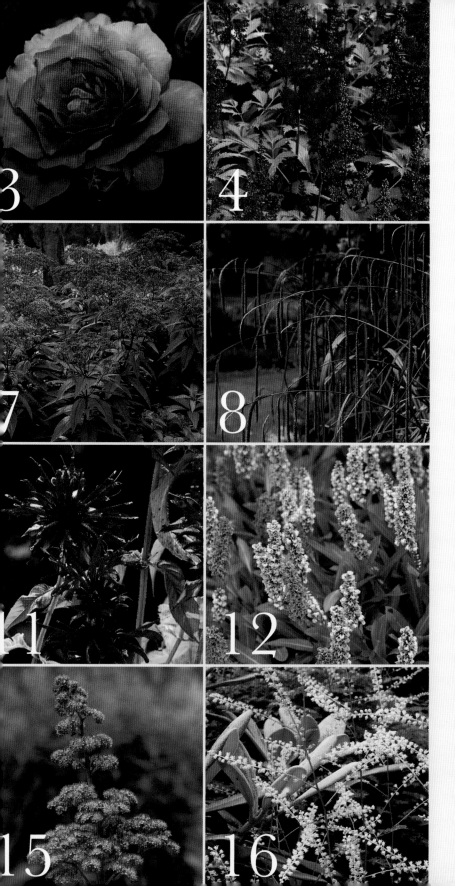

9 *Cotoneaster horizontalis*
Fishbone cotoneaster
An easy-to-grow shrub that should tolerate heavy, clay soil and partial shade. H 3 ft (1 m); S 15 ft (5 m).

10 *Digitalis purpurea*
Foxglove
A shade-loving biennial native to woodland. Purple, pink, or white flowers. H 3–6 ft (1–2 m); S to 24 in (60 cm).

11 *Monarda* 'Mahogany'
Bergamot
Hardy perennial with ragged, wine-red flowers, tolerant of most soil types but needs to be kept moist in summer. H 36 in (90 cm); S 18 in (45 cm).

12 *Persicaria affinis* 'Donald Lowndes'
Persicaria
Low-growing evergreen perennial that produces bottlebrush spikes of flowers. H to 8 in (20 cm); S 12 in (30 cm).

13 *Camassia leichtlinii* 'Semiplena'
Quamash
Semidouble, creamy white flowers. Should grow well in clay soil to which grit has been added for better drainage. H 24 in–4 ft (60 cm–1.2 m); S 4 in (10 cm).

14 *Caltha palustris*
Marsh marigold
Prefers bog conditions or very shallow water. Waxy yellow flowers in spring. H 4–16 in (10–40 cm); S 18 in (45 cm).

15 *Rodgersia pinnata* 'Superba'
Rodgersia
A perennial ideal for growing near water, or in damp woodland. Horse-chestnut-like leaves and tall clusters of flowers. H to 4 ft (1.2 m); S 30 in (75 cm).

16 *Aruncus aethusifolius*
Aruncus
Small, compact perennial that positively likes moist, heavy soil. Creamy white flowers appear in early summer. H 10–16 in (25–40 cm); S 16 in (40 cm).

Dry, free-draining soil

By late summer, free-draining, sandy soil is often very short of water, and many plants just won't survive. Some plants, however, will thrive in these trying conditions (*see panel*). Trees and shrubs, including conifers, are also good choices for this soil. Once established, their deep root systems make them pretty much drought-proof, although they will need watering for the first year or two until they have settled in. Nevertheless, even when you are growing well-adapted plants, it is still worth adding an organic soil improver to help soil structure and stability, without restricting drainage. Composted bark, garden compost, and spent mushroom compost are all good choices.

Many aromatic herbs come from the Mediterranean hillsides and enjoy dry, well-drained soil. They often have attractive foliage and pretty flowers, in addition to their culinary uses.

Sandy soil

Light, sandy soil is easy to work, but water runs freely through it, washing out nutrients. Adding plenty of organic matter adds nutrients and helps soak up and retain moisture. Applying a general-purpose fertilizer in spring will also top off nutrient levels. Rose fertilizer is a good choice because it tends to be rich in magnesium, an element often in short supply in sandy soil. Calcium is also easily washed out, so sandy soil is often acidic. You can easily check this with a test kit (*see p.53*). In severe cases you may need to add lime every five years.

Sandy soil is also prone to compaction. Again, plenty of organic matter is the answer; dig it in before planting whenever the soil is dry enough to work. Lawns on sandy soil are especially liable to suffer from speedy drainage and compaction. Fall spiking, feeding, top-dressing with organic matter, and scarifying will be needed to keep them looking good (*see pp.202–203*).

Limestone soil

Limestone soil is also very free-draining, but rich in calcium. Don't even think about trying acid-loving plants—camellias, for example—as they will never really thrive, if they survive at all. Other plants, even those adapted to limestone soil, will greatly benefit from mulching, watering, and fertilizing. Organic matter, added frequently, is vital, although needs to be used generously because it breaks down very quickly in lime-rich soils.

The best lawn grasses prefer mildly acidic soil, so lawns on limestone soil are seldom quite as good as on other types. Consider going for wildflower-rich mixes or eco-lawns, where clover in the lawn keeps it green in dry weather and adds nitrogen, saving the need for fertilizer.

How plants tolerate drought

Plants that naturally grow in dry environments or in well-drained soil have several ways of coping with the conditions. Nevertheless, a bit of extra care will work wonders. Water plants very thoroughly before and after planting, and keep them just above ground level to leave room for a generous mulch (*see pp.280–281*), which will help retain soil moisture.

Thick, fleshy leaves have large cells capable of holding moisture over a long period. *Agave americana* is a classic example, hailing from the dry deserts of the southern United States.

Hairy leaves work by trapping a layer of moist, still air close to the leaf surface so that it loses water less quickly. The pasque flower, *Pulsatilla vulgaris*, has softly hairy leaves and is available in many colors, such as the red 'Rubra'.

Long, thick taproots, such as those of verbascums, yuccas, and this *Eryngium* x *oliverianum*, reach deep into the soil in the quest for water, and store moisture and starch for lean periods.

Summer-dormant plants retreat below ground to avoid heat. Many spring bulbs, including tulips, developed this strategy to avoid the heat of the Mediterranean summer. Some other types of plants, like *Geranium tuberosum*, do the same.

Top plants for dry, free-draining soil

1 *Allium schoenoprasum* 'Forescate'
Chives
A pink-flowering chive that likes heat, sun, and fertile, well-drained, sandy soil. H 24 in (60 cm); S 3 in (7 cm).

2 *Cotinus coggygria* Purpureus Group
Smoke bush
A deciduous shrub that produces masses of tiny flowers and grows well in light, chalky soil. H 24 in (60 cm); S 3 in (7 cm).

3 *Scabiosa lucida*
Scabious
Small perennials that occur naturally in dry, sunny meadows and on rocky slopes. H 8 in (20 cm); S 12 in (30 cm).

4 *Artemisia* 'Powis Castle'
Mugwort
Drought-tolerant perennial with silvery gray foliage that prefers light, dry soil. H 24 in (60 cm); S 36 in (90 cm).

5 *Nandina domestica*
Heavenly bamboo
A tall, flowering shrub that likes light, dry soil, but must not be allowed to dry out. Small white flowers in midsummer. H 6 ft (2 m); S 5 ft (1.5 m).

6 *Penstemon* 'Apple Blossom'
Penstemon
Perennial grown for foxglovelike flowers. Prefers well-drained soil. H 18–24 in (45–60 cm); S 18–24 in (45–60 cm).

7 *Sempervivum ciliosum*
Houseleek
A dense, spreading succulent for growing in a rock or gravel garden, in crevices in walls, or in containers. H 3 in (8 cm); S 12 in (30 cm).

8 *Lavandula angustifolia* 'Munstead'
Lavender
A blue-purple-flowered variety. Lavender thrives in well-drained, sandy soil in full sun. H 15 in (45 cm); S 24 in (60 cm).

9 *Coreopsis grandiflora* 'Badengold'
Coreopsis
A mass of deep golden-yellow, daisylike flowers that, if deadheaded, will continue all through the summer. H to 36 in (90 cm); S 18 in (45 cm).

10 *Hebe* 'Bowles' Variety'
Hebe
A compact flowering shrub that will tolerate poor and slightly alkaline soil if kept moist but well-drained. H 18 in (45 cm); S 24 in (60 cm).

11 *Bergenia* 'Sunningdale'
Elephant's ears
Glossy-leaved evergreen that produces clusters of bright lilac-magenta flowers from early spring onward. H 12–18 in (30–45 cm) S 18–24 in (45–60 cm).

12 *Verbascum* 'Cotswold Queen'
Mullein
Verbascums will grow in most fertile soil but need good drainage and like full sun. H 4 ft (1.2 m); S 12 in (30 cm).

13 *Perovskia* 'Blue Spire'
Perovskia
A plant that tolerates poor, dry, chalky soil. It has silvery foliage and violet-blue flowers. H 4 ft (1.2 m); S 3 ft (1 m).

14 *Weigela* 'Looymansii Aurea'
Weigela
An easygoing, pink-flowering shrub that will grow in almost any soil but prefers partial shade. H 5 ft (1.5 m); S 5 ft (1.5 m).

15 *Centaurea cyanus*
Cornflower
With a natural habitat of meadows and grasslands, cornflowers will grow in most well-drained soil. H 8–32 in (20–80 cm); S 6 in (15 cm).

16 *Pennisetum alopecuroides*
Fountain grass
A bristle-flowered, evergreen grass that prefers light, well-drained soil and is ideal for prairie-style, perennial planting. H 2–5 ft (0.6–1.5 m); S 2–4 ft (0.6–1.2 m).

Exposed sites

Like humans, plants are predominantly composed of water. This makes them prone to dehydration—a constant threat in an exposed garden, whether by the coast, inland, or at high altitude. Wind can test plants to the limit, and only those species that are adapted to resist its drying effects—either by storing water in their leaves or roots, or reducing the loss of water through their leaves—stand a chance. On the positive side, exposed gardens usually have high light levels and excellent air circulation, reducing fungal disease. But strong sun can also fade subtle flower colors, and good air circulation can quickly turn into an eddying wind that damages plants.

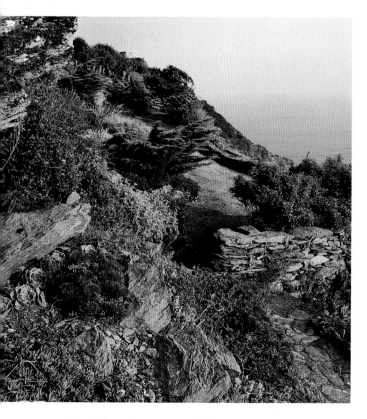

Coastal gardens enjoy a mild climate but must endure strong winds and salt spray. Low-growing species can cope especially well, and will not interfere with stunning views.

Wind damage and stunting

Exposure causes slow, stunted growth—a tree in an exposed garden can be as little as half the size of one of the same age and species in a sheltered garden. Trees and shrubs can also be "pruned" by the prevailing wind. In an exposed inland garden, very cold winds are usually the main enemy. If you garden on the coast, you should benefit from a mainly frost-free climate because sea temperatures rarely drop below freezing, and thus keep the winds coming over them warm. On the down side, salt spray borne on the breeze can "fry" leaves and often kills plants as effectively as frost.

Using plants for shelter

Minimize the effects of wind by using a shelter belt of plants. Unlike solid walls and fences, which can cause wind to accelerate and eddy through a garden, plants slow it down gently. A shelter belt can be anything from a hedge to a dense planting of trees and shrubs. One of the best hedging plants for seaside gardens is salt-tolerant *Griselinia littoralis*, while hornbeam (*Carpinus betulus*) makes a good, dense hedge for exposed inland gardens.

Roses often thrive in exposed sites because the good air circulation helps prevent fungal diseases and general damp. Choose varieties with strong flower colors, such as 'Hertfordshire', that will resist fading in high light levels.

Shelter belts or hedges filter and slow wind very effectively to protect other plants in the garden. Choose plants of an appropriate size for your garden—pine trees will grow quite large, whereas roses are more compact.

You can also use synthetic windbreak materials. These usually take the form of a closely woven fabric mesh, which can be attached to regularly spaced posts. A double layer will provide greater protection. A windbreak like this will slow the wind considerably over a short distance. The mesh can be removed as soon as the plants are settled—between three and five years. Individual plants can be cosseted in a similar way with a "cage" of mesh netting on posts, and trees or shrubs planted as small "whips" (usually one to two years old) can be given a head start if surrounded by a biodegradable plastic guard to create a warm and sheltered microclimate.

Plants for exposed gardens

Successful seaside gardens often take a cue from nature by using native plants that proliferate on the shoreline. These can provide a backdrop for more exotic ornamentals. Alternatively, provide shelter for plants that don't cope so well with exposure to the elements. Thick wind-reducing plantings on the boundaries of the garden, and a series of "garden rooms" surrounded by more hedges within, create very sheltered areas. In a mild coastal climate, this will enable you to grow tender, exotic plants.

The Royal Horticultural Society garden at Hyde Hall (*see p.72*) is an example of an exposed inland garden, perched on top of a hill among the rolling, arable landscape of mid-Essex, England. Throughout summer, the prevailing wind is a hot, dry southwesterly that can desiccate plants in no time, while in winter a cold northeasterly can cause significant wind chill. Despite this, the garden is bursting with plants, the majority of which have been selected because of their tolerance to exposure.

Top plants for exposed sites

1 *Buddleja davidii* 'Fascinating'
Butterfly bush
Large, fast-growing, deciduous shrub whose lilac-pink flowers are irresistible to butterflies. H 10 ft (3 m); S 15 ft (5 m).

2 *Prunus spinosa* 'Purpurea'
Blackthorn or Sloe
A hardy tree or shrub with sharp spines that makes a good hedge. Its edible black fruits are favored by both birds and gin drinkers. H 15 ft (5 m); S 12 ft (4 m).

3 *Crambe maritima*
Sea kale
A perennial native to coastal areas with tough, leathery leaves and large clusters of small, white flowers. Stems can be eaten as a vegetable. H 30 in (75 cm); S 24 in (60 cm).

4 *Juniperus squamata* 'Meyeri'
Juniper
An evergreen, coniferous shrub with blue-green foliage. Originally from the Himalayas, so tolerant of extreme weather. H 12–30 ft (4–10 m); S 20–25 ft (6–8 m).

5 *Othonna cheirifolia*
Othonna
Evergreen shrub with fleshy leaves and daisylike yellow flowers in summer. H 24 in (60 cm); S 3 ft (1 m).

6 *Rosa* 'Hertfordshire'
Rose
Ground-cover rose, with large clusters of flat, carmine-pink blooms, freely produced from summer to fall. H 18 in (45 cm); S 3 ft (1 m).

7 *Helichrysum italicum*
Curry plant
Small, evergreen shrub with strongly aromatic, silvery gray leaves. H 24 in (60 cm); S 3 ft (1 m).

8 *Griselinia littoralis*
Griselinia
Good as single plants but also useful as hedging or a coastal windbreak. Vigorous. H to 25 ft (8 m); 15 ft (5 m).

9 *Tamarix* x *ramosissima*
Tamarisk
Deciduous shrub with feathery leaves and tiny pink flowers. Withstands winds and sea spray. H 15 ft (5 m); S 15 ft (5 m).

10 *Potentilla fruticosa* 'Red Ace'
Cinquefoil
A compact, deciduous, flowering shrub that is fully hardy and tolerant of poor soil. H 3 ft (1 m); S 5 ft (1.5 m).

11 *Cytisus battandieri*
Pineapple broom
Pineapple-scented flowers in mid- to late summer. H 15 ft (5 m); S 15 ft (5 m).

12 *Festuca glauca* 'Elijah Blue'
Blue fescue
Tufted, evergreen grass, with spikelets of blue-green flowers in summer. H to 12 in (30 cm); S 10 in (25 cm).

13 *Glaucium flavum*
Yellow horned poppy
Branched gray stems of golden yellow or orange poppylike flowers, in summer. H 12–36 in (30–90 cm); S to 18 in (45 cm).

14 *Hippophae rhamnoides*
Sea buckthorn
Silver-green, deciduous shrub often used for windbreaks, hedges, and to stabilize sand dunes. H 20 ft (6 m); S 20 ft (6 m).

15 *Rosmarinus officinalis*
Rosemary
Best-known as a kitchen herb but can grow into large, resilient shrubs tolerant of poor soil. H 5 ft (1.5 m); S 5 ft (1.5 m).

16 *Agrostemma githago*
Corn cockle
A fast-growing annual that requires full sun and flowers best on poor soils. H 24–36 in (60–90 cm); S 12 in (30 cm).

Rock gardens

Traditionally, rock gardens have served as self-contained areas in which gardeners can grow the sort of plants normally found in high, mountainous, alpine habitats. For this reason, they are purposely constructed from rocks and stones in an attempt to mimic the bare outcrops, scree slopes, ledges, and crevices found at high altitudes. Most of the plants for which such environments are created are small and compact, and tend to be tough and drought-resistant. Many of them flower profusely, in a range of brilliant colors. Contemporary garden design, however, has broadened the definition of the term "rock garden." Drawing inspiration from Mediterranean and desert landscapes, and employing lots of hard surfaces such as paving, pebbles, river stones, and gravel, modern rock gardens are as likely to feature cacti and succulents as true alpines.

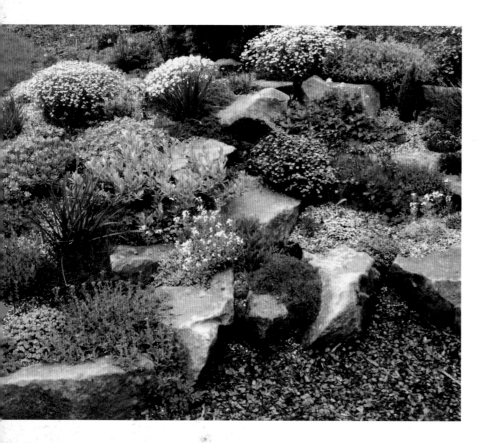

Many rock-garden plants are low-growing and deep-rooted. They form neat clumps or spread horizontally in a matlike fashion. Most have small leaves to minimize water loss due to evaporation.

Creating a rock garden

The best site for an alpine rock garden is an open, sunny, south-facing slope. Almost all rock plants grow best with lots of light and in well-drained soil. They don't do well where the soil is damp and heavy, or where there are overhanging trees. If you're constructing a rock garden from scratch, first lay a foundation of coarse rubble, such as broken bricks, to create a gradient or form a mound. Cover it with inverted sod or a sheet of polypropylene punctured to let water drain through freely. Place your rocks on top, positioning the largest ones first. Salvaged or second-hand stones are best—particularly sandstone, limestone, or tufa. Aim for a natural-looking mix of bare outcrops, miniature ravines and gullies, and plenty of crevices for planting. Infill the stones with good garden soil, and then spread a top layer of specially prepared soil comprising equal parts loam, garden compost or leafmold, and sharp sand or grit. You may want to leave some areas as scree beds, covering them with a mix of coarse grit, gravel, or stone chips.

Choosing plants for rock gardens

Some rock-garden plants are true "alpines," and some aren't. Those that are actually come from alpine regions, where they grow above the tree line, having evolved to withstand the extreme weather conditions found at high altitudes. Most are dwarf or low-growing and hug the ground to avoid buffeting from strong winds. Their leaves tend to be small, fleshy, and often covered by woolly hairs in order to help them retain moisture that would otherwise evaporate in hot sun or constant wind.

Nonalpines include dwarf trees and shrubs, plants that originate on cliffs and shores in coastal areas, a wide range of miniature bulbs, and even cacti and succulents. In general, all share the same dislike of being waterlogged and a preference for free-draining, moderately fertile soils.

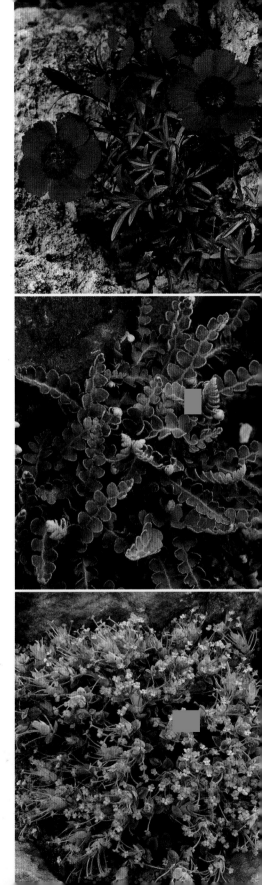

(top) **The Alpine pink** *Dianthus alpinus* 'Joan's Blood' bears magenta-pink flowers in summer.

(center) **The rusty-back fern** *Asplenium ceterach* is a dwarf variety that rarely grows taller than 6 in (15 cm).

(bottom) **Marjoram or oregano** is an herb well-suited to rock gardens. *Origanum amanum* has funnel-shaped, pink flowers.

Top plants for rock gardens

1 *Limnanthes douglasii*
Poached egg plant
Bright flowers from summer to fall. Once established, it will self-seed freely. H 6 in (15 cm); S 6 in (15 cm).

2 *Campanula poscharskyana*
Campanula
Low-growing perennial that produces masses of star-shaped, violet flowers. H to 6 in (15 cm); S to 24 in (60 cm).

3 *Armeria maritima*
Sea thrift
Seaside plants with grasslike foliage and small rounded flowerheads. H to 8 in (20 cm); S to 12 in (30 cm).

4 *Aubrieta deltoidea*
Aubretia
Often seen cascading over walls, aubretia is one of the earliest and most colorful spring-flowering perennials. H 2 in (5 cm); S 24 in (60 cm) or more.

5 *Silene schafta*
Campion or catchfly
A useful rock-garden plant that does not flower until late summer and into fall. H 10 in (25 cm); S 12 in (30 cm).

6 *Thymus doerfleri* 'Bressingham'
Thyme
A ground-hugging, aromatic, evergreen shrub that will spread naturally in crevices. H 6 in (15 cm); S 18 in (45 cm).

7 *Gentiana septemfida*
Gentian
A small, spreading perennial grown primarily for the intense blue or purple-blue flowers that appear in late summer. H to 6–8 in (15–20 cm); S to 12 in (30 cm).

8 *Sedum spathulifolium* 'Cape Blanco'
Stonecrop
Bright yellow, star-shaped flowers above a mat of rosette-shaped, silver-green leaves. H 4 in (10 cm); S 24 in (60 cm).

9 *Saxifraga sancta*
Saxifrage
Tufts of bright green leaves from which clusters of small yellow flowers appear in spring. H 2 in (5 cm); S 8 in (20 cm).

10 *Narcissus* 'Tête-à-tête'
Daffodil
A dwarf variety that produces up to three golden yellow flowers per stem early in spring. H 6 in (15 cm).

11 *Gypsophila repens* 'Dorothy Teacher'
Baby's breath
A compact, alpine perennial with blue-green foliage and tiny flowers that are pale pink when new but darken over time. H 2 in (5 cm); S to 16 in (40 cm).

12 *Viola wittrockiana* Crystal Bowl Series
Pansy
Compact plants in a wide range of clear colors. Summer-flowering. H to 5 in (12 cm); S to 12 in (30 cm).

13 *Anemone blanda* 'Violet Star'
Anemone
A low-growing perennial with relatively large flowers that are a deep, dark violet color. H 6 in (15 cm); S 6 in (15 cm).

14 *Geranium cinereum* 'Ballerina'
Geranium
A dwarf hardy geranium that produces attractive, red-veined pink flowers with dark centers from late spring onward. H to 6 in (15 cm); S to 12 in (30 cm).

15 *Ajuga reptans* 'Multicolor'
Bugle
A small, creeping perennial with dark bronze-green leaves splashed with cream and pink. H 6 in (15 cm); S 24–36 in (60–90 cm).

16 *Juniperus communis* 'Compressa'
Juniper
Slow-growing dwarf conifer whose restrained height keeps it in proportion with other rock-garden plants. H to 32 in (80 cm); S 18 in (45 cm).

Choosing and buying plants

If you find yourself bewildered by the huge choice of plants available, look for the tried-and-tested star performers from each group of plants. A good garden center or mail-order nursery should have information about which plants have shapely forms, plenty of flowers, or show good disease resistance, and grow reliably in your hardiness zone.

Where to buy your plants

Your local garden center can be a good place to buy plants, since most have a wide range of well-grown stock, but be aware of possible pitfalls. First, garden centers tend to put plants in full flower on prominent display, to entice gardeners into impulse buying. This is where research comes in handy. Stick to your list as much as possible and resist these temptations—you may find you have no space or no suitable site or soil for a hastily purchased plant. Many garden-center staff are not horticulturally trained, and so any advice they offer may not be authoritative. The expert staff are often on duty on weekends when the stores are busiest, so seek them out if you need advice. Lastly, garden centers usually don't grow plants, but bring them in from a number of suppliers, so the quality may vary.

Specialist nurseries usually raise their plants on-site, and their staff can offer growing advice and help you to identify the best cultivars for the conditions in your garden. Many nurseries offer mail-order catalogs, which enable you to buy a wider range of plants. Plants are also available over the Internet, but remember to check that suppliers' websites are secure and their business is trustworthy.

A good plant is a healthy specimen that will grow quickly and strongly. Look for new stems or buds: a multistemmed clematis like the one on the left is better than a single-stemmed one.

Look under the pot; if there are no or few roots growing through the drainage holes, the plant is probably not rootbound.

Slide the plant out of the pot to check that the roots are pale, plump, and not congested, and that the soil is moist.

Reject a weedy pot; weeds are a sign of neglect. They stress the plant as they compete for food and water.

Choosing your plants

Sometimes it is tempting to buy plants in flower because you can see what the flowers look like, but root growth ceases while plants are blooming, so they may take longer to establish. If you are thinking of buying large plants for instant impact in your garden, remember that mature specimens are slower to recover from the shock of planting than smaller, younger ones. Large plants also have more leaves from which to lose water, and tend to dry out before their roots can establish and take up moisture. Young plants planted at the same time often overtake larger ones after a year or so.

Health checks

Make sure that you buy a sturdy, healthy specimen with a balanced shape and multiple stems. Leaves should also be free from signs of pests or diseases. Most plants at garden centers and nurseries are container-grown. Check the root ball; if there is a solid mat of roots, or if they coil around the base or sides of the pot, the plant has been in it for too long and may suffer from a lack of nutrients.

You usually get what you pay for, so go to a well-run nursery or garden center for healthy, top-quality plants. However, even in the best establishments, it's still worth checking the plants over. Reject any plant that looks sickly or shows signs of disease or pest infestation.

When to plant

Although it is usually best to plant your purchases right away, there are times when this is not possible. In these cases, care for the plants until you can plant them. Container-grown plants can be kept in their pots for a few weeks before planting out, provided you keep them well watered during dry periods.

If you buy tender bedding plants in early spring, before the threat of frost has passed, keep them in a frost-free place, such as a greenhouse or cool conservatory, or on a windowsill, until warmer weather arrives. Make sure you keep their soil moist and deadhead them regularly. In a frost-free greenhouse, you can plant bedding in hanging baskets or larger containers and grow them on so they fill out before being set outside for the summer.

4. Perennials, Annuals, & Biennials

These plants are the mainstay of the traditional flower garden, and will probably provide you with most of the flowers in your beds and borders from early spring right through to the end of fall. Perennials are long-lived and, although they may die down in fall, provided they are hardy enough to survive the winter they will come up again and produce new growth the following spring. They may well be with you for many years, so unless you're prepared to move them, give some thought to where best to site them before planting. Annuals, in contrast, only last for a year and either self-seed or are sown or planted afresh each spring. Biennials have a two-year cycle, flowering only in their second year.

A mixed border needs a little planning. Think ahead about where to place your plants according to how large they grow and when they bloom. Use annuals to fill spaces and to take over from early-flowering bulbs.

Growing perennials

Most hardy herbaceous plants do best if planted in fall, when the soil is still warm and in time for winter rain to help new roots grow. Tender types prefer spring planting. There are times when you should avoid planting, such as summer or winter—new plants suffer in long spells of dry, very wet, or cold weather. Strong wind, fierce sun, and frost can all damage exposed roots. Also, avoid planting soon after heavy rain or a period of waterlogging, and don't dig or walk on clay soil when it's wet, since this can cause compaction, and squeezes out oxygen needed by plant roots.

Preparing the planting site

Weeds abhor a vacuum, and any clear soil is likely to be colonized by them. If left to grow, they will dramatically reduce the amount of water, nutrients, and light that your new plants receive, just when they need it most. Take some time to clear weeds properly before planting. Use a fork to pry deep-rooted perennial weeds out of the soil; if you leave any roots, they may reshoot.

Some ornamental plants, particularly those that form dense ground cover, such as geraniums, hog the border in much the same way as weeds. Make sure that you place new plants a decent distance away from them, or cut back the ground cover until the newcomers are established. Large hedges and trees may also compete with new plants for water and light. Additionally, avoid planting closer to walls than about 18 in (45 cm), because the ground at the foot of a wall can be extremely dry—this area is called a rain shadow.

Delphiniums are classic herbaceous border plants. Some varieties grow very tall and tend to become top-heavy, especially after rain, so they will probably need supporting.

Weeding thoroughly is essential before planting a border. Neither new annual seedlings nor reemerging perennials will thrive if weeds are competing with them for light, water, and nutrients.

Planting a perennial

Prepare the soil of the planting area to get your plant off to a flying start (*see pp.112–113*). Add organic matter to improve the soil's structure and encourage new root growth—the farther the roots spread, the greater the area from which they can obtain water and nutrients. Water the plant well about an hour or two before planting, since a dry root ball is difficult to wet when planted.

1 **Stand the plant in its pot** in position in the border. Do a visual check—will it have enough room to spread to its mature height and width, or will it be overwhelmed by neighboring plants?

2 **Dig in plenty of organic matter**, such as garden compost or well-rotted farmyard manure, over and beyond the planting area. Dig a planting hole about twice as wide and as deep as the pot or root ball.

3 **Knock the plant out of its pot** and gently tease some roots free from the root ball—this encourages them to spread into the surrounding soil, especially if the roots are congested. If you see any dead or damaged roots, trim them off with pruners.

4 **Stand the plant** in the hole. Ensure that the top of the root ball is level with the soil surface; if needed, remove or add soil to get the level right. Draw soil around the root ball with your fingers to fill in the hole, making sure that the level of the plant doesn't change.

5 **Use your heel** to firm the soil gently around the plant. This removes any air pockets and makes sure that the roots are in contact with the soil. Double-check that the plant hasn't become lopsided.

6 **Water thoroughly after planting** to settle the soil around the roots and eliminate any air pockets. Apply a thick mulch to help keep in the moisture, and water your new plant in dry periods.

Supporting perennials

There is a misconception that herbaceous plants must be both sheltered and staked. This is not always the case: bear in mind that gardens full of movement are more dynamic and interesting: while woody plants will not bend much in the breeze, flowers and grasses will billow attractively. Many tall plants are self-supporting, including foxgloves (*Digitalis*), mulleins (*Verbascum*), and *Verbena bonariensis*. Choose carefully, and you can grow a range of plants even in fairly windy sites—they often develop sturdier stems, more resistant to wind damage. Plants grown in a sheltered spot are more likely to suffer in a sudden blast of wind than those that are exposed all season long.

That said, you may want to grow some herbaceous plants with delicate or weak stems, which are prone to splay out due to the weight of their flowerheads or when beaten down by strong wind or rain. In exposed areas, supports are almost always necessary; insert them in spring, when leafy growth begins, as plants that have flopped never recover their former glory. Provided the support is a little shorter than the eventual height of the plant, it will soon be hidden by the foliage (though remember that some materials actually have a charm of their own).

Choosing suitable supports

A clump of bamboo thinned annually will yield a good supply of canes to be used as supports. Cut when young, the stems will be pliable enough to bend into hoops and semicircles. If you have space, you could also grow a hazel or willow to provide a supply of twiggy stems and thicker stakes for building rustic tripods.

Canes and pea sticks will be adequate for many perennials. You can lift plants that have flopped with canes and string, but if you bunch the stems tightly, they could look worse than before. For large-flowered, tall plants, such as dahlias, peonies, and chrysanthemums, supports that allow the stems to grow through them are more effective. Metal grids on long spikes can be raised as the plants grow. For very tall dahlias and delphiniums, tie each stem to a sturdy single stake using garden string or raffia.

Where a border flanks a path or lawn, hold plants back with metal or wooden-log edging, or make your own from freshly cut bamboo canes bent into arcs. Several of these can be used to form a low temporary fence or to keep bushy growth in check, preventing it from swamping lower plants.

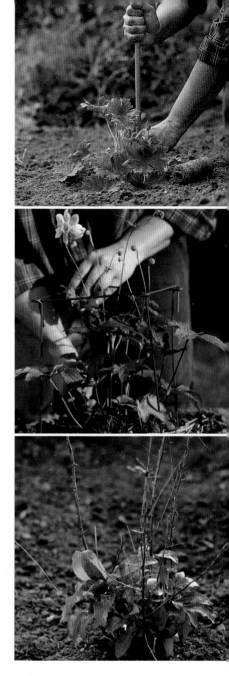

(top) **Prevent delphiniums from flopping** by staking them when they are young. To avoid eye injuries, use cane tops or corks to cover the ends of canes.

(middle) **Long-lasting metal stakes** can be linked together to encircle clumps of different sizes. Dark-colored supports will be the least visible.

(bottom) **Twiggy sticks** provide a subtle and inexpensive way to support growing plants.

Deadheading perennials

Picking off the dead flowerheads not only tidies up a plant, but also channels its energy into growth and producing new flowers, rather than into seed production. As a result, deadheading will prolong the flowering display of some plants, such as sweet peas (*Lathyrus*), pelargoniums, and verbenas.

What to deadhead

Although not an exact science, there are a few guidelines:
■ Large flowers, such as those of some pelargoniums, can be snapped off individually. The soft stems of most perennials are easily pinched through.
■ If the tall flowering stems of delphiniums, lupines, and foxgloves (*Digitalis*) are cut off, new smaller heads might sprout lower down.
■ Dainty plants with small flowers such as lobelias are best trimmed using scissors.
■ For repeat-flowering roses, cut off blooms with pruners at the cluster point, either one by one, or just above a leaf.

Shearing back

An easy way to deadhead some plants is to trim them back with shears. Trim after flowering for more flowers, fresh foliage, or both. Try this with border campanulas, catmint (*Nepeta*), hardy geraniums, knapweeds (*Centaurea*), border salvias, and pulmonarias.

In early spring, shear back growth of winter-flowering heathers (*Erica carnea*), ling (*Calluna*), periwinkles (*Vinca*), St. John's-wort (*Hypericum calycinum*), and ornamental grasses, taking care not to cut into the new shoots. Also shear off old leaves on epimediums in late winter, before they flower.

LEAVE TO SEED

Not all plants need deadheading. Some will not produce more flowers, and may develop seedheads if flowers are left in place. These may be very attractive, especially in winter, and the scattered seed could result in a crop of seedlings the next year. Try leaving the flowerheads on the following plants:

■ Achillea
■ Astilbe
■ Clematis like *C. tangutica*, *C. orientalis*, and their hybrids
■ Eryngium (*above*)
■ Ornamental grasses
■ Poppies
■ Sedum
■ Teasel

(far left) **Cosmos will bloom** almost continuously throughout summer and up to the first frost if you continue to deadhead it. Take the long flower stems back to the ferny foliage below.

(left) **Shearing catmint** back after it has flowered in summer will stimulate the plant into producing more fresh foliage and a second, smaller flush of blooms.

Perennials for winter and spring interest

1 *Brunnera macrophylla* 'Dawson's White'
Brunnera
The white in the name refers to the leaf edges. The flowers, appearing in spring, are bright blue. H 18 in (45 cm); S 24 in (60 cm).

2 *Anemone blanda* 'Radar'
Anemone
Low-growing, clump-forming anemone; in spring, has magenta-colored flowers with white centers. H 6 in (15 cm); S 6 in (15 cm).

3 *Arum italicum* 'Marmoratum'
Lords and ladies
Attractive marbled, green leaves are welcome in winter; followed by flowers in summer, and orange-red berries through to fall. H 12 in (30 cm); S 6 in (15 cm).

4 *Hepatica nobilis* var. *japonica*
Hepatica
Tiny, low-growing plant whose white, pink, or blue flowers open as early as late winter or early spring. H 3 in (8 cm); S 6 in (15 cm).

5 *Bergenia* 'Sunningdale'
Elephant's ears
Early-flowering evergreen that produces clusters of bright lilac-magenta flowers from early spring onward. H 12–18 in (30–45 cm); S 18–24 in (45–60 cm).

6 *Helleborus torquatus* 'Dido'
Hellebore
'Dido' has slightly ragged, purple and lime-green flowers and narrow, deciduous leaves. H 16 in (40 cm); S 18 in (45 cm).

7 *Primula veris*
Cowslip
Delicate clusters of small, scented, yellow flowers held on single, upright stems. H 10 in (25 cm); S 10 in (25 cm).

8 *Aubrieta deltoidea*
Aubretia
Often seen cascading over walls and rock gardens, aubretia is one of the earliest and most colorful spring-flowering perennials. H 2 in (5 cm); S 24 in (60 cm) or more.

Perennials for fall interest

1 *Catananche caerulea* 'Bicolor'
White cupid's dart
Daisylike, white flowers with purple centers appear in midsummer and last well into fall. H 20–36 in (50–90 cm); S 12 in (30 cm).

2 *Ligularia dentata* 'Desdemona'
Ligularia
Large, daisylike orange flowers and heart-shaped, leathery leaves, brownish green on top and maroon-purple beneath. H 4 ft (1.2 m); S 24 in (60 cm).

3 *Inula hookeri*
Inula
Flat, yellow flowers with delicate, narrow petals and dark yellow centers. Flowers into mid-fall. H 30 in (75 cm); S 18 in (45 cm).

4 *Kniphofia triangularis*
Red-hot poker, torch lily
The flower spikes are shorter than other varieties, but appear later and last into fall. H 4 ft (1.2 m); S 24 in (60 cm).

5 *Phlomis russeliana*
Phlomis
Yellow flowers from late spring to early fall; they form pretty dried seedheads in winter. H 3 ft (1 m); S 24 in (60 cm).

6 *Liriope muscari*
Lilyturf
Spikes of lavender or violet-blue flowers from early to late fall, and long, dark-green leaves. H 12 in (30 cm); S 18 in (45 cm).

7 *Physalis alkekengi*
Chinese or Japanese lantern
Grown less for its summer flowers than for the papery red lanterns enclosing orange-scarlet berries that appear in fall. H 24–30 in (60–75 cm); S 36 in (90 cm).

8 *Salvia patens* 'Cambridge Blue'
Salvia
Intensely blue, hooded flowers are sparse but last from midsummer to mid-fall. H 18–24 in (45–60 cm); S 18 in (45 cm).

Perennials for shade

1 *Aquilegia formosa*
Columbine
Delicate red, orange, and yellow flowers.
Happy in full sun or in full shade.
H 24–36 in (60–90 cm); S 18 in (45 cm).

2 *Ophiopogon planiscapus* 'Nigrescens'
Lilyturf
Low-growing evergreen with grasslike,
purple-black leaves, lilac flowers in
summer, and blue-black berries in fall.
H 9 in (23 cm); S 12 in (30 cm).

3 *Hosta* 'Francee'
Hosta
Large, heart-shaped, olive-green leaves
with irregular white edges. Lavender-
blue flowers in summer. H 22 in (55 cm);
S 3 ft (1 m).

4 *Epimedium grandiflorum* 'Crimson
Beauty'
Barrenwort, bishop's miter
Ground-cover plant for a shady border.
Copper-tinted green leaves and crimson
flowers. H 12 in (30 cm); S 12 in (30 cm).

5 *Pulmonaria* 'Mawson's Blue'
Lungwort
Spreading, ground-cover plant with dark
green leaves and deep blue flowers in spring.
H to 14 in (35 cm); S to 18 in (45 cm).

6 *Pachysandra terminalis*
Pachysandra
Spreading, shade-tolerant perennial with
glossy, evergreen leaves and small white
flower spikes in early summer. H 8 in
(20 cm); S indefinite.

7 *Aruncus dioicus* 'Kneiffii'
Goatsbeard
Tiny, creamy white flower plumes stand
up above delicate, fernlike, green leaves.
H 4 ft (1.2 m); S 18 in (45 cm).

8 *Bergenia* 'Morgenröte'
Elephant's ears
Leathery-leaved, clump-forming evergreen
with deep carmine flowers; thrives in
partial shade beneath trees. H 12–18 in
(30–45 cm); S 18 in (45 cm).

Perennials for cut flowers

1 *Alstroemeria ligtu* hybrids
Peruvian lily
Funnel-shaped, lilylike flowers in a wide range of colors, from pinks and reds to yellows and oranges. H 18–24 in (45–60 cm); S 2–3 ft (0.6–1 m).

2 *Aster novi-belgii* 'Lady in Blue'
Michaelmas daisy
Masses of daisylike flowers produced from late summer to mid-fall. H 12 in (30 cm); S 20 in (50 cm).

3 *Paeonia officinalis* 'Rubra Plena'
Peony
Large, double, vivid pink-crimson flowers with satiny, ruffled petals in early to mid-summer. H 30 in (75 cm); S 30 in (75 cm).

4 *Dahlia* 'David Howard'
Dahlia
Miniature variety with rounded, bronze-orange flowers and dark-bronze foliage. H 30 in (90 cm); S 24 in (60 cm).

5 *Delphinium* 'Fenella'
Delphinium
A traditional, old variety producing tall spikes of purple-tinged, gentian-blue flowers with black eyes. H to 5 ft (1.5 m); S 30 in (75 cm).

6 *Helenium* 'Crimson Beauty'
Helen's flower
Daisylike flowers with drooping petals in deep copper-red that turn brownish as they age and prominent, domed centers. H 36 in (90 cm); S 24 in (60 cm).

7 *Lychnis chalcedonica*
Jerusalem or Maltese cross
Flat heads of small, cross-shaped flowers that are a brilliant vermilion in color in early and midsummer. H 3–4 ft (1–1.2 m); S 12–18 in (30–45 cm).

8 *Gaillardia* x *grandiflora* 'Dazzler'
Blanket flower
Large daisylike flowers, up to 6 in (15 cm) across with a domed orange-red center and bright orange-red petals with yellow tips. H 24 in (60 cm); S 26 in (50 cm).

Growing annuals and biennials

You can achieve fantastic results quickly by sowing hardy annuals directly into the soil in spring, either to create an entire annual display or to fill gaps in beds and borders. It works out much cheaper than buying summer bedding in trays. Three weeks before sowing, weed and fork over the area; two weeks later, clear any weeds. This reduces the amount of weeding you need to do later, as well as eliminating competition for the water and nutrients that seedlings need. Biennials can be treated in much the same way as annuals; because they are left in the ground the winter after sowing, though, they may need protection from frost.

Sowing for success

Annuals and biennials look more natural if sown in informal swaths, or drifts, that merge into one another. To obtain this effect in a bed or border, draw out irregularly-shaped areas, one for each annual, in the soil with a cane. Then mark out straight rows (*see p.113*) within the drifts and sow one type of seed in each. Sowing in rows will make it easier to distinguish the annual and biennial seedlings from weed seedlings. Then you can easily remove weeds by hoeing between the rows.

Once you have sown the seeds, don't forget to label them. In dry weather, water the seedlings using a watering can with a fine spray—a spout causes runnels in the soil and puddling, which can wash seedlings out of the ground, and in some soil leaves a hard crust on the surface.

Half-hardy annuals and biennials usually need to be sown in containers so they can develop undercover (*see pp.294–297*); they can be planted out once the weather warms up. Check the seed packet for more details. Remember that biennials will not flower until their second year; some will need protection from frost during winter (known as overwintering) using cloches or horticultural fleece.

Hardy annuals provide an easy way to introduce a splash of color into your garden. Here, orange pot marigolds add zing to the soft blues and purples of love-in-a-mist and cornflowers.

COLLECTING SEEDS

Annuals produce seedheads in a variety of shapes, such as pods or papery capsules, and most are easy to collect for sowing early the following spring. It is not worth collecting seed from F1 hybrids—the seedlings won't look like the parent plant.

On a warm, dry day, when the seedheads have turned brown (*below*, love-in-a-mist), snip them off and lay on sheets of paper towel or newspaper to dry.

When they are completely dry, shake the seeds out onto a piece of paper. Pick out any chaff, and store the seed in a labeled paper bag or envelope (plastic bags encourage mold). Store them in a cool, dry place out of bright light.

How to sow annuals and biennials

Before sowing, prepare the soil well, removing all the weeds and forking it over. Most annuals and biennials like free-draining soil, so if you have heavy clay, dig in some coarse sand or grit to open it up. Choose an open, sunny site, not too close to large trees or shrubs, which will reduce germination rates.

Always follow the recommendations on the seed packet for correct planting depths and spacing. Sow as thinly as possible, and once the seeds have germinated and the seedlings have produced a few leaves, thin them out by removing all but the strongest, leaving the correct space between each young plant.

1 **Rake the soil** to level it, and clear away any large stones. Use the head of the rake to break down lumps to create a crumbly soil.

2 **Use a bamboo cane** to create some straight drills in which to sow the seed—press the cane lightly into the soil, as shown.

3 **Transfer a little seed** to the palm of your hand, and gently tap it with your finger to trickle the seed gradually into the drill.

4 **Cover the seeds** by gently raking a fine layer of soil over the drills. Then firm the soil lightly with the head of your rake.

5 **Water well**, using a watering can with a fine spray. A sprinkling is less likely to disturb the seeds or cause a soil crust to form.

6 **Protect seeds** from being scratched up by birds and cats by covering the area with some twiggy sticks or a layer of netting.

Easy annuals from seed

1 *Papaver somniferum*
Opium poppy
Pink, red, mauve, or even white flowers give way to seedheads that can be either cut for dried arrangements or left to self-seed. H to 4 ft (1.2 m); S to 12 in (30 cm).

2 *Lathyrus odoratus*
Sweet pea
A wide range of flowering annuals, most are climbers and many are highly scented. Flowers in almost every color except yellow. H 6–8 ft (2–2.5 m); S to 3 ft (1 m).

3 *Helianthus* 'Triomphe de Gand'
Sunflower
Mid-sized sunflower with golden-yellow flowers up to 5 in (12 cm) in diameter. H 5 ft (1.5 m); S 4 ft (1.2 m).

4 *Nigella damascena*
Love-in-a-mist
Good as long-lasting cut flowers; the seed capsules can be dried for flower arrangements. Self-seeds freely. H to 20 in (50 cm); S to 9 in (23 cm).

5 *Eschscholzia californica*
California poppy
Fragile, poppylike flowers open fully only in sun and vary in color from yellow, orange, and gold to red, pink, and white. Almost indestructible. H to 12 in (30 cm); S to 6 in (15 cm).

6 *Lagurus ovatus*
Hare's-tail
A compact, annual grass with pale green leaves and fluffy, hairy seedheads. Sow in groups or drifts in spring. H 20 in (50 cm); S 12 in (30 cm).

7 *Callistephus chinensis* Ostrich Plume Series
China aster
Sow during spring for feathery pink, crimson, or white flowers from late summer until late fall. H to 24 in (60 cm); S 12 in (30 cm).

8 *Calendula officinalis*
Pot marigold
Daisylike flowers range in color from bright yellow and orange to cream and apricot. Will continue flowering until the first fall frost. H 12–30 in (30–75 cm); S 12–18 in (30–45 cm).

9 *Tropaeolum majus*
Nasturtium
Some climb, while others scramble. All grow vigorously and produce masses of red, orange, or yellow flowers. H 3–10 ft (1–3 m); S 5–15 ft (1.5–5 m).

10 *Cosmos bipinnatus* Sensation Series
Cosmos
Flowers well in to late summer, so sow in situ in late spring to fill gaps in a border left by early-flowering plants. H 36 in (90 cm); S 18 in (45 cm).

11 *Nicotiana* 'Lime Green'
Tobacco plant
Bright, lime-green flowers have a wonderful evening and nighttime fragrance. Flowers from midsummer to fall. H 24 in (60 cm); S 10 in (25 cm).

12 *Ipomoea purpurea*
Common morning glory
A climbing annual with trumpet-shaped flowers that may be blue-purple, magenta, pink, or white. Needs full sun. H 18 ft (5.5 m); S 10 ft (3 m).

5. Bulbs

Regardless of the size of your garden, there is always space for bulbs. They discreetly die down when not in bloom, and their compact size means that they can easily be tucked in among other plants. When they do perform, they offer a high ratio of flower to foliage. If you plan ahead, you could have bulbs flowering in your garden nearly year-round. Bulbs can be left to naturalize in lawns or to carpet shaded woodland areas in spring. They also provide the early season's show in your borders, before herbaceous plants have stirred into growth, and make excellent companions for perennials and deciduous shrubs, filling the gaps between these plants. This chapter covers not only true bulbs but also corms, rhizomes, and tubers.

A mixed planting of early-flowering, bright red 'Showwinner' tulips and white and purple crocuses creates a startling blaze of spring color.

Growing bulbs

Bulbs are easy to grow, as long as you follow a few simple rules. In the wild, most bulbs grow in climates with hot, dry seasons, and prefer light, free-draining soils in full sun. Bulbs from woodlands need moist, rich, but free-draining soil, and dappled sun or part shade. In short, if you know where your bulbs come from, it's easier to provide a home for them in the garden. For example, woodland bulbs, such as bluebells, colchicums, cyclamen, and snowdrops, come into growth when the weather is sunny and wet—this will be when overhanging trees are leafless, since the foliage reduces the amount of light and rainwater reaching the bulbs. The bulbs come into leaf, flower, and set seed between late fall and spring, and are dormant again by the time the trees are in full leaf.

What is a bulb?

It can be confusing when you discover that the word "bulb" is often used as a blanket term for any plant that has an underground food-storage organ. So as well as true bulbs (as in snowdrops and lilies), there are three other forms: corms (crocuses), rhizomes (irises), and tubers (cyclamen). Each type of bulb has evolved to cope with distinct growing conditions.

True bulbs are made of leaves layered as in an onion, with a papery skin. Lily bulbs are looser in form, and lack a papery skin.
Corms are the thickened base of the stem; they have 1–2 buds at their apex. Tiny cormlets may grow around the base.
Rhizomes are swollen stems, which usually grow horizontally near the soil surface, and have several buds along them.
Tubers come in two types. Root tubers (as in dahlias) have buds at the stem base. Stem tubers (as in cyclamen) have surface buds.

(clockwise from top left)
Daffodils, dahlias, irises, and gladioli

IDENTIFYING BULBS

Getting to grips with what the different types of bulbs look like will help you to determine their planting needs.

clockwise, from top left:
True bulb (e.g., daffodils, tulips, and lilies)
Tuber (e.g., dahlias and cyclamen)
Rhizome (e.g., irises and lily-of-the-valley)
Corm (e.g., gladioli and crocuses)

A succession of flowers from bulbs can be enjoyed through much of the year, not just in spring. Try starting with snowdrops in late winter, followed by lilies in summer and nerines in fall.

Planning a year-round display

The late winter and early spring show is dominated by bulbs with flowers in clear yellows and whites, such as trilliums, winter aconites, and snowdrops. These are soon followed by the first daffodils, like *Narcissus* 'February Gold'. The pretty, scented pheasant's-eye daffodils are among the last of the season to bloom. Early irises, hyacinths, grape hyacinths, and ipheions belong to the blue brigade that cheers spring gardens. Crocuses, of course, encompass all three colors.

It is not until the tulips emerge that the color spectrum broadens. Tulips come in every color except blue, and range from the dainty (*Tulipa sylvestris*, great for naturalizing) to the seriously baroque. The parrot tulip 'Rococo' has fiery red, fringed petals with green streaks.

As spring turns to summer, alliums (ornamental onions) decorate our borders. Their distinctive flowerheads, in globes or pendent clusters, range from the cheerful golden *Allium moly* and tall 'Purple Sensation' to the giant spheres of metallic, starry flowers of *Allium christophii*, which are great for drying. More irises add dusky hues of blue, amber, rust, and purple.

Fewer bulbs perform in midsummer, but they include some stunners. Lilies are elegant and stately; many have strong perfumes. Gladioli add height. Eucomis, with its flowerheads of greenish or reddish, starry flowers topped by a pineapple-like tuft, makes a wonderful architectural plant for late summer. Finally, in the fall there are crocuslike colchicums and vivid pink nerines.

Choosing and buying bulbs

Most bulbs are available for purchase in their dormant state, so buy spring-flowering bulbs in late summer or fall and summer-flowering ones in spring. Don't leave it too late; if you buy bulbs soon after they arrive at the retailer, you'll get the pick of the healthiest and most vigorous.

Choose bulbs that are big, firm, and plump; plants from dried-up bulbs will not thrive. Reject any with blemishes—indications of pest damage or disease—or signs of rot or mold, or any that are missing their papery skins or have started sprouting. Look for bulbs that are labeled "from cultivated stock" or "nursery-propagated" to avoid buying any that are collected from the wild.

Planting bulbs

Here are a few tips you should follow when planting to get the most out of your bulbs:

■ Most bulbs should be planted 2–3 times the depth of the bulb; the exception is for tulips, which should be planted 3–4 times the depth.

■ Space bulbs at distances 2–3 times their width.

■ Plant corms and tubers with their growth buds upward—they are not as distinct as on true bulbs.

■ Plant scaly bulbs, such as lilies, on their sides to stop them from accumulating moisture in between their scales and rotting.

■ If your soil is cold, wet, or poorly drained, grow bulbs in pots.

■ If your soil is light and dry, add well-rotted organic matter to prevent the roots from drying out.

Bulbs in mixed borders

When planting spring bulbs in borders, you may be tempted to plant them close to the front because they flower early in the season. However, since most other plants in the border won't be very visible, you can spread bulbs around in little clusters or drifts, from the front to the back. Then, as their foliage dies down, they will be hidden behind the emerging growth of shrubs or perennials. Later-flowering bulbs are often better scattered in between other plants, which also help to disguise their unsightly dying foliage.

PLANTING BULBS IN A BORDER

Most bulbs prefer free-draining soil, as they like to be fairly dry when dormant; fork some sand into the planting area in heavy soil. Bulb planters take out a plug of soil for each bulb, but can be laborious on stony soil or over large areas. Instead, dig out an entire planting area.

1 **Position the bulbs** in the hole with their pointed tips upward. Discard any bulbs that show signs of disease or rotting.

2 **Fill in the hole** with soil, firming as you go with your fingers, taking care not to damage the bulbs' growing tips.

3 **Chicken wire** over the planted area will prevent animals from digging them up. Remove it as soon as the first shoots appear.

Planting bulbs in grass

It you want to create a natural-looking display of bulbs in a lawn, make life easy for yourself by adapting your planting technique to the size of the bulbs.

To plant small bulbs, cut an H-shaped cut in the sod and fold back the flaps (*top*). If necessary, dig out the soil to the recommended depth for the bulb type. Place bulbs randomly, growing point upward. Replace the soil, then fold back the sod and firm.

To plant large bulbs in grass, start by scattering the bulbs randomly over the ground. Use a bulb planter to make a hole, then place the bulb inside (*bottom*). Fill in the hole with soil from the bottom of the core, then replace the circle of turf, firming in gently.

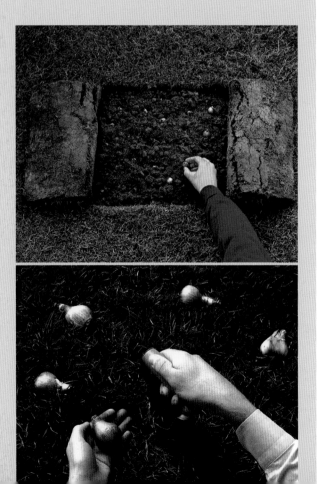

Planting "in the green"

Winter aconites, snowdrops, and anemones have tiny bulbs that dehydrate very quickly and often fail to produce decent plants. If you buy these bulbs, soak them overnight in water before planting to help kickstart them into life. It is best, though, to buy plants "in the green," which means they have been lifted directly after flowering while the foliage is still fresh. This gives them a chance to reestablish before becoming dormant. Although plants in the green are more expensive, they are more reliable. If you have clumps in the garden, lift the bulbs as soon as they have flowered, tease them apart, and replant where you want them. Make sure that the pale bases of the leaves are below the soil.

Bulb aftercare

While they are in growth, bulbs need fertilizing, watering, and deadheading. Tall-stemmed bulbs may also need staking. After flowering, most bulb foliage dies back. Some gardeners bend the foliage over and tie it up to make it look neat, but this stops nutrients from the leaves from getting to the bulb and helping to form flower buds for next year. Let the leaves die down naturally until they are dry and yellow (about five weeks), and then cut them off.

To keep bulbs flowering well, divide them every 3–4 years. Using a fork, pry out a dormant clump, tease apart, discard any diseased bulbs, and replant. Tulips may stop blooming if they're not lifted after flowering each year. After lifting, clean the bulbs, store in paper bags in a cool, dry place, then replant them in fall. Dahlias, gladioli, and tuberous begonias should be lifted and stored over winter.

Lifting and storing in winter

Except in mild areas where frost is light or nonexistent, lift tender bulbs and tubers over winter. They can be kept in any cool, frost-free shed, greenhouse, or conservatory, maintaining a minimum temperature of 40–45°F (4–7°C). Cut down the stems of begonias and lift the tubers just before the frosts start. Dry them off and dust with sulfur before packing them into trays of dry compost or bark.

Lift gladioli in mid-fall when the leaves are beginning to turn yellow. Snap off the stems and dry off the bulblike corms. You'll find there is a withered old corm under the new one; pull this off and discard it. You will also find baby corms, which you can grow on like seeds. Dust the new corms with sulfur dust and store them in shallow trays either in a cool, dry, airy shed or in a room indoors.

Chocolate cosmos (*Cosmos atrosanguineus*) should be lifted in fall as a precaution in very cold areas. Dig up tubers before the frosts start, and store under cover in trays of barely moist potting mix. Check all stored bulbs and tubers regularly for signs of rot throughout the winter, and discard any that have succumbed.

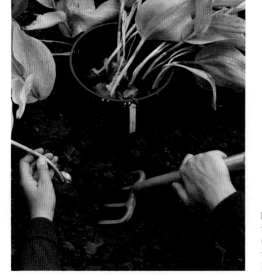

Lift bulbs with a fork once the plant's leaves turn yellow. Clean off the soil, remove the foliage, and leave the bulbs indoors to dry overnight.

STORING DAHLIAS OVER WINTER

1 Cut old stems back to a height of about 6 in (10 cm) above the ground. Fork the soil gently to loosen it, and carefully lift out the tubers.

2 Store tubers upside-down somewhere frost-free until they have dried out completely. Then up-end them, cover them with bark or vermiculite, and keep them dry until spring.

3 Plant out tubers in spring and cover with soil so the crown at the base of the stem, where new shoots will appear, is about 1–2 in (2.5–5 cm) below ground.

Bulbs for spring

1 *Gladiolus tristis*
Gladiolus
Aromatic, pale yellow or cream flowers on thin, arching stems in spring. Gladioli grow from corms. H 18 in–5 ft (45 cm–1.5 m); S 2 in (5 cm).

2 *Iris* 'George'
Iris
A vigorous but short variety that grows from bulbs. Velvety, rich purple flowers. H 5 in (13 cm).

3 *Narcissus* 'Suzy'
Daffodil
A mid-spring daffodil with large, open flowers in primrose yellow with bright orange centers. H 16 in (40 cm).

4 *Chionodoxa* 'Pink Giant'
Glory of the snow
Not "giant" at all but a small, low-growing bulb with delicate, pretty pink flowers. H 4–8 in (10–20 cm); S 2 in (5 cm).

5 *Muscari armeniacum*
Grape hyacinth
Spikes of tightly clustered, tiny blue flowers in spring. Perfect for containers and rock or woodland gardens. H 16 in (40 cm); S 2 in (5 cm).

6 *Crocus minimus*
Crocus
A deep lilac- or purple-colored crocus that does not flower until late spring. H 3 in (8 cm); S 1 in (2.5 cm).

7 *Hyacinthus orientalis* 'Ostara'
Hyacinth
Large, upright spikes of violet blue flowers. Good for borders or containers. H 8–12 in (20–30 cm); S 3 in (8 cm).

8 *Fritillaria meleagris*
Snake's-head fritillary
Nodding, bell-like, purple and white flowers excellent for naturalizing in grass or meadow gardens. H to 12 in (30 cm); S 2–3 in (5–8 cm).

3

4

7

8

11

12

15

16

9 *Anemone pavonina*
Anemone
A Mediterranean variety that likes full sun and blooms in spring. Flowers may be red, pink, or purple. H 10 in (25 cm); S 6 in (15 cm).

10 *Galanthus* 'Atkinsii'
Snowdrop
Single, nodding, white flowers appear as early as late winter and into early spring. H 8 in (20 cm); S 3 in (8 cm).

11 *Narcissus* 'Satin Pink'
Daffodil
An unusual variety with pure white petals and a pink-flushed central cup. Flowers in mid-spring. H 18 in (45 cm).

12 *Eranthis hyemalis*
Winter aconite
Bright yellow flowers in late winter and early spring. Aconites grow from small, knobby tubers. H 2–3 in (5–8 cm); S 2 in (5 cm).

13 *Erythronium* 'Pagoda'
Dog's-tooth violet
Sulfur-yellow flowers in spring, backed by glossy, deep green leaves with bronze mottling. Suited to moist, shady woodland. H 6–14 in (15–35 cm); S 4 in (10 cm).

14 *Tulipa* 'Ballerina'
Tulip
Sweetly scented, flame-colored blooms in blood-red and orange-yellow. H 24 in (60 cm).

15 *Ornithogalum dubium*
Star-of-Bethlehem
Unusual variety with waxy, yellow-orange flowers instead of the usual white. H 6–12 in (15–30 cm); S 6 in (15 cm).

16 *Camassia leichtlinii*
Quamash
Tall spikes of star-shaped, creamy white flowers. Good for cutting. H 24 in–4 ft (60 cm–1.2 m); S 4 in (10 cm).

Bulblike plants for summer and fall

1 *Dahlia* 'Arabian Night'
Dahlia
Large, double, rich burgundy-red flowers from early summer, from tubers. H 4 ft (1.2 m); S 20 in (50 cm).

2 *Iris latifolia*
English iris
Midsized, narrow-leaved iris with flowers in blue, violet, or white. H 10–24 in (25–60 cm).

3 *Lilium henryi*
Lily
Flowers in late summer, with deep-orange blooms spotted with black markings. H 3–10 ft (1–3 m).

4 *Roscoea cautleoides*
Roscoea
Useful as a plant that likes damp, shady sites and flowers all summer and into fall. It grows from tubers. H 22 in (55 cm); S 6 in (15 cm).

5 *Lilium candidum*
Madonna lily
Sweetly scented, pure white flowers in midsummer. H 3–6 ft (1–2 m).

6 *Allium cernuum*
Nodding onion
Stiff, upright stems support small, drooping, deep pink, bell-shaped flowers. H 12–24 in (30–60 cm); S 2 in (5 cm).

7 *Colchicum speciosum* 'Album'
Fall crocus
Small white flowers appear in fall before the leaves. Corms can be planted in grass. H 7 in (18 cm); S 4 in (10 cm).

8 *Tigridia pavonia*
Tiger flower
Short-lived exotic needing full sun. Irislike flowers in summer. Lift bulbs in winter. H 5 ft (1.5 m); S 4 in (10 cm).

9 *Crocus ochroleucus*
Fall crocus
Tiny, late-summer-flowering crocus with creamy-white flowers with yellow throats. H 2 in (5 cm); S 1 in (2.5 cm).

10 *Fritillaria camschatcensis*
Black sarana, chocolate lily
The dark purple-black flowers appear in early summer, but beware: they have a notoriously unpleasant odor. H to 18 in (45 cm); S 3–4 in (8–10 cm).

11 *Begonia* 'Herzog von Sagan'
Begonia
Large, yellow flowers with pink, frilled margins. Lift the tubers in fall before frost. H to 36 in (90 cm); S 18 in (45 cm).

12 *Galtonia viridiflora*
Galtonia
Arching stems support nodding, green-and-white flowers in late summer. H to 3 ft (1 m); S 4 in (10 cm).

13 *Nerine bowdenii*
Nerine
Small but flamboyant, lilylike flowers in bright pink appear in fall, when most other colourful blooms are fading. H 18 in (45 cm); S 3 in (8 cm).

14 *Scilla peruviana* 'Alba'
Squill
Tight, conical clusters of small, star-shaped, white flowers in early summer. H 6–12 in (15–30 cm); S 2–4 in (5–10 cm).

15 *Canna* 'Endeavour'
Canna
Tall stems of bright red, irislike flowers from midsummer to early fall. Cannas grow from rhizomes. H 5–7 ft (1.5–2.2 m); S 20 in (50 cm).

16 *Cyclamen hederifolium*
Cyclamen
Traditionally grown under trees, the pink flowers appear in mid- and late fall, before the leaves. Grows from tubers. H 4–5 in (10–13 cm); S 6 in (15 cm).

6. Shrubs

Shrubs are vital furnishings for the garden. They provide a permanent structure, adding seasonal interest. They can also be used to define areas of the garden, and to disguise eyesores, such as compost piles or bins, as well as neighboring yards. Shrubs are incredibly versatile and there is one to suit every design and location, whether your garden is large or small. They range from dwarf, ground-covering plants, suitable for the front of a border, to large architectural specimens that grow to a couple of yards tall and wide and make great screens or backdrops.

A flowering shrub such as *Hydrangea paniculata* 'Unique' provides a double whammy: attractive green foliage all spring and summer, plus beautiful, conical, white flowerheads in August and September.

Growing shrubs

Use shrubs to help define your garden style. For a modern or minimalist design, consider mass plantings of one plant, or two contrasting plants, such as the evergreen *Viburnum davidii* with its small white flowers followed by steely blue berries, teamed with clipped golden privet, *Ligustrum* 'Vicaryi'. In a more traditional setting, use a wider range of plants for diversity and interest. Some shrubs, such as *Viburnum plicatum* 'Mariesii', with its tiers of horizontal branches, have such a striking appearance that they can be used to provide a focal point at the end of a vista, or a centerpiece in a lawn or gravel garden.

Shrubs for structure

Ideal as background plants, shrubs provide solidity and structure, creating a sense of permanence in a planting plan. Avoid planting in a uniform line against a fence; instead, use plants of different heights and shapes strategically in beds and borders. Use large dark specimens behind light-colored flowers; small shrubs, such as dwarf boxwood, thyme, or euonymus to edge the front of a plan; and those with dramatic foliage, such as *Fatsia japonica*, *Sambucus* *racemosa* 'Sutherland Gold', or a tree peony (*Paeonia delavayi*) to provide focal points.

Remember that many shrubs have pretty flowers and berries; seasonal features should be considered carefully when making planting plans. For example, while the white-flowered *Choisya* 'Aztec Pearl' will set off the oval blue flowerheads of *Ceanothus* 'Blue Mound' brilliantly, the orange blooms of a kerria matched with pale pink montana clematis 'Elizabeth' will create a sickly mix.

(left) **The red fall berries** of cotoneaster are a good meal for birds stocking up for winter. Site one near a window to watch them feeding. The white spring flowers also attract insects.

(right) **Nectar-rich plants**, such as the butterfly bush, *Buddleja davidii*, will attract butterflies and moths into your garden with mauve, pink, red, or white summer flowers.

(opposite) **The unusual shape** of *Viburnum plicatum* 'Mariesii' makes it an eye-catching focal point in a border. This large shrub has horizontally layered branches that are laden with white flowers in spring.

Year-round interest

To create an exciting shrub border, compile a list of plants that perform at different times of the year.

■ **Winter and early spring** can make gardens appear bare, so choose plants that flower at this time. The yellow flowers of forsythia and pink flowering currants (*Ribes sanguineum*) kick-start spring, together with the early magnolias. Certain shrubs that flower in winter and early spring have a wonderful perfume—such as witch hazel (*Hamamelis*), daphne, and winter boxwood (*Sarcococca confusa*). The corkscrew hazel (*Corylus avellana* 'Contorta') sports wild, twisted stems, and dogwoods (*Cornus*) brighten up winter gardens with colorful bark. Evergreens with different leaf shapes and textures will help to increase visual contrast.

■ **In spring and summer**, shrubs that flower include berberis, lilac (*Syringa*), and scented osmanthus and philadelphus; smaller shrubs make colorful fillers in the border. For summer color, plant buddlejas, hydrangeas, escallonias, fuchsias, and hypericum. Summer-flowering heathers will thrive if planted in acidic soil.

■ **Fall** will often bring a cold snap after a warm summer, producing fantastic foliage color. Winning plants for this time of the year include Japanese maples, deciduous cotoneasters, and azaleas, dogwoods (*Cornus*), and the smokebush (*Cotinus*). Birds soon devour certain fruits and berries; to extend the season of interest, combine shrubs with a few whose fruit is less attractive to wildlife, such as some crab apples (*Malus*), yellow-berried cotoneasters, and roses.

Choosing and buying shrubs

At the garden center, look for healthy plants in clean, damp soil that show no sign of pests or diseases. Reject plants that look to be in poor health, as they may be carrying a disease that will affect your other plants. Don't be tempted by the "sales" corner—the plant is usually only there because it has been standing around too long, and is unlikely to do well once planted.

■ **Leaves** should not be discolored, pale, or wilting. Look for specimens with bright, new leaves or shoots, as this shows that they are growing well.

■ **Roots** should not be poking through the holes at the base or growing in circles indicating the plant is potbound; tap the rootball out of its pot to check. A healthy root system means that the plant should quickly establish after planting.

■ **Top-heavy plants** should be avoided; their roots are likely to have become congested.

■ **Dead leaves** are a sign of neglect or disease. If diseased plants and their soil are brought into the garden, the problem may spread to other plants.

■ **Weeds** growing on the soil are a sign of neglect, and will have deprived it of water and nutrients. They may also be carrying diseases that can affect the plant.

(left) **Leaves bearing holes** could be a sign that the plant is infected by pests or diseases.

(right) **A healthy root system**—that isn't potbound—means that the plant should take off quickly once planted.

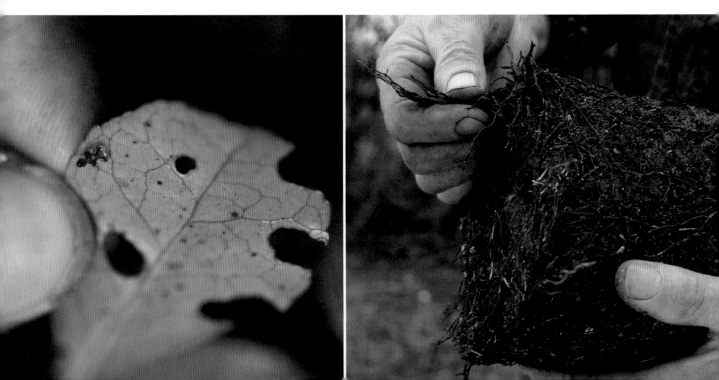

Planting a shrub

If you have just bought a container-grown shrub, first water it well by plunging it—pot and all—in water for about an hour, then allow it to drain. To remove the rootball from the pot, turn the pot over and hold the shrub firmly with the fingers of one hand between the stems at soil level, then gently squeeze the sides of the pot, or tap the base, until it slides off. Carefully tease out any roots that are curling around the rootball.

1 **Dig a planting hole** that is as deep and twice as wide as the rootball of the shrub (here, a viburnum). Place the plant into the hole and lay a pole across the top to make sure that it is at the same depth as it was in its original container. Adjust the depth of the hole if necessary.

2 **Set the shrub in the hole**, and then backfill around the rootball with your hands, firming the soil with your heel. At the same time, create a slight saucer-shaped depression within the soil surrounding the plant—this will encourage water to collect naturally over the root area.

3 **Prune lightly only if necessary**: cut out any stems that are dead or unhealthy, and prune any that are growing toward the center of the plant back to a healthy, outward-facing bud or shoot. Water the plant well, and then apply a mulch, making sure that it does not touch the stems.

Transplanting a shrub

If you decide that a shrub is in the wrong place, you can simply move it. The younger the shrub, the easier and more successful the move should be. The best time to transplant a deciduous shrub is in the fall; move evergreens in the spring, just before the new growth emerges. Prune the shrub back by a third before transplanting—this will compensate for root loss, and should make it easier to handle.

1 **Mark out a circle** around the outer edge of the roots using a spade. The roots of shrubs normally do not spread out farther than the extent of the stems before they were pruned.

2 **Dig a trench around the circle** and use a fork to loosen the soil around the roots. With a spade, dig under the rootball so that it can be lifted out of the soil, cutting through woody roots if necessary.

3 **Tilt the plant to one side** and feed a piece of burlap or a ground sheet under it. Then rock the shrub to the other side and pull the material through so that the plant is sitting on top of it.

4 **Enlist the assistance** of someone else to help you carry the shrub to its new location in the garden. This is especially important with a large, heavy rootball like this one.

5 **Dig a hole** that is twice as wide and the same depth as the rootball at the new site. Carefully lower the shrub into the new hole.

6 **Fill in with soil** around the roots, ensuring that there are no air gaps. Firm the soil with your foot. Water well, and apply a mulch.

Pruning shrubs

Keep an eye on your shrubs throughout the year, cutting out dead, diseased, and damaged stems to keep the plants healthy. Remove any stems that are crossing and rubbing against each other, all-green shoots on variegated plants, and suckers on grafted plants. Cutting out badly placed stems and reshaping plants will improve their appearance. Some pruning methods increase growth, fruiting, and flowering, as well as stimulating the production of young, decorative stems.

When to prune

As a general rule of thumb, prune late-summer and fall-flowering plants, which usually bloom on the current year's stems, in early spring. Spring and early-summer flowering plants bloom on the previous year's wood, and should be pruned after flowering, so that the new stems have time to ripen before winter. To renovate most deciduous trees and shrubs, prune in winter when the plants are dormant. For the majority of evergreens, prune in spring, just as the new growth resumes.

Bear in mind that pruning deciduous plants in winter results in vigorous regrowth in spring. Pruning in spring and early summer produces much thinner growth, while summer pruning reduces the leafy canopy and the plant's food resources, resulting in relatively weak regrowth.

Mophead hydrangeas (*Hydrangea macrophylla*) will flower on stems produced the previous year. In mid-spring, prune old stems by up to 12 in (30 cm), down to pairs of fat, healthy buds—these will produce the flowering shoots.

To encourage new stems on multistemmed plants such as *Viburnum* x *bodnantense*, cut out any old weak stems at the plant's base. If the plant is overgrown and flowering is poor, cut down all of the stems in late spring.

Light pruning

If you are not familiar with your shrubs, prune them lightly, and see how they respond during the growing season. Prune newly-planted shrubs cautiously, as they need to grow to develop their natural beauty—although you may wish to encourage a good shape with a little pruning. For example, boxwood (*Buxus*) or yew (*Taxus*) can be clipped lightly into a sphere. Other plants, like heathers, just need shearing over to remove spent flowers, and to promote neat growth. Tip pruning, where the shoot tips are removed, can be carried out on young shrubs to encourage a bushy habit.

Many plants that should be pruned cautiously will respond to renovative pruning when they become too large for their site, their stems have become congested, or flowering is poor. In these cases, cut back the stems to near ground level when the plant is dormant, or buds are just breaking, in late winter or early spring.

Prune young shrubs, such as this mahonia, in mid-spring; this will stimulate the growth of more flowering stems, which will bloom in the coming fall/winter. Prune off the old flowering stems, cutting just above a leaf or sideshoot.

Moderate pruning

Cutting shrubs back to half their size works for those that resent being pruned to a low framework, but flower on new wood, such as sun roses (*Cistus*). Prune shrubs that flower on shoots produced the previous year, such as broom, after flowering. Remove the old flowering stems and shorten new stems to encourage more sideshoots—they will bloom the following year.

Hard pruning

Cutting back to soil level works for plants that send up shoots from below the ground, such as brambles (*Rubus*). The resulting canes are either colorful, or will flower and fruit prolifically. Leave a low framework of stems, 8–12 in (20–30 cm) high, from which new shoots can arise. Plants that produce young, colored stems, such as dogwoods (*Cornus*) and willows (*Salix*), can be pruned in this way in late winter.

Old wood tends to be unproductive, channeling energy away from flowering young stems. Remove it with a clean cut just above the new stem. Make a slanted cut so that rain water will not collect around the base of the new wood and rot it.

Pruning an early-flowering shrub

Shrubs that flower before midsummer, such as forsythia, kerria, and deutzia (*shown here*), should be pruned after they have flowered. Their blooms develop on stems that were made the year before, therefore pruning soon after flowering gives the plants time to develop new stems that will bloom the following year. Deutzias can become tall and leggy if left unpruned, but regular trimming keeps them bushy and compact, and encourages more stems of sweetly-scented flowers to develop.

1 **Inspect your plant**: this deutzia is five years old, and has become too tall, while the stems shooting up from the base are congested. Some flower buds are also suffering from frost damage.

2 **Cut out any wood** that is dead, diseased, and damaged. Then use sharp pruners to remove one in three of the congested stems, targeting the old and weak growth.

3 **Shorten the remaining stems** to a pair of strong, healthy buds, or new shoots, as shown here. Pay particular attention to crowded shoots in the center of the plant.

4 **Remove any stems that are crossing** and rubbing against each other. Also prune out shoots that are growing toward the middle of the plant.

5 **Reduce the height of the shrub** if necessary: take down the tallest stems, cutting back to healthy, outward-facing shoots or buds.

6 **The pruned shrub** is shorter and the congestion has been reduced. New growth will soon appear from the base and below pruning cuts, resulting in more flowers.

Pruning for good foliage

Hazel, elder, willow, and colored-stemmed dogwoods can all withstand hard pruning. When grown for their foliage effects, as with this variegated elder, or for their red or golden shoots, as with many dogwoods and willows, all the old stems should be pruned in late winter or early spring in order to encourage new growth.

1 **Elder is a vigorous plant**—most of the growth seen here was made during the previous year. In alternate years all the stems can be pruned back in early spring to a low framework near its base.

2 **Prune each stem** back to two or three pairs of buds above the base of the previous year's wood. Although you will get the best foliage by pruning in this way, you are also removing the flowering stems.

3 **Cut old, congested wood** in the center of the plant right down to the ground. Also remove any stems that are badly positioned, or growing toward the middle.

4 **Make smooth, clean cuts**, using loppers on all branches that are more than 1/2 in (1 cm) in diameter. Use a curved pruning saw on very thick branches, or where you need to make a cut in an awkward spot.

5 **Pruning will encourage vigorous growth**, despite the finished result looking sparse. Now the flowering stems have been removed, this spring-flowering plant will not bloom or produce berries this year.

6 **By early summer**, the elder's stems will have grown by 3 ft (1 m) or more, and the fresh, beautifully variegated leaves will unfurl to make a compact, eye-catching feature in the garden.

Shrubs for spring color

1 *Rhododendron* 'Irohayama'
Azalea
Low-growing, evergreen azalea with pale flowers that have pink- or lavender-edged petals. H 2 ft (60 cm); S 2 ft (60 cm).

2 *Leucothoe fontanesiana* 'Scarletta'
Leucothoe
Leaves are dark red-purple in color when young but turn dark green in summer then bronze in winter. H 3–6 ft (1–2 m); S 10 ft (3 m).

3 *Ceanothus* 'Concha'
California lilac
Large evergreen shrub covered with dense, heavy clusters of vivid, dark-blue flowers in late spring. H 10 ft (3 m); S 10 ft (3 m).

4 *Paeonia delavayi*
Tree peony
Tall, upright deciduous shrub form of peony with dark red flowers that can each grow to 4 in (10 cm) in diameter. H 6 ft (2 m); S 4 ft (1.2 m).

5 *Kerria japonica* 'Golden Guinea'
Kerria
Lovely, bright spring-flowering shrub with broad, hypericum-like golden-yellow flowers. H 6 ft (2 m); S 8 ft (2.5 m).

6 *Photinia* x *fraseri* 'Red Robin'
Photinia
Large evergreen shrub that can grow to the size of a small tree. New leaves are scarlet-red, but turn green as they age. H 15 ft (5 m); S 15 ft (5 m).

7 *Chaenomeles* x *superba* 'Crimson and Gold'
Flowering quince
Thorny, deciduous shrub that produces bright red flowers followed by yellow fruits. H 3 ft (1 m); S 6 ft (2 m).

8 *Kolkwitzia amabilis* 'Pink Cloud'
Beauty bush
Deciduous shrub that in late spring is completely covered in masses of deep-pink flowers. H 10 ft (3 m); S 12 ft (4 m).

Shrubs for summer and fall color

1 *Potentilla fruticosa* Princess
Cinquefoil
Low-growing, deciduous shrub with long-lasting pale-pink flowers that may fade to white in the sun. H 2 ft (60 cm); S 3 ft (1 m).

2 *Kalmia latifolia*
Calico bush
A dense bushy shrub bearing distinctive pink flowers from crimped buds in summer. H 10 ft (3 m); S 10 ft (3 m).

3 *Hydrangea macrophylla* 'Maculata'
Hydrangea
Lacecap, commonly sold as 'Blue Wave'; the blue color of the flowers is only reliable in acidic soil. H 6 ft (2 m); S 8 ft (2.5 m).

4 *Helianthemum* 'Wisley Primrose'
Rock rose, sun rose
Compact evergreen shrub with gray-green leaves and in summer pale yellow flowers with darker centers. H 8–12 in (20–30 cm); S 12–18 in (30–45 cm).

5 *Phlomis fruticosa*
Jerusalem sage
Evergreen shrub with gray-green, sage-like leaves and clusters of hooded, golden-yellow flowers. H 3 ft (1 m); S 5 ft (1.5 m).

6 *Euonymus europaeus* 'Red Cascade'
Spindle tree
Deciduous shrub or small tree with an extraordinary mixture of scarlet-crimson leaves and fuchsia-pink fruits in fall. H 10 ft (3 m); S 8 ft (2.5 m).

7 *Fuchsia* 'Andrew Hadfield'
Fuchsia
Small shrub with generous displays of single carmine-red flowers through summer and into fall. H 8–18 in (20–45 cm); S 8–12 in (20–30 cm).

8 *Leycesteria formosa*
Himalayan honeysuckle
A thicket-forming deciduous shrub with green stems. Drooping flowers are followed by purple berries. H 6 ft (2 m); S 6 ft (2 m).

Shrubs for winter color

1 *Mahonia* x *media* 'Charity'
Mahonia
Upright and spiny-leaved evergreen, architectural, with large, spiky clusters of scented flowers. H to 10 ft (3 m); S to 6 ft (2 m).

2 *Leucothoe fontanesiana* 'Rainbow'
Switch ivy
Evergreen whose dark green leaves are mottled cream and pink in winter. Clusters of white flowers in late spring. H 5 ft (1.5 m); S 6 ft (2 m).

3 *Cornus alba* 'Sibirica'
Dogwood
A deciduous shrub with bright red leaves in fall and even more vibrant red stems in winter. H 10 ft (3 m); S 10 ft (3 m).

4 *Daphne bholua*
Daphne
Upright shrub bearing clusters of fragrant pinkish-white flowers in winter, followed by fleshy fruits. H 2–6 in (5–15 cm); S 3 ft (1 m) or more.

5 *Skimmia japonica* 'Bronze Knight'
Skimmia
Vigorous evergreen shrub with dark, glossy pointed leaves and clusters of dark-red winter buds. H to 20 ft (6 m); S to 20 ft (6 m).

6 *Ilex aquifolium* 'Madame Briot'
Holly
Bushy, evergreen shrub or small tree with spiny, dark-green leaves edged with gold and bright red berries. H 30 ft (10 m); S 15 ft (5 m).

7 *Euonymus fortunei* 'Emerald 'n' Gold'
Evergreen bittersweet
A bushy, evergreen shrub bearing white-edged, bright green leaves, tinged pink in winter. H 24 in (60 cm); S 36 in (90 cm).

8 *Hamamelis* x *intermedia* 'Jelena'
Witch hazel
Tall deciduous shrub with orange flowers on bare branches in midwinter. Good fall leaf color, too. H 12 ft (4 m); S 20 ft (6 m).

Evergreen shrubs

1 *Viburnum tinus* 'Variegatum'
Viburnum
Dense, compact shrub with pointed green leaves edged with creamy yellow. Clusters of red flowers in late winter and spring. H 10 ft (3 m); S 10 ft (3 m).

2 *Pittosporum tobira*
Pittosporum
Dark-green, glossy leaves are dense enough for a line of shrubs to act as a windbreak hedge. H 6–30 ft (2–10 m); S to 20 ft (6 m).

3 *Fatsia japonica*
Japanese aralia
Large, architectural plant with huge, hand-shaped glossy green leaves. Clusters of white flowers followed by black berries. H 5–12 ft (1.5–4 m); S 5–12 ft (1.5–4 m).

4 *Origanum* 'Kent Beauty'
Marjoram, oregano
Low-growing, trailing subshrub. In summer produces pale- and rose-pink flowers, rather like hops. H 4 in (10 cm); S 8 in (20 cm).

5 *Lavandula stoechas*
Lavender
Compact, mound-forming shrub with long, thin, gray-green leaves. Dark purple flower spikes with distinctive "ears" or bracts. H 2 ft (60 cm); S 2 ft (60 cm).

6 *Laurus nobilis* f. *angustifolia*
Sweet bay, bay laurel
Large shrub or small tree that can be clipped into formal topiary shapes. Shiny oval leaves can be used as an herb. H to 40 ft (12 m); S to 30 ft (10 m).

7 *Erica carnea* 'Vivellii'
Heath
Low-growing, spreading evergreen with purple-pink flowers from late winter to spring. Makes a good ground cover plant. H 6 in (15 cm); S 14 in (35 cm).

8 *Euphorbia characias*
Spurge
An upright shrub, and a striking architectural feature plant. Flowers in spring and early summer. H 4 ft (1.2 m); S 4 ft (1.2 m).

Shrubs for fragrance

1 *Viburnum* x *burkwoodii* 'Anne Russell'
Viburnum
Compact deciduous shrub whose clusters
of pink buds produce fragrant white
flowers in mid- to late spring. H 6 ft
(2 m); S 5 ft (1.5 m).

2 *Trachelospermum jasminoides*
Star jasmine
Evergreen, woody climber with oval leaves,
and fragrant white flowers in summer.
H to 30 ft (9 m); S to 30 ft (9 m)

3 *Sarcococca confusa*
Christmas box, sweet box
Dense, dark-green evergreens that
bloom in winter with intensely fragrant
white flowers. H 6 ft (2 m); S 3 ft (1 m).

4 *Choisya* 'Aztec Pearl'
Mexican orange blossom
Compact evergreen; scented flowers in late
spring, and again in late summer, especially if
deadheaded. H 8 ft (2.5 m); S 8 ft (2.5 m).

5 *Osmanthus* x *burkwoodii*
Osmanthus
Evergreen with glossy, dark-green leaves
and white flowers that have a fragrance
like jasmine. H 10 ft (3 m); S 10 ft (3 m).

6 *Cytisus battandieri*
Broom
Tall, deciduous shrub with silver-green
leaves and clusters of yellow, pineapple-
scented flowers in summer. H 15 ft
(5 m); S 15 ft (5 m).

7 *Philadelphus* 'Virginal'
Mock orange
Powerfully fragrant, pure-white double
flowers appear on this dark-green
deciduous shrub in early or midsummer.
H 10 ft (3 m); S 8 ft (2.5 m).

8 *Daphne mezereum*
Daphne
A deciduous shrub that produces purple-
pink flowers in early spring before the
leaves appear. Fragrant but toxic. H 10 ft
(3 m); S 8 ft (2.5 m).

Shrubs for walls

1 *Escallonia* 'Langleyensis'
Escallonia
Fast-growing evergreen or semievergreen with glossy leaves and pink flowers. Makes a good hedge. H 6 ft (2 m); S 10 ft (3 m).

2 *Fremontodendron* 'California Glory'
Flannel flower
Upright, spreading evergreen best grown against sunny walls. Deep yellow flowers from late spring to fall. H 20 ft (6 m); S 12 ft (4 m).

3 *Jasminum nudiflorum*
Jasmine
Sprawling, straggly shrub that positively needs wall training and regular trimming. Tolerates north- or east-facing walls. H 10 ft (3 m); S 10 ft (3 m).

4 *Pyracantha* 'Watereri'
Firethorn
Spiny evergreen with white flowers and red berries; can be fan-trained or espaliered against walls or fences. H 8 ft (2.5 m); S 8 ft (2.5 m).

5 *Euonymus fortunei* 'Emerald Gaiety'
Evergreen bittersweet
Bushy, spreading shrub with bright green leaves whose white edges turn pink in winter. H 3 ft (1 m); S 5 ft (1.5 m).

6 *Cotoneaster horizontalis*
Fishbone cotoneaster
A deciduous shrub whose branches spread sideways in a fishbone pattern. Red leaves and bright red berries in fall. H 3 ft (1 m); S 15 ft (5 m).

7 *Garrya elliptica*
Garrya
Large, pollution-resistant evergreen with tough, leathery leaves and long gray-green catkins in mid- to late winter. H 12 ft (4 m); S 12 ft (4 m).

8 *Forsythia suspensa*
Forsythia
Deciduous shrub with golden yellow flowers in early to mid-spring, before leaves appear. H 10 ft (3 m); S 10 ft (3 m).

7. Climbers

Climbers produce long, flexible stems that they use to twine around or hook onto their support. Others cling on with specially adapted suction pads or aerial roots. Using this ability, they will scramble over plants—or anything else—to get to the best light. Use this to your advantage by planting climbers where they will disguise any eyesores in the garden, or brighten up dreary walls and fences. In a small garden, climbers are real assets, giving height without taking up too much ground space; use their foliage and flowers to dress up trellises, walls, and other garden structures, or let them climb through trees and shrubs to prolong the interest of these natural supports.

Most clematis can be trained to climb up the trunk of a tree, although some—like this *Clematis alpina*—may need some help from twine or canes until they establish their grip.

Growing climbers

Most climbers are easy to grow. They are inherently vigorous, as it is in their nature to scramble and spread upward and outward in pursuit of as much light as possible. However, woody varieties can take a few years to establish. Before they reach their required height and spread, you can fill the space with annual climbers for instant results. Sweet peas, morning glories, and climbing nasturtiums are all good choices for sunny sites, although the latter also tolerates some shade. Annual climbers are also useful for embellishing a vegetable garden, as their root systems are less invasive than those of woody or perennial plants, and they will not interfere with crop production. Sweet peas are ideal here, adding scent and encouraging pollinating insects, as well as providing a bonus crop of cut flowers.

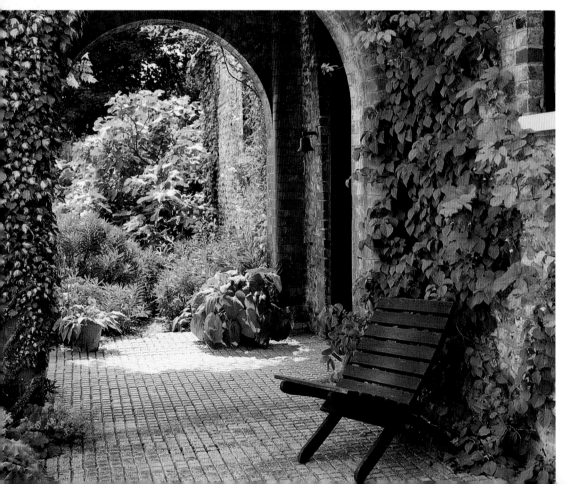

Leafy climbers are the perfect plants to create a cool retreat. Here, ivy and *Hydrangea anomala* subsp. *petiolaris* scale the house walls, softening the brickwork. Both are self-clinging, and need no additional wires or supports to climb, but be aware that they can damage old masonry.

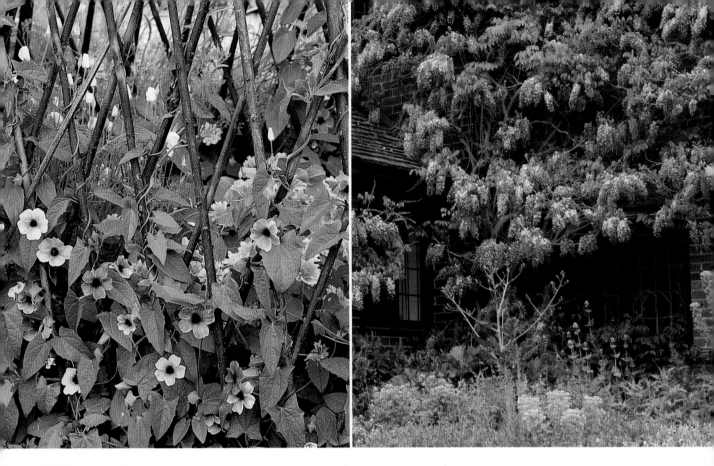

(left) **Annual climbers** such as these black-eyed Susans (*Thunbergia alata*), and also morning glories, sweet peas, and nasturtiums, are perfect for filling in gaps while a woody climber establishes, or for a wigwam support in a border.

(right) **Wisteria** dripping with scented flowers is a stunning sight in spring, but remember that it is very vigorous, needs strong support, and must be pruned regularly (*see p.157*).

Choosing climbers

While some climbers are quite small, reaching up to around head-height, others can extend to the top of large trees or over your house, so check the final heights of your chosen plants when making your plans. Also look for mature specimens in other people's gardens or parks to see how they perform.

To plant a few climbers together so that they intermingle, be sure their pruning requirements are compatible. A late-blooming large-flowered clematis, such as the dark purple 'Jackmanii Superba', makes a good match with one of the viticella types, such as the rich red 'Mme. Julia Correvon' or dark purple 'Etoile Violette', as both are pruned back to about 12 in (30 cm) in early spring (*see p.156*). But neither makes a good match with early-flowering types, such as *Clematis alpina*, which can be left or pruned after flowering, from mid- to late spring. When pruning the late-flowering variety, you might remove the wrong stems and remove the flowers from your spring performer, too. Likewise, plant climbers with similar support requirements together; understanding how they climb will help you provide the best supports (*see pp.152–3*).

Where to plant climbers

In the wild, many climbers scramble up through trees and shrubs to the light at the top. To imitate these conditions in your garden, ensure that the climber has its head in the sun, and use other plants around its base to shade the roots.

Climbers will also grow up established trees with light canopies, such as old fruit trees or robinias; light filters through the branches and encourages the climber to work its way up through the canopy. Good candidates for this type of display include rambling roses, such as blowsy pink 'Albertine' and creamy 'Bobby James', and summer-flowering, large-flowered clematis such as 'Perle d'Azur', which will start to bloom as the rose finishes.

For walls and fences supporting wall shrubs or roses, fix horizontal wires 18 in (45 cm) apart. For leaf or stem twiners, add vertical wires as well, or use large-mesh galvanized sheep or pig wire.

(clockwise from top left) **Honeysuckle, clematis, roses, and Virginia creeper.**

How climbers climb

■ **Stem twiners** (as on honeysuckle and wisteria) wind around their supports, and can be trained along wires or up posts.

■ **Stem roots** (as on ivies) are produced on certain plants to help them cling to vertical supports, such as walls and fences. They can damage old walls.

■ **Leaf-stalk and tendril twiners** (as on clematis and sweet peas) have thin, flexible leaf stalks or tendrils that twine on contact with wires, trellis, or other plant stems.

■ **Adhesive pads** (as on Virginia creepers) adhere to walls and posts, so they do not need wires, trellises, or canes for support.

■ **Hookers** (as on roses and brambles) use the thorns along their stems to hoist themselves up over their support.

Around conifers, plant just outside the edge of the canopy, and use canes to guide the stems up to the lowest branches; plant a little closer to the trunk of deciduous trees. Try to plant on the windward side of the tree, so that unsecured young shoots are blown toward the stem.

South-facing walls can be too hot for some climbers; choose a sun-lover, such as a passion flower, wisteria, trachelospermum, or a vine (*Vitis*). The soil will also be dry next to a sunny wall, so plant about 18 in (45 cm) away from it; then mulch in spring, and water in dry weather.

Plant clematis and roses where they will receive the cooler morning or early evening sun, because both dislike the intense heat of a south wall, unless it is partially shaded.

Supports for climbers

The method by which your plant climbs (*see panel, left*) will influence the type of support it requires, and its vigor will determine how large and strong the support needs to be.

On walls, the least obtrusive support to add is galvanized wire; on the other hand, fancy trellises can be used to add decorative appeal to plain surfaces. Plastic and metal ties must be checked and loosened regularly, particularly on woody climbers. Twine or raffia, with some "give," are better.

On arbors and arches, fix vertical wires to run up and down opposite sides of the posts. Train and tie in your climber in a corkscrew fashion when the stems are young and flexible.

Homemade bamboo cane tripods will support annuals and most perennials. Wigwams, pyramids, and obelisks must be sturdy enough to withstand the weight and vigor of the climber.

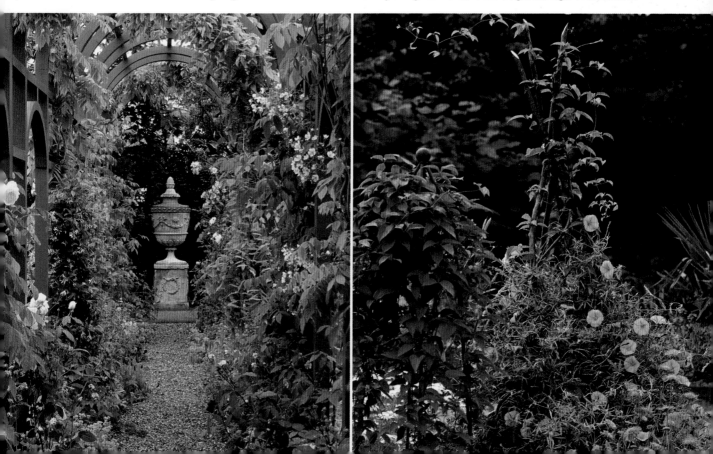

Planting against a wall or fence

Attach supports before you prepare the soil, or it will become compacted. With freestanding supports like arches and obelisks, dig over the area before erecting them, rather than negotiating around the uprights later. Vine eyes are invaluable for attaching wires to vertical surfaces. The wire can be pulled taut by giving the vine eye a few more turns once the wire is in place.

1 **Water the plant** well an hour before planting, or submerge it in a bucket of water. Allow to drain. Then dig a hole about 18 in (45 cm) from the fence, not right up against it in the dry "rain shadow." Check that the hole is deep enough for the plant.

2 **Use bamboo canes** arranged in a fan shape and leaning into the fence to form a temporary support on which to guide the climber's stems up to the permanent wires. The canes can be removed later.

3 **Lean the plant** against the canes; make sure it is still level with the soil (except for clematis, which should be about 4 in/10 cm below the surface level). Backfill the hole with a trowel, then firm in with your fists.

4 **Untie the plant** from its original cane and remove this, then fan out the main stems and tie into the canes, using soft twine in a loose figure-eight. Tying just above the cane's joints should prevent the twine from slipping down.

5 **Fluff up the soil**, then draw it up to form a circular ridge around the climber's base, creating a saucer-shaped depression. Drench the soil with water. The hollow will retain the excess water, allowing it to seep into the root area. Water the new climber regularly from then onward, especially if planting in spring.

6 **Apply a mulch** around the plant, but do not allow it to touch the stems. Once the stems reach the wires, train the outermost ones horizontally along the lower wires, and the central ones up and along the upper ones—this will ensure good coverage.

Pruning climbers

Climbers stand on other plants' shoulders to reach the light, then hog as much of it as they can. As a result, they may grow up out of sight, leaving their trailing bare stems behind—not ideal in a small garden. An easy remedy is to cut them back severely, either in late winter, as for many late-summer- or fall-flowering clematis, or every few years, as for honeysuckle. Climbers that flower early in the year and bloom on stems made the previous year should be trimmed after flowering.

When to prune climbers

Different types of climbers require pruning at different times of year—often depending on when they flower and whether the flowers appear on new or old stems.

Clematis fall into three main groups: those that flower in late winter or spring; those that flower in early summer; and the later-flowering types that bloom from midsummer to fall. For the best flowers, each should be pruned in a different way (*see below*).

Some woody climbers, including actinidia, parthenocissus, and wisteria, should be pruned in winter when dormant, like many trees and shrubs, although wisteria needs further pruning in summer for the best results (*see panel, right*).

Early-flowering clematis (including *Clematis montana, C. armandii, C. cirrhosa,* and *C. macropetala*) need little pruning. After flowering, give them a light trim, cutting back too-long or unproductive stems to a healthy bud. Renovation is possible for old, straggly plants: cut back all stems almost to the ground, but do not repeat this for at least three years.

Early- to midsummer flowering clematis can be left to their own devices, unless the plant needs restricting, when a trim after flowering will help. For renovation of old, tangled plants, cut back to buds near soil level in late winter. You may either lose that year's flowers, or the plant may flower later in the summer as a result.

Late-flowering clematis, which do not flower until late summer or fall, are pruned in late winter or early spring when the buds are starting to swell. Prune them down to a pair of plump, healthy buds about 12 in (30 cm) from the base. Alternatively, if you are dealing with a vigorous type, it can be cut down to the ground.

Pyracantha can be trained up a wall or a fence like a climber. New berries are formed at the base of stems made the previous year, so take care not to prune them off.

Pruning and training wall shrubs

Certain shrubs, while not actual climbers, can be treated almost as if they were by growing them against fences, walls, and trellises. Use the same pruning methods as for freestanding plants, but tie in stems during the summer in order to guide growth over the surface to be covered. At the same time, shorten any shoots that are growing away from the wall to make sure the shrub stays neat and narrow.

Pyracantha, cotoneaster, and ceanothus make excellent wall shrubs; all flower in spring at the base of stems made the previous year. Make sure that the wall is in good condition before fixing a trellis to it, as any repairs will be difficult once the plant is established. When pruning, take care not to cut back too hard into the old wood if you want blooms and berries. Shorten all new sideshoots in midsummer, leaving two to three leaves to encourage flower formation the following year, and to make any berries more visible.

PRUNING AN ESTABLISHED WISTERIA

Wisteria is a special case, where shortening the sideshoots promotes the formation of flower buds. You will need to prune twice: once in summer, and again when the plant is dormant in winter. For large plants, you may need a sturdy ladder to reach the top.

1 In summer, after flowering, prune back the sideshoots to within five to seven leaves from the main stem, and tie in new growth.

2 In winter, shorten the new stems that have formed after you pruned in summer. Take these back to leave two buds. The short sideshoots that are left will produce lots of spring blooms.

Climbers for flowers and foliage

1 *Tropaeolum speciosum*
Flame nasturtium
A perennial, climbing variety of nasturtium with vermilion flowers in summer followed by small blue berries. H 10 ft (3 m).

2 *Solanum crispum* 'Glasnevin'
Solanum
Fast-growing climber with small, oval green leaves and clusters of purple-blue flowers with yellow centers in summer. H 20 ft (6 m).

3 *Rhodochiton atrosanguineus*
Rhodochiton
A leaf-stalk-twining climber with heart-shaped, green leaves and dark purple and red pendantlike flowers. H 10 ft (3 m).

4 *Vitis coignetiae*
Vine
Relative of the grapevine with unpalatable fruits. Grown for its huge leaves and vibrant fall color. H 50 ft (15 m).

5 *Eccremocarpus scaber*
Chilean glory flower
Fast-growing climber with dramatic tubular flowers; grows well as an annual in temperate climates and may overwinter in warm areas. H 10–15 ft (3–5 m).

6 *Hedera helix* 'Eva'
Ivy
A variegated ivy with small but dense foliage heavily splashed with white. Good for lightening a gloomy wall. H 4 ft (1.2 m).

7 *Actinidia kolomikta*
Actinidia
The pink- and white-splashed leaves are the main attraction, although on young plants leaves are green. H 15 ft (5 m).

8 *Passiflora caerulea* 'Constance Elliott'
Passion flower
Fast-growing climber with long, green leaves and exotic, scented white flowers in summer and fall. H 30 ft (10 m).

Climbers for scent

1 *Jasminum officinale* 'Argenteovariegatum'
Jasmine
Late summer-flowering, hardy, twining jasmine, with variegated leaves edged in cream. H 40 ft (12 m).

2 *Wisteria floribunda* 'Alba'
Wisteria
Large, woody, deciduous climbers that can live for many years once established. White, hanging flower clusters up to 2 ft (60 cm) long. H 30 ft (10 m).

3 *Lonicera periclymenum* 'Serotina'
Honeysuckle
Powerfully scented flowers in mid- and late summer. Both flowers and berries are very popular with wildlife. H 22 ft (7 m).

4 *Solandra maxima*
Chalice vine, cup of gold
Vigorous evergreen climber with fragrant, trumpet-shaped, golden-yellow flowers. Needs a warm spot. H 23–30 ft (7–10 m).

5 *Trachelospermum jasminoides*
Star jasmine
Woody evergreen that needs a sunny, sheltered wall. Pure white, scented flowers in mid- to late summer. H 28 ft (9 m).

6 *Lathyrus odoratus*
Sweet pea
Vigorous tendril climbers available in hundreds of varieties. Flowers in shades of red, pink, mauve, blue, and white—often scented. H 6 ft (2 m).

7 *Akebia quinata*
Chocolate vine
Large, twining, woody climber with spice-scented, cocoa-colored flowers sometimes followed by long fruits. H 30 ft (10 m).

8 *Beaumontia grandiflora*
Herald's trumpet
The shape of the scented, white flowers gives this evergreen climber its common name. It flowers from late spring to summer. H 15–50 ft (5–15 m).

Climbers for shady walls

1 *Hedera helix* 'Dragon Claw'
Ivy
Most ivies are suitable for a cold wall.
This quick-growing, curly-leaved variety
is also known as 'Curly-Q'. H 6 ft (2 m).

2 *Schizophragma integrifolium*
Schizophragma
Large, heavy, deciduous climbers
related to hydrangeas, with similar
foliage and clusters of creamy-white
flowers. H 40 ft (12 m).

3 *Vitis coignetiae*
Vine
Dark green leaves turn a vibrant,
saturated red in fall. Sadly, the small,
black grapes taste unpleasant.
H 50 ft (15 m).

4 *Hedera hibernica*
Ivy
A fast-growing ivy with triangular, dark-
green leaves that will grow almost
anywhere. H 30 ft (10 m).

5 *Hydrangea petiolaris*
Climbing hydrangea
A wall-climbing variety with large, white
flowerheads and leaves that turn from
green to gold in fall. H 50 ft (15 m).

6 *Lonicera* x *americana*
Honeysuckle
Deciduous honeysuckle that grows well
in shade. Extremely fragrant flowers
followed by small, red berries. H 22 ft
(7 m).

7 *Hedera pastuchovii* var. *cypria*
Ivy
A wall-climbing ivy originally from Cyprus
with triangular green leaves marked with
gray-green veins. H 10 ft (3 m).

8 *Lathyrus latifolius*
Everlasting pea
Perennial climber with slender, blue-
green leaves and strings of small, pink-
purple flowers. H 6 ft (2 m).

Fast-growing climbers

1 *Allamanda cathartica*
Golden trumpet
Vigorous evergreen grown largely for its bright yellow flowers from summer to fall. H 25–50 ft (8–15 m).

2 *Ipomoea coccinea*
Scarlet morning glory
A quick-growing, twining climber grown as an annual. Bright red and yellow flowers in summer. H 10 ft (3 m).

3 *Passiflora caerulea*
Blue passion flower
Vigorous climber that flowers from summer into fall, then produces edible but uninteresting, orange-yellow fruits. H to 30 ft (10 m).

4 *Fallopia baldschuanica*
Fallopia
Also known as the "mile-a-minute plant," its name says it all. Useful for quickly covering ugly walls—or entire buildings. H 40 ft (12 m).

5 *Parthenocissus tricuspidata*
Boston ivy
Vigorous form of Virginia creeper whose leaves turn wonderful fiery shades of orange, red, and purple in fall. H 70 ft (20 m).

6 *Cobaea scandens* f. *alba*
Cup-and-saucer vine
A wall-climbing variety with large, white flowerheads and leaves that turn from green to gold in fall. H 50 ft (15 m).

7 *Humulus lupulus* 'Aureus'
Golden hop
A perennial climber with beautiful golden-yellow foliage and scented flowers in summer. H 20 ft (6 m).

8 *Parthenocissus henryana*
Chinese Virginia creeper
Long, slender leaves are green with clearly marked gray or even pinkish veins; they turn bright red before dropping in fall. H 30 ft (10 m).

Early- and midsummer-flowering clematis

1 *Clematis* 'Vyvyan Pennell'
Unusual, double flowers with a lilac-colored, velvety texture in early summer.
H to 8–10 ft (2.5–3 m).

2 *Clematis* 'White Swan'
Compact variety with beautiful, semidouble white flowers. Blooms in late spring. H to 6 ft (2 m).

3 *Clematis armandii*
Strong-growing evergreen with tapering, glossy, green leaves and fragrant, white flowers in spring.
H 10–15 ft (3–5 m).

4 *Clematis* 'Blue Ravine'
Large, open, violet-blue flowers. Blooms in late spring and again in late summer. H to 10 ft (3 m).

5 *Clematis macropetala*
Deciduous, hardy clematis whose blue or violet, semidouble flowers appear from spring to early summer.
H to 6–10 ft (2–3 m).

6 *Clematis* 'Niobe'
Large, single, deep red flowers up to 6 in (15 cm) in diameter throughout summer. H to 10 ft (3 m).

7 *Clematis* 'Fireworks'
Very large, 8-in (20-cm) purple flowers with dark magenta bars down the center of each petal. H 10 ft (3 m).

8 *Clematis montana* var. *grandiflora*
Very vigorous with dark-green leaves and large white flowers in late spring and early summer. H 30 ft (10 m).

Late-flowering clematis

1 *Clematis* 'Bill MacKenzie'
Perhaps the best-known yellow clematis. Open, bell-shaped flowers followed by fluffy seedheads. H to 22 ft (7 m).

2 *Clematis* 'Polish Spirit'
Single, velvety, rich purple-blue flowers bred by Brother Stefan Franczak, a Jesuit monk from a Warsaw monastery. H 12 ft (4 m).

3 *Clematis* 'Perle d'Azur'
Small, azure-blue flowers from midsummer to fall. H 10 ft (3 m).

4 *Clematis rehderiana*
Shade-tolerant clematis with unusual tubular, scented, yellow flowers from midsummer to late fall. H 22 ft (7 m).

5 *Clematis* 'Huldine'
Cup-shaped, white and mauve flowers appear after the height of summer and last into fall. H 10–15 ft (3–5 m).

6 *Clematis* 'Jackmanii'
Late-flowering variety with velvety, deep purple flowers. A traditional cottage-garden classic. H 10 ft (3 m).

7 *Clematis* 'Purpurea Plena Elegans'
An old variety with rosy purple, double flowers that last for several weeks. H 10 ft (3 m).

8 *Clematis tangutica*
Unusual among clematis in having yellow flowers. Late-blooming, with conspicuous fluffy gray seedheads. H 20 ft (6 m).

8. Roses

Guaranteed to bring a note of romance into your garden, the rose has, for many centuries, been one of the most sought-after garden flowers. With thousands of different types to choose from, think first about how you want to use yours. There are dwarf roses for patios and pots, large shrubs to fill gaps at the back of the border, and giant ramblers that will scramble over buildings and arbors or scale trees. Consider flowering times, too; you can opt for roses that flower once a year and usually bear fruits, or others that bloom throughout summer.

A large shrub rose such as 'Buff Beauty', with its wonderful apricot-colored flowers, can fill a warm, sunny corner of the garden with fragrance throughout the summer.

Growing roses

Traditionally, roses were grown in their own gardens, but few people today have the space to plant formal rose beds. Mixing roses with other plants prolongs the season of interest, disguises the bare stems left after pruning, and attracts insects that devour aphids. Blackspot or mildew are also less prevalent in a mixed environment. While a little blackspot or mildew will not kill the plant, they are unsightly when they affect a whole bed. Try to hide the diseased foliage using other plants rather than apply pesticides that harm the environment and wildlife.

Types of roses

Roses come in many shapes and forms; because many are sold when dormant and pruned back, it is hard to imagine them in bloom. Get to know the different types and their pruning needs (*see pp.170–173*) before buying. As well as the main kinds described here, the flower shape may also appear on the label—single, with the central boss of stamens visible; semidouble, with an extra ruff of petals; or double, with a rounded mass of over 30 petals.

■ **Shrub** roses are varied in character; a few flower only once, such as some old garden roses and wilder species, while others put on a longer show. Modern shrubs like 'Sally Holmes' (*pictured*) flower repeatedly.
■ **Climbers** tend to have stiff stems with either single flowers or flowers held in clusters. 'Climbing Iceberg' (*pictured*) has showy double white flowers from summer through to fall.
■ **Ramblers** are vigorous climbers, with long, flexible stems and flowers that are borne in one burst in summer. 'Sander's White Rambler' (*pictured*) is rampant, with double, scented white flowers.
■ **Floribunda** bush roses, such as 'The Queen Elizabeth' (*pictured*), bear sprays of flowers. Like the hybrid teas, they flower best and most continuously if you cut off the dead flowers.
■ **Hybrid tea** bush roses will produce large flowers if pruned hard. 'Precious Platinum' (*pictured*) is vigorous, and bears fully double scarlet-crimson flowers.

(opposite page, clockwise from top left)
Shrub, floribunda, rambler, hybrid tea

(right) **Climber**

PLANTING A ROSE

Before planting the rose, prune off any dead, diseased, or crossing stems and damaged roots. Prepare the site by digging a hole deep enough to hold the plant, and forking some well-rotted organic matter into the bottom.

1 Lay a cane across the hole to make sure the planting depth is correct. The graft union (the bulge at the base of the stem) should be 1 in (2.5 cm) below the soil level—this will help to prevent suckers from growing.

2 Refill the hole with soil, stepping the soil down gently with your foot to remove any air pockets. Rake the soil, then water it thoroughly.

Shape and foliage

Because many roses can be quite ungainly when not in flower, look for those with a good overall shape. Species roses, such as *Rosa xanthina* f. *hugonis*, are graceful, outward-arching plants. 'Geranium' makes a handsome shrub, with its brick-red single flowers, followed by bottle-shaped rosehips in late summer. Other shapely shrubs include 'Marguerite Hilling', with large, bright pink single flowers throughout the summer, and 'Nevada', which produces creamy flowers.

Some roses also have interesting foliage, such as *Rosa glauca*, with bluey-green leaves offset by dark red stems. A few roses have scented foliage, which can become quite powerful on warm summer evenings when the atmosphere is slightly humid. Try *Rosa primula*, the leaves of which smell of incense, or *Rosa rubiginosa* with its apple-scented foliage.

Choose easy-care shrub roses for a low-maintenance garden. 'Alba Maxima', for example, needs little pruning, tolerates some shade, and bears masses of creamy-white blooms.

(far left) **Deadhead hybrid teas** by cutting back the spent flowers to a healthy sideshoot or strong outward-facing bud.

(left) **Deadhead floribundas** by cutting back whole trusses of flowers to a healthy sideshoot, leaf, or bud to promote new flowering stems.

Choosing and buying roses

With such a huge range of roses available, making a choice can be daunting. Consider how much time you want to commit to caring for your plants. As a rule, hybrid teas and floribunda roses, such as Freedom and The Times Rose, respectively, tend to be the most demanding, requiring careful pruning and being intolerant of crowding by other plants—this is why they were traditionally grown in separate rose beds.

If you have less time to spare, choose slightly tougher shrub roses. These include the old garden roses, such as albas and hybrid musks; English roses, including Redouté and Cordelia; rugosa roses, which are among the toughest, most undemanding roses available; all the species roses, like *Rosa pimpinellifolia*, *R. canina*, and *R. glauca*, as well as a large range of modern shrub and groundcover roses such as 'Marguerite Hilling', Bonica, and the Flower Carpet roses in their various colors.

A problem in small yards is the lack of sunlight, as roses are sun-lovers. It is especially important to plant roses that flower more than once in the season in a sunny, south-facing position. If your garden receives sun for only part of the day, opt for once-only flowering types. The lovely alba roses come into this group and include beauties such as the creamy-white 'Alba Maxima' and double-flowered, pale pink 'Great Maiden's Blush', both of which have the typically healthy, pale gray-green foliage that gives this group of old roses their distinctive character.

Roses are often bought by mail order, as specialist rose nurseries offer an extensive choice. The downside is that you cannot select the actual plant you want, although most of these firms have an excellent reputation and should respond immediately if you feel a rose has arrived in poor condition.

ROSEHIPS

Although some roses only flower once, in summer their blooms are followed by colorful rosehips. These add sparkle to fall and winter gardens, as well as providing a valuable food source for birds and other wildlife. All roses produce hips, although albas, rugosas, *R. moyesii*, and the dog rose, *R. canina*, provide the most dramatic displays.

Hips vary in shape as well as vigor: many rugosa roses, such as *Rosa rugosa* 'Alba', 'Nyveldt's White', and 'Fru Dagmar Hastrup' bear chubby, round red hips, while others, such as the vigorous rambler *Rosa filipes* 'Kiftsgate', produce sprays of little red buttons. To preserve hips, don't deadhead the flowers, and give your roses plenty of water throughout the growing season to swell the fruit.

Pruning bush roses

Bush roses include hybrid teas and floribundas, both of which need to be cut back hard each year to encourage new growth. But do not prune floribundas quite as ruthlessly as hybrid teas, as this will reduce the number of flowers.

Pruning hybrid tea roses

1 **Remove any shoots** that are dead, diseased, weak, or crossing shoots from the center of the bush to leave an open symmetrical framework from which new shoots can arise.

2 **Reduce the main stems** to 8–12 in (20–30 cm) above the ground, cutting back to a healthy, outward-facing bud—hybrid tea roses respond well to drastic pruning. After a few weeks, new shoots will appear, eventually producing an abundance of blooms.

To prune floribunda roses, cut the main shoots back to about a third of their length, and trim any remaining healthy sideshoots by about one- to two-thirds.

Pruning old-fashioned roses

Old-fashioned roses, such as albas, mosses, and damasks, are pruned lightly in summer after the first flush of flowers (*see right*). To renovate old specimens, cut back all but the strongest young stems to the ground, and prune those that remain, taking them back by one third of their length. Renovate after flowering or in the spring—if you choose spring, you will lose the forthcoming season's flowers.

Gallica roses are pruned in much the same way as other old-fashioned roses, but cut the sideshoots back to the main stem, or to a shoot close to the main stem.

1 **Remove any wood** that is dead and diseased, then cut back the main stems and sideshoots by one-third to a healthy, outward facing bud.

2 **When fall arrives**, cut back any extra-long whippy stems that could be vulnerable to damage by strong winter winds.

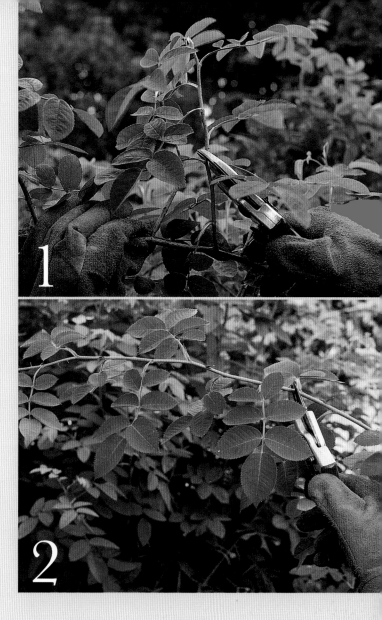

Pruning climbers and ramblers

Climbers and ramblers are best pruned in late summer, when you can see the different kinds of shoots more easily, although they will respond well to pruning in winter, too.

Each year, ramblers make lots of new growth that flowers the following year. To prevent your rose from becoming a tangled mess, cut out the oldest stems near the ground in early fall, and retain young stems, tying them in to replace the old ones. On the remaining older wood, shorten the sideshoots to two to four healthy buds from the main stem. The young stems will flower the following year, while more new shoots will grow from the base of the plant.

(top) **For rambling roses**, prune the sideshoots back to 2–4 healthy buds from the main stem.

(bottom) **Tie in the new growth** to wires or other supports.

Pruning a climbing rose

After planting a climber, do not prune back the long stems. Instead, tie them to canes and tie the canes in a fan shape to horizontal wires fixed to your support. Train young flexible sideshoots horizontally along the wires as they grow. When established, you can prune each year to keep the plant neat, and to encourage plenty of flowering shoots.

1 **Retain old wood**, except for any diseased, dead, or weak growth, which should be cut down to the ground or to a healthy bud.

2 **Only prune the sideshoots**, reducing them to about two-thirds of their original length, and cutting to a bud facing in the right direction.

3 **Tie in the newly-pruned stems** horizontally to their support. This encourages more flowering sideshoots to form along the stems.

4 **Prune back any too-long stems** that are protruding beyond the support, and sideshoots growing away from it.

Roses for pergolas and arches

1 *Rosa* **'Albertine'**
A popular rambler with arching, branching stems and clusters of coppery-pink, scented flowers. H 15 ft (5 m); S 8 ft (2.5 m).

2 *Rosa* **'Phyllis Bide'**
A vigorous climber for training up walls or pillars. Small, double flowers are buff-pink flushed with yellow. H 8 ft (2.5 m); S 5 ft (1.5 m).

3 *Rosa* **'New Dawn'**
Easy to grow; will tolerate a north-facing site. Fragrant, pale, blush-pink flowers in summer. H 15 ft (5 m); S 15 ft (5 m).

4 *Rosa* **Handel**
Modern climber, quite compact, and lovely for an obelisk or arch. Makes good new growth from the base each year. H 10 ft (3 m); S 7 ft (2.2 m).

5 *Rosa* **Laura Ford**
Upright climber with dense clusters of semidouble, bright yellow flowers touched with pink. H 7 ft (2.2 m); S 4 ft (1.2 m).

6 *Rosa* **'Compassion'**
Strongly scented, bushy climbing rose with dark-green leaves and double blooms in salmon-pink tinted with apricot. H 10 ft (3 m); S 8 ft (2.5 m).

7 *Rosa* **'Climbing Iceberg'**
A climbing version of the popular floribunda bush rose. Plenty of sweet-scented flowers, and not too thorny. H 12 ft (4 m); S 10 ft (3 m).

8 *Rosa* **Summer Wine**
Strong, upright climber with large, semiglossy leaves and coral-pink flowers in summer. H 10 ft (3 m); S 7 ft (2.2 m).

Roses for mixed beds

1 *Rosa*
Baby Love
Dwarf modern bush rose with small, bright-yellow flowers. Excellent for the front of a border or as a low hedge. H 32 in (80 cm); S 24 in (60 cm).

2 *Rosa*
'Ballerina'
Compact shrub rose with multiple clusters of single, pale-pink flowers with white centers. H 3–4 ft (1–1.2 m); S 4 ft (1.2 m).

3 *Rosa*
Bonica
A low shrub rose, excellent for ground cover; has a long flowering season followed by bright-red hips. H 3 ft (1 m); S 4 ft (1.2 m).

4 *Rosa*
'Roseraie de l'Haÿ'
Rugosa rose with wrinkled leaves; a large, dense shrub. Flowers almost continuously until late fall. H to 6 ft (2 m); S 6 ft (2 m).

5 *Rosa*
'Madame Hardy'
Vigorous Damask rose with dark-green leaves and fully double, scented, white blooms, each with a distinctive green eye. H 5 ft (1.5 m); S 4 ft (1.2 m).

6 *Rosa*
'Constance Spry'
Vigorous, sprawling shrub rose that needs hard pruning or training as a climber. Large, myrrh-scented, pink flowers. H 6 ft (2 m); S 5 ft (1.5 m).

7 *Rosa*
'Complicata'
Large, old-fashioned Gallica shrub rose with cascades of open, pink flowers. Good in wilder, more informal gardens. H to 7 ft (2.2 m); S to 8 ft (2.5 m).

8 *Rosa*
'Charles de Mills'
Suitable for hedging at the back of a border. An upright Gallica rose with large, fully double, magenta-pink flowers. H 4 ft (1.2 m); S 3 ft (1 m).

Roses for scent

1 *Rosa* 'Arthur Bell'
Bush rose with bright green, glossy leaves and clusters of fragrant, double yellow flowers. H 3 ft (1 m); S 24 in (60 cm).

2 *Rosa* Breath of Life
A climber with large, scented, fully double flowers colored a pinkish-apricot. H 9 ft (3 m); S 7 ft (2.2 cm).

3 *Rosa* Gertrude Jekyll
An English shrub rose, in the old garden style but repeat-flowering. Deadhead for a continuous show of flowers. H 5 ft (1.5 m); S 3 ft (1 m).

4 *Rosa* Valencia
A hybrid tea, vigorous and usually healthy, with long, sturdy stems that are excellent for cutting. Very strong, sweet scent. H 30 in (75 cm); S 26 in (65 cm).

5 *Rosa* 'Félicité Parmentier'
Old garden rose in the alba group, with a single flush of beautiful, fragrant, pale-pink flowers. H 4 ft 6 in (1.3 m); S 4 ft (1.2 m).

6 *Rosa* Baronne Edmond de Rothschild
A hybrid tea bush rose that produces large, scented, fully double, ruby-red flowers with petals that have pale pink undersides. H 3 ft (1 m); S 30 in (75 cm).

7 *Rosa* 'Penelope'
Bushy shrub rose with large clusters of scented, pale creamy-pink blooms from summer to fall. H 3 ft (1 m); S 3 ft (1 m).

8 *Rosa* Fragrant Cloud
Large, vigorous hybrid tea. The scented flowers, which fade to purple with age, are often borne in clusters. H 30 in (75 cm); S 24 in (60 cm).

Roses for patios

1 *Rosa*
'Nathalie Nypels'
A modern bush rose bearing clusters of sweet-scented, rose-pink flowers. H 30 in (75 cm); S 24 in (60 cm).

2 *Rosa*
Laura Ashley
A miniature climber with mauve and pink flowers. Sometimes used as ground cover, but also ideal for a hanging basket. H 24 in (60 cm); S 4 ft (1.2 m).

3 *Rosa*
Anna Ford
A dwarf bush rose perfect for containers. Clusters of semidouble, rich orange-red flowers with yellow centers. H 18 in (45 cm); S 18 in (45 cm).

4 *Rosa*
Cider Cup
Miniature floribunda rose with clusters of warm orange-apricot-pink flowers, dark leaves, and a fruity scent. H 30 in (75 cm); S 24 in (60 cm).

5 *Rosa*
Ferdy
A cluster-flowered shrub rose. Masses of small, double, coral-pink flowers throughout summer. H 32 in (80 cm); S 4 ft (1.2 m).

6 *Rosa*
Baby Masquerade
Dense, miniature bush rose with small, rosette-shaped flowers that start off yellow, then turn pink and crimson. H 16 in (40 cm); S 16 in (40 cm).

7 *Rosa*
Little Bo-Peep
An excellent miniature rose for containers, dense and bushy, and covered with flowers all season. H 32 in (80 cm); S 3 ft (1 m).

8 *Rosa*
Warm Welcome
A miniature climber, good on a wigwam or obelisk-style support in a tub, flowering from top to bottom. H to 8 ft (2.5 m); S to 5 ft (1.5 m).

9. Grasses, Bamboos, & Ferns

Planting grasses, bamboos, and ferns is a way of introducing striking and sometimes unexpected architectural elements into a garden. What these plants may lack in terms of brightly colored flowers, they make up for in shape and texture. Grown either singly or in groups, they create form and structure. They add movement, too, as their tall stems, canes, fronds, and flowerheads sway and rustle in the wind. And they are certainly not monochromatic; they display a huge range of color, from an infinite variety of subtly different greens to blue, gray, silver, bronze, and gold. Don't overlook them.

Bamboo canes are sometimes reason enough on their own for choosing and growing the plant. Those of *Phyllostachys aureosulcata* f. *spectabilis* are a spectacular golden-yellow.

Growing grasses

For many centuries, grasses have been a key component in European gardens, although until relatively recently these were limited to lawns or meadows. Since the latter part of the 20th century, ornamental grasses have been used more and more in our gardens. Even though they do not have the pretty, colorful flowers of most garden plants, they bring structure, height, texture, fall color, winter silhouettes, and—most important of all—movement. Some, such as *Stipa gigantea* and molinias, stand well into fall with their stems glowing golden orange, and grasses like miscanthus and calamagrostis remain attractive throughout the winter months and into the spring.

The winter garden will look much more interesting if it has some grasses, because they don't die down in fall like other herbaceous plants. The birds can also feast on the seedheads.

Choosing grasses

Grasses usually fall into one of two groups: clumpers or spreaders. Some naturally form perfectly behaved clumps, whereas others can take over your garden with their creeping rootstocks. So choose carefully. There is now a large selection of grasses available that do not self-seed or spread wildly. If in doubt, check with your supplier, or take a close look at how the plant is growing. If it makes a neat, dense clump or tussock, it should not run; if you see shoots coming up all over the pot without forming a tight clump, beware. In light sandy soils in particular, grasses, such as variegated gardener's garters (*Phalaris arundinacea*), can become invasive and need to be regularly weeded out.

Sound and movement add an extra dimension to a bed or border when grasses rustle in the wind. Intersperse them among traditional flowering plants for contrasts of color and shape.

Where to plant grasses

You can use grasses as solitary feature plants, or scattered through other plants, or in larger drifts or swaths. How you do it depends on the type of grass you choose and the effect you wish to achieve. Try large drifts of *Miscanthus sinensis* 'Kleine Silberspinne'—although not the tallest grass, it is still impressive. *Calamagrostis* x *acutiflora* 'Karl Foerster' also looks good in a mass. You could use it to create a hedgelike screen, or add depth to a bed or border by scattering it through a planting of smaller flowering perennials.

Since many grasses stand through fall, you can create a beautiful effect by siting them carefully. The flower spikes and orange stems of *Molinia caerulea* 'Windspiel' or 'Transparent' glow if they catch the late afternoon sun in fall. As its name suggests, 'Transparent', like other molinias, is almost translucent. If you position it at the front of a planting, it creates a see-through screen, and the feathery plumes brush your face as you walk past.

PLANTING GRASSES

The ideal time to plant grasses is during spring or fall when the grass is warm; winter is sometimes an option, but only if the soil isn't rock-hard or waterlogged. Water a plant well before planting by placing the pot in a pail of water. Prepare a hole four times larger than the pot; set the pot in the hole to check that the soil level will be at the same height once planting is complete.

1 Carefully slide the plant out of its pot. Tease out some of the roots to help the plant establish successfully in the soil.

2 Top off the planting hole with soil, and use your foot to firm it. Then water the plant thoroughly.

Naturalistic grass planting

Designers in Germany and North America have developed a way of planting perennials and grasses that mimics the plants' natural growth habits. Plants are chosen from a natural habitat with conditions similar to those in the garden. For example, if your garden is partly shaded, you should choose plants that originate from woodland margins, which will thrive in light shade with a few hours of sun each day.

Plants are placed how they would occur naturally. For example, grasses with creeping or spreading roots are planted in drifts and groups. Those that scatter themselves by means of seed are dotted around. Any bare soil is covered with ground-cover plants or mulch to suppress weeds. The result is a community of plants that are allowed to grow and evolve naturally. Caring for such a scheme involves less maintenance than traditional gardening, since plants are not supported or deadheaded, but simply tidied up when they are past their best.

Keeping grasses looking good

Ornamental grasses need little attention to keep them looking good. Most evergreen grasses, including sedges and rushes, only need a trim to remove damaged leaves and old flower stems. The best time to do this is in late winter, before fresh spring growth emerges. Grasses that turn straw-colored in fall should be cut down to the ground in late winter, after you have enjoyed their frosted foliage. New growth will soon emerge.

Most grasses will grow in poor soil and thrive on neglect—give them too much water, food, and fuss and they'll die. Large grasses, such as pampas, are an exception, and need an occasional feeding with a general-purpose fertilizer to keep them vigorous. Grasses seldom need watering, except after planting and while they establish, but if their leaves roll up, it's a sign they need a drink.

(opposite, clockwise from top left)

Clear debris, such as old stems, using a spring-tined, or grass, rake. Work from the center of the clump and comb out any debris.

Gravel is an attractive and effective mulch for grasses; it will conserve moisture and suppress weeds.

Cut back old stems close to the ground, using pruners or shears. If the grass has sharp edges, wear eye protection and gloves.

Use loppers on thicker grasses, such as miscanthus, where the stems are more like canes. You may even need to use a saw.

Grasses for leaf color

1 *Festuca glauca*
Blue fescue
Dense, tufted evergreen grown for steely blue leaves. Flowers in early to midsummer. H to 12 in (30 cm); S 10 in (25 cm).

2 *Holcus mollis* 'Albovariegatus'
Striped Yorkshire fog
A creeping, perennial grass with flat, soft leaves in blue-green with creamy white edges. Forms a carpetlike ground cover. H 8 in (20 cm); S 18 in (45 cm).

3 *Miscanthus sinensis* 'Variegatus'
Variegated miscanthus
Tall grass with narrow, variegated leaves in pale-green and creamy white stripes. H to 6 ft (1.8 m); S 10 in (25 cm).

4 *Imperata cylindricata* 'Rubra'
Japanese blood grass
Small, slow-growing, perennial grass; blood-red leaves increase in intensity as fall approaches. H 12 in (30 cm); S 12 in (30 cm).

5 *Molinia caerulea* subsp. *caerulea* 'Variegata'
Striped purple moor grass
Small, deciduous grass whose leaves are striped cream and turn clear yellow in fall. Purple flower spikes. H 18–24 in (45–60 cm); S 16 in (40 cm).

6 *Hakonechloa macra* 'Aureola'
Hakone grass
Dense mounds of brightly colored, pale-green leaves flushed with red in fall. Good for growing in containers. H 14 in (35 cm); S 18 in (45 cm).

7 *Helictotrichon sempervirens*
Blue oat grass
Forms large, dense, rounded tussocks of evergreen, tightly rolled, silvery blue-green leaves. H to 4 ft (1.4 m); S 24 in (60 cm).

8 *Miscanthus sinensis* 'Zebrinus'
Zebra grass
Horizontal white or yellow bands appear on the leaves in summer. Maroon or copper-colored flower plumes. H to 4 ft (1.2 m); S 4 ft (1.2 m).

Grasses for flowers

1 *Pennisetum setaceum* 'Purpureum'
Fountain grass
Tropical, deciduous grass often grown as an annual. Dark purple leaves and crimson flowers. H 24 in (60 cm); S 24 in (60 cm).

2 *Stipa gigantea*
Giant feather grass, golden oats
Upright stems carry spectacular, oatlike flowers that ripen from purple-green to gold. H to 8 ft (2.5 m); S 4 ft (1.2 m).

3 *Miscanthus sinensis* 'Grosse Fontäne'
Miscanthus
Its name translates as "large fountain." Tall flower spikes in midsummer; the long, arching leaves turn golden-brown in fall. H 5 ft (1.7 m); S 4 ft (1.2 m).

4 *Pennisetum alopecuroides* 'Hameln'
Fountain grass
Small, evergreen grass with distinctive, bristly flowerheads often compared to foxtails or bottlebrushes. H 20 in (50 cm); S 20 in (50 cm).

5 *Cortaderia selloana* 'Silver Comet'
Pampas grass
Slightly kitsch, perhaps, but dramatic nevertheless. This variety has large white plumes and white striped leaves. H 8–10 ft (2.5–3 m); S 5 ft (1.5 m).

6 *Deschampsia cespitosa* 'Goldtau'
Tufted hair grass
Compact variety with a cloudlike mass of tiny flowers that change color from silvery-red to golden yellow in late summer. H to 30 in (75 cm); S to 30 in (75 cm).

7 *Panicum virgatum* 'Dallas Blues'
Blue switchgrass
A perennial prairie grass originally from Texas. Blue-green foliage fades to golden-yellow in fall. Large heads of delicate flowers. H 8–10 ft (2.5–3 m); S 5 ft (1.5 m).

8 *Briza maxima*
Greater quaking grass
Despite its name, quite a compact grass. Grown for its unusual, hoplike flowerheads. H 18–24 in (45–60 cm); S 10 in (25 cm).

Growing bamboos

As relatives of grasses, bamboos are not strictly woody plants, but from a gardening point of view, we tend to treat them as such because their tough woody canes live for many years. The absence of flowers, fruit, or other seasonal features is made up for by their graceful, swaying stems, and fine leaves that rustle in the breeze. The canes of some are unusually colored, ranging from gray-green and yellow to inky black. As a bonus, after a few years you can harvest your own bamboo canes to use as plant supports.

Where to plant bamboos

Bamboos range in height from relatively small ones at 4–6 in (10–15 cm) tall, to giants that will tower above a house. They also vary considerably in terms of hardiness. The majority prefer moist soil, although *Pseudosasa japonica* tolerates shallow soil over chalk, while most *Fargesia*, *Sasa*, and *Phyllostachys* tolerate shade.

Some, such as *Pleioblastus*, tend to spread rampantly, but others, such as *Phyllostachys*, remain in a manageable clump; ask for advice when purchasing, and if choosing an invasive type, make sure you have sufficient space, or use a root barrier. Bamboos often spread less in moist situations than in dry.

The majority of bamboos die after flowering, but don't let this put you off growing them, as it may not happen in your lifetime. You can also avoid this by buying young plants, such as offspring of *Fargesia murielae*, which last flowered in the 1990s.

An elegant backdrop where space is tight, fargesias form an erect clump rather than spreading over and shading out any shrubs and plants in front of them.

(left) **Bamboo screens** lend a contemporary look to modern garden designs. Here, their crossed stems and feathery foliage are made more dramatic by the red background and uplighting.

(right) **A see-through bamboo screen** creates a delicate divide, segregating the garden into two distinct areas. The advantage over a wall or a fence is that the bamboo stems don't block out as much light as they would planted thickly.

Bamboo screens and backdrops

Bamboos are a versatile group of garden plants. Architectural types, such as the elegant *Fargesia murielae* and *Fargesia nitida*, or the fuzzier-looking *Chusquea culeou*, look spectacular both as a main focal point in a bed, or standing alone in a hard landscape setting, such as a gravel or courtyard garden. As well as this, bamboos are particularly suited to modern designs. Try planting one species *en masse* in geometric-shaped beds in order to create a contemporary look, or use them in a row to create a dramatic screen, either as a boundary or to divide up the garden into separate rooms. For a screen or feature, consider bamboos with interesting stems, such as the black-caned *Phyllostachys nigra* or one of the yellow-stemmed types, such as *Phyllostachys bambusoides* 'Castilloni'.

Bamboo effects

Although not strictly woody plants—bamboos are actually perennials—their permanent woody canes mean that they can be used like shrubs in the garden. The tall types, such as *Phyllostachys* or *Fargesia*, create elegant screens when planted in a row, and shorter bamboos, including sasa and *Pleioblastus variegatus*, make good ground cover. Most bamboos, except very tall varieties, work well in containers, although many enjoy damp soil conditions and thus need frequent watering when grown in pots. Alternatively, use bamboos in geometric beds in contemporary gardens, or to define and enhance Asian garden designs.

Bamboos in containers

One way to prevent a bamboo from spreading is simply to keep it potted. Always use pots big enough for the roots, and never let the plants dry out. For smaller bamboos, pots should be at least 16 in (40 cm) in diameter; they need to be 36 in (90 cm) or more across for larger plants. Containers in contemporary designs and materials work really well with bamboos.

One of the best small bamboos for containers is the light, ferny *Pleioblastus pygmaeus*, or, for something taller, try *Arundinaria gigantea* subsp. *tecta*, with its yellowish stems, which reaches about 6 ft (1.8 m) in height.

Feed the plants throughout the growing season (a slow-release fertilizer is ideal) and make sure they do not get too crowded by cutting out about one in three of the canes each year.

Controlling a bamboo's spread

Some bamboos are particularly invasive, and they need to be kept in check to prevent them from taking over the rest of the garden.

There are a number of ways to control the spread of bamboos. Confining your bamboo plants to a container (*see panel, left*) is probably the simplest method, as the roots cannot spread beyond the container walls.

If you prefer your plants to stay in the soil, construct a simple barrier around them to restrain the roots. The barrier can be made of overlapping slates, steel, or nonperishable plastic, and should be at least 16 in (40 cm) deep. Bury it vertically in the ground, with about 3–4 in (8–10 cm) protruding above the surface, so that it encircles the bamboo. If possible, seal any seams in the barrier to prevent the roots from escaping.

Some gardeners prefer to dig around the clump annually using a spade, and slice off and dig out roots going beyond their allotted space (*see panel, right*).

A simple barrier sunk into the soil around the root area will prevent the bamboo from encroaching on other plants' space.

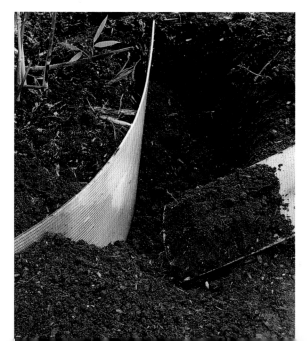

Cutting back bamboos

Running bamboos spread by sending out rhizomes (or underground shoots) into the surrounding soil. The way to control them is to dig a trench about 12 in (30 cm) wide and deep all around the clump in order to reveal the rhizomes. Then sever them close to the root ball and dig them out of the ground. When they are young and still fairly soft, you should be able to slice through them easily with a sharp spade. As they age, they harden and you may have to use pruners or loppers.

1 **Use a spade blade** to slice through any rhizomes that have grown into the trench area. If they are particularly tough, it may help to sharpen the blade before you do so using a sharpening stone. Alternatively, cut them away using pruners.

2 **Remove the pieces of rhizome** from the soil by tugging them out by hand. If they go particularly deep into the ground, use a fork to uncover and remove them. Either dispose of them, or pot them up to create new bamboo plants.

3 **Refill the trench** with the soil you removed earlier. If any further shoots start to spread out beyond the root-ball area, cut them off immediately. This process will probably need to be repeated next season to keep the plant in check.

Ornamental bamboos

1 *Phyllostachys aureosulcata* f. *aureocaulis*
Golden bamboo, fishing pole bamboo
Medium-sized to large bamboo that can spread vigorously in warm climates. Upright, bright golden-yellow canes. H 6–30 ft (2–10 m); S indefinite.

2 *Sasa palmata* f. *nebulosa*
Sasa palmata
Vigorous, spreading bamboo with 14–16-in- (35–40-cm-) long, glossy, bright green leaves. H to 6 ft (2 m); S indefinite.

3 *Phyllostachys vivax* f. *aureocaulis*
Golden Chinese timber bamboo
A sturdy-stemmed, fast-growing bamboo with butter-yellow canes, sometimes green-striped. Can grow tall. H to 30 ft (10 m); S indefinite.

4 *Fargesia nitida*
Fountain bamboo
Slender, purple-green canes topped by narrow, mid-green leaves. Compact and slow-growing. H to 15 ft (5 m); S 5 ft (1.5 m).

5 *Pseudosasa japonica*
Arrow bamboo
Spreading bamboo that will form tall thickets in warm climates. Young canes are olive green, but pale beige when mature. H to 20 ft (6 m); S indefinite.

6 *Phyllostachys nigra*
Black bamboo
Canes become almost jet-black by their third year. A neat clump-former. H 10–15 ft (3–5 m); S 6–10 ft (2–3 m).

7 *Chusquea culeou*
Chilean bamboo
Distinctive, thick canes with white, papery sheaths in the first year, and prominent, swollen "knuckles" or nodes. H to 20 ft (6 m); S 8 ft (2.5 m).

8 *Phyllostachys viridiglaucescens*
Phyllostachys
Hardy, evergreen clump-forming bamboo with greenish-brown canes that arch at the base. H 20–25 ft (6–8 m); S indefinite.

9 *Yushania maculata*
Yushania maculata
Upright, spreading bamboo with narrow, green leaves; canes turn from blue-gray to olive green. H to 12 ft (4 m); S indefinite.

10 *Fargesia murielae*
Umbrella bamboo, Muriel's bamboo
Compact, elegant, arching bamboo with cascades of delicate leaves and canes that turn from green to yellow as they mature. H 12 ft (4 m); S 5 ft (1.5 m).

11 *Sasa veitchii*
Veitch's bamboo
Spreading bamboo with purple canes and broad, dark-green leaves that have white, parchmentlike margins in fall. H 5 ft (1.5 m); S indefinite.

12 *Phyllostachys nigra* f. *henonis*
Henonis bamboo
Bright green canes turn yellow-green when mature. Glossy, evergreen leaves, which are downy and rough when young. H 30 ft (10 m) S 6–10 ft (2–3 m).

13 *Semiarundinaria fastuosa* var. *viridis*
Narihira bamboo
Tall, upright, clump-forming bamboo with green canes—ideal for woodland gardens. H to 22 ft (7 m); S 6 ft (2 m).

14 *Thamnocalamus spathiflorus*
Thamnocalamus
A fast-growing, clump-forming bamboo. The stems turn an unusual pinkish-brown as they age. H to 30 ft (10 m); S 20 ft (6 m).

15 *Fargesia murielae* 'Simba'
Umbrella bamboo 'Simba'
So-called dwarf variety but may still grow to a good size. Compact and clump-forming evergreen. H 6 ft (2 m); S 5 ft (1.5 m).

16 *Pleioblastus variegatus*
Dwarf white stripe bamboo
Small, bushy, spreading bamboo with clearly striped, green and white leaves. H 2$^1/_2$–5 ft (0.75–1.5 m); S 4 ft (1.2 m).

Growing ferns

Ferns are unlike all other plants. For a start, they don't flower, so their appeal has much more to do with form and texture than with dramatic differences in color. They also reproduce completely differently. Instead of setting seed, most produce spores. These are contained in tiny capsules on the undersides of the leaves. When the spores are released, they may—if conditions are right—produce small growths that will eventually grow into new, young plants. It is possible to propagate ferns yourself, by collecting spores and growing them on in pots kept in a propagator, but it's hit-or-miss and can take almost two years before you have plants mature enough to plant out. It's easier to propagate them by division (*see pp.298–9*). Some ferns are hardy and will happily grow outdoors; others are tender and are best protected or moved indoors in winter.

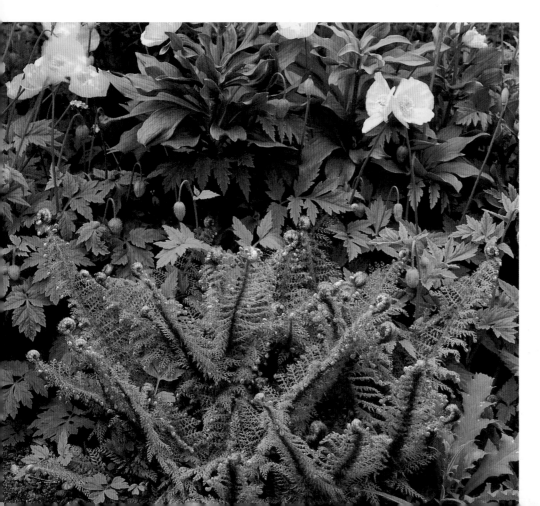

Ferns planted in a mixed border look wonderful in spring as their tightly coiled new fronds gradually unfurl—although they will do much better if the bed is in at least partial shade.

Tender, subtropical tree ferns such as *Dicksonia antarctica* can be grown outdoors in sheltered, mild-climate gardens, but they are not hardy and their trunk or crown may need wrapping in fleece or straw to be sure they survive the winter.

A damp, north-facing yard can create a real challenge for growing anything except ferns and other shade-tolerant, moisture-loving plants.

Where to plant ferns

Ferns are a godsend for any gardener struggling with a shady, damp area where few other plants are happy. Many ferns positively dislike full sun, since their fronds are prone to scorching in the heat. They much prefer humidity, and most will thrive in full or partial shade, in boggy corners, beside ponds and streams, and beneath the branches of overhanging trees. The most important things are to keep them moist at all times, to plant them in rich, fertile soil that has had plenty of well-rotted organic matter dug into it, and to protect them from wind. Ferns tend to be slow-growing and may take some time to establish themselves. Thereafter, most are tough survivors and should require little more than the removal of dead foliage in spring when new fronds start to emerge.

Ferns tend not to be overly picky about the pH level of the soil, and most will grow happily if it is neutral to alkaline. There are one or two exceptions, however: so-called hard ferns (*Blechnum*) prefer acidic soils, as does the small, delicate parsley fern (*Cryptogramma crispa*). If you have naturally alkaline soil, it may be easier to grow these in containers filled with bark-based compost or special ericaceous (lime-free) potting mix mixed with sharp sand or grit.

Tree ferns can be grown outdoors only in warm regions. They are tender, subtropical plants originating from the South Pacific, Australasia, South and Central America, and South East Asia. In temperate northern climates, they must be brought indoors in winter, or the trunks from which their long fronds sprout must be wrapped in a watertight covering of straw or fleece.

Hardy ferns

1 *Dryopteris filix-mas*
Male fern
Deciduous fern forming large, shuttlecock-like clump of upright, arching, mid-green fronds. H 4 ft (1.2 m); S 3 ft (1 m).

2 *Osmunda regalis*
Royal fern
Large, deciduous fern with bright green fronds. Fertile fronds have rust-brown, flowerlike spires. H 6 ft (2 m); S 12 ft (4 m).

3 *Matteuccia struthiopteris*
Ostrich fern, shuttlecock fern
Tall, sterile, green fronds up to 4 ft (1.2 m) in length surrounding shorter, brown fertile ones, arranged in the shape of a shuttlecock. H 5 ft (1.7 m); S to 3 ft (1 m).

4 *Polystichum setiferum*
Soft shield fern
Evergreen fern with arching, lance-shaped fronds; will form large clumps in deep shade with lots of moisture. H 4 ft (1.2 m); S 36 in (90 cm).

5 *Asplenium scolopendrium*
Crispum Group
Hart's-tongue fern
Glossy green fronds with distinctive wavy or undulating, frilled edges. H 12–24 in (30–60 cm); S 12–24 in (30–60 cm).

6 *Polypodium vulgare*
Common polypody
Low-growing, spreading fern with leathery, dark green fronds. Good for ground cover—and will tolerate sun. H 12 in (30 cm); S indefinite.

7 *Dryopteris affinis*
Golden male fern
Slightly shorter than the standard filix-mas, with a dark spot where each pinna (part of the frond) joins the golden-brown midrib. H 36 in (90 cm); S 36 in (90 cm).

Tender ferns

1 *Platycerium bifurcatum*
Common staghorn fern
Long, arching, lobe-shaped, antlerlike
fronds give this fern its common name.
H 3 ft (1 m); S 3 ft (1 m).

2 *Nephrolepis exaltata*
Sword fern
Tufted, evergreen or semievergreen fern
with long, widely arching fronds. H to
7 ft (2 m); S to 7 ft (2 m).

3 *Pteris cretica* var. *albolineata*
Cretan brake
Evergreen fern with attractive, variegated
fronds that have white central bands on
each individual pinna. H 18 in (45 cm);
S 12 in (30 cm).

4 *Adiantum raddianum* 'Gracillimum'
Maidenhair fern
Extremely delicate fern with finely
divided, almost cloudlike fronds. Needs
warmth and humidity. H to 32 in
(80 cm); S 12 in (30 cm).

5 *Asparagus densiflorus* 'Myersii'
Foxtail fern
Erect, foxtail-like fronds of dense,
feathery stems, 2–16 in (30–40 cm)
long. H to 3 ft (1 m); S 20 in (50 cm).

6 *Blechnum gibbum*
Hard fern
Tall, evergreen fern with long, straight,
deeply divided, bright green fronds that
spring up from a trunklike rhizome.
H to 36 in (90 cm); S to 36 in (90 cm).

10. Lawns, Meadows, & Gravel Gardens

A lawn can have a magical effect on a yard. The open area of green it provides is soothing both to look at and to walk on. Lawns are very flexible, as they can be cut to any shape from a rectangle to sinuous curves that provide open areas and link seamlessly to other parts of the yard. Most yards, even small ones, are likely to have a lawn. A traditional lawn should be an even green with a crisp edge; otherwise it is unlikely to enhance the beauty of your garden. Look at your lawn closely: does it pass muster, or is it scruffy around the edges and marked with brown patches? Is the grass fairly uniform, or are there assorted broad-leaved weeds, mossy or bare areas under trees, or coarse grasses sprouting in clumps?

A new sod lawn is an expensive but instant option; there is no waiting for seeds to germinate or young grass to establish itself.

What kind of lawn?

An attractive lawn does not have to be closely cut and evenly striped. Such an effect needs a lot of work, and the fine grasses that give the smooth appearance will not tolerate heavy wear. If your lawn is well used, coarser grasses cut a little higher will suit your purposes much better. Grass does not have to be cut to a uniform height: you could leave an area to grow long and flower. This looks appealing and attracts wildlife, especially if planted with wild flowers and bulbs.

Size and shape

It is easier to mow and edge a simple shape. If your lawn has awkward corners, you could cut them out or broaden tight curves. For small gardens, a geometric shape works best; rectangular, round, or oval lawns are ideal. On small lawns, neat edges are important and weeds are very noticeable. Large lawns are easier to manage in many ways. Weeds are less obvious, and wear and tear makes less impact. Riding mowers can be used, and gently curving shapes are easy to handle.

Steeply sloping banks can be mown with a hand mower, but a walled terrace or ground-cover planting may look better and be easier to manage than grass. Gently undulating lawns are not a problem, but if your lawn has humps that are scalped by mower blades, leaving bare patches, and hollows that fill with lush long grass, leveling the ground is advisable. Grass paths are feasible where wear is light. Make them of mowable width, at least 36 in (90 cm); calculating the width in multiples of your mower blade will make mowing much easier. Remember the edges—are you prepared to trim them? Is there a hard edge? A hard edge of bricks, flagstones, treated lumber, or a metal strip set below the level of the grass allows the mower to pass over the edge freely, saving a great deal of work.

(opposite, clockwise from top left)
A neat patch of green for summer use describes most lawns. An even green requires some work, but a few weeds won't matter.

To encourage wildlife, cut the lawn only in late summer and late fall. Sow wild flowers to create a mini-meadow.

For a playground, use a coarser lawn mix with rye grass. The grass should not be cut too short, and needs regular care.

A perfect green lawn to set off the garden needs a high proportion of fine grasses. Paths and summer watering are essential.

(right) **If a grass path** is used year-round, consider laying stepping stones or replacing it with paving.

Caring for your lawn

To keep a lawn dense, green, and springy, you need to weed and feed it, rake off debris and dead grass, and every so often get air into the soil after the wear and tear of summer. However, mowing is the most important job and this must be done regularly while the grass is growing. Grass clippings don't need to be a waste product; they can either be used as a mulch on the grass to reduce evaporation, or added to the compost bin, where they will break down.

(top) **Rotary mowers** are good for utility lawns and long grass; some have a mulching facility or roller to leave stripes.

(bottom) **String trimmers** are useful for long grass and where the lawn abuts a wall. On some, the head can be turned to trim edges vertically.

Mowing

Regular mowing encourages dense growth. Mow little and often, removing no more than a third of the grass blade at each cutting. If you routinely let the grass grow long and then cut it hard, the quality of the lawn will deteriorate.

Grass will grow fastest in warm, moist conditions, when a fine lawn may need cutting two or three times a week. A weekly cut is usually sufficient for a utility lawn; remember that coarse-leaved grasses do not tolerate close mowing. In hot, dry weather mow less frequently and allow the grass to grow longer than normal in order to conserve moisture. Don't waste the clippings: mix them into the compost pile, except for the first two or three cuts after applying lawn weedkiller; these clippings should always be discarded.

Clean your mower after every use, removing any grass and wiping the blade with an oily rag. Instructions come with every machine, and it is worth taking note of these. Regularly oil moving parts, and keep the blade sharp or it will tear the grass. It is easy to remove and sharpen the blades of a rotary mower, using an oilstone or diamond sharpener or file. There are gadgets available to sharpen the blades of cylinder mowers, but these are not always very effective. It may be better to have the blades professionally reground. On some models they can easily be replaced when they become worn or damaged.

Mowing tips

■ Mow in spring, summer, and fall, and occasionally in winter if the grass is growing.

■ Do not mow when the lawn is very wet, frozen, or during drought conditions in summer.

■ Brush off any worm castings before mowing, or they will be flattened and smother the grass.

■ Collect clippings. If left they will encourage earthworms and worm casts, and build up a layer of "thatch." The exception is during hot summers, when the clippings can be left as a mulch to conserve soil moisture.

■ For a rectangular lawn, first mow a wide strip at each end, for turning the mower. Then mow up and down in straight strips, slightly overlapping the edges of each strip.

■ For a curved or irregular shape, start by mowing a strip around the edge, then mow straight up the center. Mow each half as for a rectangular lawn.

■ If a mower jams while you're using it, make sure you unplug it or remove the spark plug lead before investigating.

Plants spilling out of borders shade out grass and make mowing awkward. Cut back sprawling stems or lay a hard paved edge to help keep edges neat.

Watering

Grass loses its springiness and starts to discolor when it is short of water. New lawns and high-quality lawns must be watered. Water as soon as you notice that the grass does not spring back after being walked on. Utility lawns can be left; the tougher grasses in these lawns will turn brown as they become dormant, but will recover and turn green when rain arrives. If at all possible, it is easier and less wasteful to wait for rain.

Lawn sprinklers are the usual method of watering, but are wasteful. To reduce evaporation, run them in the morning or evening, or during the night. Soaker hoses can be used, but need to be moved across the lawn by about 8 in (20 cm) every half hour. For large high-quality lawns, consider installing pop-up sprinklers or investing in a robotic watering device that moves automatically after an area is soaked.

Fertilizing

A starved lawn will turn a pale yellowish green. To avoid this, feed your lawn at least once a year with the lawn fertilizer appropriate to the time. Check that you are buying what you need and always follow the manufacturer's instructions.

■ **Spring and summer fertilizers** are high in nitrogen to encourage rapid, lush growth and good color. Apply in spring or early summer.

■ **Fall fertilizers** are high in potassium to toughen up the grass for winter. Apply in early fall.

Lawn fertilizers come in granular and liquid formulations. Liquid fertilizers are watered on. They are fast-acting and most suitable for small lawns. The granular forms have a longer-lasting effect but need watering in if there is no rain within two or three days. They must be spread evenly, so invest in a wheeled spreader if your lawn is large; this will need to be adjusted so that the fertilizer is applied at the correct rate.

Fall lawn care

The droughts and wear of summer can leave lawns hard and patchy. Improve them by scratching out dead grass "thatch" and opening up compacted soil to allow the roots to breathe and rain and nutrients to penetrate. This helps grass to grow deeper and survive drought. Rake up leaves and brush off worm castings; where grass is covered for any time, it turns yellow and may die.

1 **Use a spring-tined rake** to vigorously scratch out or "scarify" thatch. Treat moss and make sure it is dead before scarifying; raking live moss spreads the problem around.

2 **Aerate the lawn** every 2–3 years. This is easiest when the soil is moist. Drive in a fork, or on heavy soils use a hollow-tiner to remove cores of soil, every 4 in (10 cm).

3 **Apply top-dressing** directly after aerating, spreading the mixture evenly over the surface—one bucketful will cover approximately 6 sq yd (5 sq m). Make top-dressing using 3 parts sandy loam, 6 parts horticultural sand, and 1 part peat substitute (such as composted bark or coir).

4 **Work the top-dressing** well into the grass and the air holes using the back of a rake or a stiff broom. To make the job easier, allow the mixture to dry slightly before brushing it in.

5 **Apply a fall lawn fertilizer** at the rate recommended on the package. For an even spread, scatter half the fertilizer in one direction and the other half at right angles to it.

6 **If the lawn looks sparse**, sprinkle it with some seed. Choose a seed type to match the rest of the lawn and use about half the amount recommended for sowing a new lawn.

1

4

Lawn edges

If not repaired, damaged edges will continue to deteriorate, and like any bare patch, they also provide an open invitation for weeds to establish. Reseeding a damaged edge is rarely effective, so try tackling the problem using this simple technique.

1 **Cut out a rectangle** of sod around the damaged area. Cut a generous area, or the sod will fall apart as you lift it out. It might help to stand on a board and cut against it to get a straight edge.

2 **Undercut the rectangle** with a spade. Try to cut the sod to as even a thickness as possible, with at least 1 in (2.5 cm) of soil.

3 **Lightly fork over** the newly exposed soil to break up the surface and to encourage rerooting. Add soil if necessary and firm well.

4 **Lay the piece of sod again**, turning it around so that the broken edge faces inward, and the cut edge aligns with the edge of the lawn. Check the fit and level, and make any adjustments. Butt up the edges, pressing down the replaced section firmly.

5 **Fill the hole with top-dressing** (*see pp.202–203*) and work it into the seams to help them knit together. You can reseed the hole if it is large, using an appropriate grass seed. Water, and keep an eye on the repair until the grass has started to regrow, weeding and watering if required.

6 **To maintain a neat edge**, recut it whenever it starts looking untidy; this is easiest when the soil is moist but not wet. Lay a plank on the lawn to stand on and cut against, or use a taut length of string as a guide. Sever the grass roots with a spade or edger where they are spreading into the bed or border. When you have finished working in one direction, work back in the other, pressing against the cut surface to firm it.

What's wrong with my lawn?

All lawns inevitably develop discolored patches or problems from time to time, often caused by adverse weather conditions. Keep an eye out for the first signs of trouble, because prompt treatment will usually prevent permanent damage to your lawn. If the same problems keep reappearing time and again, look at the underlying conditions in your garden; tackling the causes will be far more effective in the long run than repeatedly treating the problems they create.

Lack of light

Grass growing in light or dappled shade can thrive, but the deep shade from trees can often be too much. First of all, the grass will become thin, and then moss is likely to develop. It may be possible to open up the tree canopy by carrying out judicious pruning in order to let more light penetrate. Shade-tolerant seed mixes are available, but they are fine grasses that do not cope well with heavy wear or close cutting. Consider using alternative ground covers in shady areas, such as moss, shade-loving plants, or bark mulch.

Waterlogging

Poorly drained lawns are beset with problems as grass roots die due to lack of oxygen. If water sits on your lawn after rain, it can point to a high water table or to poor drainage.

An impervious layer of compacted soil—otherwise know as "hardpan"—below the surface can often result in poor drainage. It is possible to relieve compaction and penetrate the hardpan by spiking if it is not too far below the surface (*see pp.202–203*); smeared layers of hardpan near the surface are common. If the problem lies deeper, more drastic and expensive action

Scorch/yellow patches may be due to fertilizer that was unevenly distributed or not watered in, or to dog urine. If you see a dog urinating on the lawn, water the area thoroughly immediately.

Snow mold is most common in late fall and winter. It is a sign of poor aeration and too much nitrogen. Scarify and aerate the lawn, and do not use spring lawn fertilizers in fall.

Drought causes yellowish, strawlike patches; the whole lawn may be affected. Let the grass grow longer and leave cuttings on the lawn to reduce evaporation. Water or wait for rain.

Worm castings, left by earthworms, are small, muddy mounds on the lawn in spring or fall. These are unpleasant, but not damaging, and are nutrient-rich. Brush them into borders before mowing.

Fairy rings appear as lush grass in spring. Underneath are fungi living on matter like old tree roots; toadstools appear in fall. Fertilize, aerate, and water the lawn to keep them in check.

Mole hills are unsightly. Ultrasonic devices or smoke in the tunnels may drive the moles away, but trapping and releasing them elsewhere is more likely to be effective.

will probably be required. Solving the problem may involve either digging drainage trenches or laying a system of drainage pipes. Of course, it could be easier to abandon all thoughts of establishing a lawn in these circumstances, and instead grow a variety of plants that thrive in moist conditions (*see pp.80–83*).

Lawns over clay soil can often be especially problematic, as winter wet leads to dead patches and moss growth, while in summer the roots of the grass may fail to reach moisture deep in the soil. One way of overcoming this is to copy the method of making golf greens, and lay the lawn on a layer of coarse sand.

Start by improving the soil using generous additions of organic matter as well as some careful cultivation. Then spread a layer of horticultural sand 2–3 in (5–8 cm) deep over the surface and place the sod on top. The grass should root through the sand into the fertile clay below and make good growth. During summer the roots will be able to extract moisture from the moist soil below the sand, and in winter excess water will drain through the sand, which should result in a lawn surface that is far less wet.

Weeds

Rare is the lawn without a weed; weed seeds are either blown into your garden or brought in by birds. A good lawn-care regimen will deal with many weeds: regular mowing exhausts them, and healthy, strong-growing grass will crowd them out. Mowing the lawn too short, letting it grow too long, or failing to fertilize can all provide an opening. Weeds will move into bare patches where grass has been worn away or weeds have been dug out by hand; prevent this by reseeding. If you cannot match the seed mix to the existing lawn, it will soon blend in.

Rake the lawn before mowing to lift weed stems into the path of the blade, and use a mower bag to prevent weeds from spreading. For difficult weeds, use a suitable lawn weedkiller, or apply a weed-and-feed formulation in spring.

Moss in a lawn is a sign of bad growing conditions, such as low fertility, compacted or poorly drained soil, and shade; it is also a problem in acidic soils. Fall lawn care and spring fertilizing will help (*see pp.201–3*). Test the soil, and if the pH is low, apply lime in winter in the form of ground chalk at the rate of $1^1/_2$ oz per sq yd (50 g per sq m).

Lawn weeds

Typical lawn weeds fall into two types: some are low-growing wild flowers, while others are undesirable coarse grasses or grasslike plants.

They all share an ability to survive regular mowing. Once they have germinated, they spread through the lawn by creeping stems, runners, or through seed in grass clippings; early action is the best way to contain the problem.

Dandelions have deep taproots and if their tops are cut off, more small plants grow again from any part of the root left in the soil. Creeping buttercups do just that, and creep to form mats. Daisies do the same, but to many they are a delight and not a weed; similar views are held about clover. Some weeds may be encouraged, especially in wildlife-friendly long grass; others smother lawn grasses and need controlling.

1 **White clover** (*Trifolium repens*) Mat-forming weed indicating poor, slightly alkaline soil; its roots contribute nitrogen. Use a lawn weedkiller.

2 **Annual meadow grass** (*Poa annua*) This is a tufted grass that spreads by seeding; dig out plants by hand before they flower.

3 **Creeping buttercup** (*Ranunculus repens*) The creeping stems form mats. Weedkiller is not reliable; you may have to dig this out by hand, so try to catch it early.

4 **Moss** This indicates poor conditions, especially in acidic soil. Use moss killer in spring or fall, but it is likely to return if the underlying cause is unresolved.

5 **Self-heal** (*Prunella vulgaris*) A mat-forming weed that is best dealt with by use of a lawn weedkiller. This could be left in meadow grass.

6 **Slender speedwell** (*Veronica filiformis*) Control the mats of tiny leaves by feeding the lawn to encourage growth and scarifying in fall.

7 **Dandelion** (*Taraxacum officinale*) Use a spot weedkiller or dig out the taproot. Deal with dandelions before they have a chance to seed.

8 **Pearlwort** (*Sagina procumbens*) This is a creeping weed that forms low mats of grassy leaves. It can be controlled with a lawn weedkiller.

9 **Lesser yellow trefoil** (*Trifolium dubium*) An annual weed that is often quickly spread by mowing without a bag. Control with lawn weedkiller.

10 **Field woodrush** (*Luzula campestris*) A clump-forming, grass-like plant that prefers acidic soil. Dig out by hand; apply lime in winter in the form of ground chalk.

11 **Yorkshire fog** (*Holcus lanatus*) A coarse-leaved, creeping grass; slash repeatedly with a knife to weaken bad patches, or dig out and reseed.

12 **Broad-leaved plantain** (*Plantago major*) A solitary plant with a taproot, which spreads by seed. Dig out the roots by hand or use a spot weedkiller.

13 **English daisy** (*Bellis perennis*) Leave the rosettes if you like a daisy-spangled lawn. If not, dig out the roots by hand.

14 **Mind-your-own-business** (*Soleirolia soleirolii*) Forms mats of tiny leaves, thriving in damp sites. Lawn weedkillers do not effectively suppress it; rake it out.

15 **Yarrow** (*Achillea millefolium*) The mats of ferny leaves thrive in dry soil; they will also stay green in dry weather. Dig it out by hand or use lawn weedkiller.

PREPARING THE SOIL

Dig over the area, plus an extra 6 in (15 cm) all around, removing weeds and adding soil improvers (see pp.202–203). In heavy clay or wet soil, mix grit into the topsoil to improve drainage. In light, sandy soil, add 3–4 in (8–10 cm) of bulky organic matter during digging; this will help to retain moisture and nutrients.

1 After digging and leveling, while soil is moist but not wet, use the back of a fork to break down the soil surface until it is fine and crumbly, then rake level. Step down the site with the weight on your heels to eliminate soft spots that might later sink, giving an uneven surface. Repeat at right angles.

2 Rake off stones and debris; if soil is stony, rake again at right angles. After leaving for at least five weeks to allow soil to settle, lightly hoe off any seedling weeds. A few days before laying sod or sowing, lightly rake in a balanced organic or compound granular fertilizer at the recommended rate.

Making a new lawn

If you want a new lawn, you have the choice of laying sod or sowing seed. Whichever method you choose, the site must be well drained, level, and cleared of weeds. This means preparing the soil thoroughly, at least five weeks and ideally several months in advance, to give it time to settle.

Creating the right environment

■ Kill or clear all perennial weeds, plus the old grass if you are replacing a badly neglected lawn. The easiest way is to use a glyphosate weedkiller, although more than one application may be needed.

■ Cultivate the soil, first skimming off any existing sod. If you prefer not to use a weedkiller, you can dig out weeds by hand during cultivation.

■ A good lawn requires 8–12 in (20–30 cm) of well-drained topsoil; the subsoil should also drain well. With these conditions the grass will root deeply, reducing the need for watering. Where the depth of topsoil is irregular, the lawn will dry out more quickly in shallow areas and develop brown patches. If your topsoil is shallow, it is worth buying enough to achieve an even depth.

Seed or sod?

■ **Seed** costs less than sod, and the wide choice of grasses means you can satisfy your requirements more exactly, but it will be up to a year before the lawn can take heavy use.

■ **Sod** gives you an instant lawn, usable in about eight weeks, when the sod has taken root. However, good-quality sod, like good-quality carpet, is not cheap.

Buy sod from a reputable specialist. Sod from good suppliers is specially grown in fields and lifted to order. If you can inspect the sod to check the quality, so much the better. Usually there is a choice between high-quality ornamental sod, containing only fine grasses, and utility grade, which has a proportion of hardwearing rye grasses. Some suppliers will grow special sod to order, but this is more expensive and takes about 18 months.

Laying a sod lawn

The best time to lay sod is early fall or early spring. Sod should not be left lying around, so get to work immediately; otherwise, unroll each piece of sod and lay grass side up on paving or plastic sheeting, watering if necessary. It will keep for a few days like this.

Sod should be laid on soil that is moist, but not wet. Lay the first row of sod along one edge of the site, tamping down each piece with the back of a garden rake. This will eliminate air pockets and bring the sod into close contact with the soil, encouraging it to root.

Keep the lawn well watered, or sod will shrink and curl. In dry weather, water up to twice a week at first—this encourages rooting.

Do not disturb the sod before it has rooted; try to keep off it for at least three weeks. To check rooting, try peeling back one corner of the sod; if it does not lift easily, the grass has rooted. Once this has happened, you can mow the lawn as necessary, but set the blade high. Avoid all but the lightest use until the lawn has been down for eight weeks.

1 **Make a tight seam** with the adjacent piece of sod. To do this, raise the edges slightly, push them together so they are almost overlapping, and press down firmly with your thumbs. Tamp down once more along the seams to prevent the edges from lifting.

2 **Continue to lay the pieces in rows**, arranged so the joints are staggered, like bricks in a wall. Protect the sod that has already been laid by working on a plank to lay the next row. Continue until the site is covered, firming by tamping down with the back of a rake. Do not use small pieces of sod at the edges; they will quickly dry out. Use a full-size roll of sod at the edge, and put the smaller piece in the gap behind it.

3 **Scatter fine sandy loam**, or good topsoil mixed with horticultural sand, over the surface. Brush it well into the seams to fill any gaps and encourage the pieces of sod to knit together.

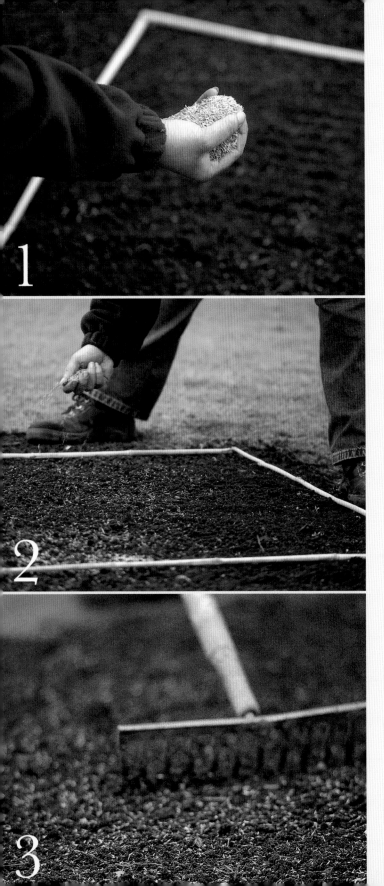

Seeding a lawn

The best time to sow a lawn is in early fall when the soil is warm and moist. The next best time is spring, but the soil may be cold after winter, which will delay germination. Scatter seed by hand; a seed distributor may be useful to cover large areas. Sow the seed over a slightly greater area and cut a clean edge a year after sowing when the lawn is established.

1 **Prepare the ground**. If hand sowing, divide the site into 3-ft (1-m) squares with string or canes. Stir the seed to mix evenly. Weigh out seed for 1 sq yd (1 sq m), following the directions on the package. Pour into a plastic cup, mark the level, and use it as your measure. As a guide, 1 oz (30 g) is roughly a handful.

2 **For even distribution**, scatter half the seed over the square in one direction, and half at right angles to it. Use the same crisscross method if sowing by machine. Repeat for each square. When all the seed is sown, remove the strings or canes.

3 **Seedlings should appear** within 14 days. Water regularly. Mow for the first time, on a high setting, when seedlings have reached 2 in (5 cm). For fall-sown lawns, maintain this height until growth slows. The following spring you can gradually lower the blade height.

Alternatives to grass

If you decide your lawn is too small, too rough and weedy, too steep, or too much trouble, there are some practical, low-maintenance alternatives. Choose soft play bark for a children's play space, pave it for an all-weather entertaining area with raised beds, or create a sunny gravel garden.

Ground-cover options

In a sunny, well-drained garden, spread gravel 1 in (2.5 cm) deep over a geotextile membrane; this will suppress weeds and create a seaside mood. If you plan to lay down paving, it needn't stay dull and gray. Leave out a slab here and there to make room for a small tree or low shrub, and plant small ferns or creeping Jenny in moist, shady cracks.

Plants such as cyclamen, hellebores, or *Vinca minor* grow well under trees. Some, like lilyturf (*Liriope*) and ajuga, even put up with dry soil. Once they have settled they will take care of themselves, especially if you use mulch to suppress weeds and retain soil moisture. While grass might not tolerate a very shady, damp area, this is the perfect environment for moss to establish; let it spread, don't walk on it too often, and plant early-flowering bulbs like snowdrops (*Galanthus*) or lily of the valley (*Convallaria majalis*).

(top) **Cyclamen** is quite happy growing in the shade cast by trees, providing ground cover and brightening up a shady spot.

(bottom) **Moss** often grows naturally in damp shade where grass struggles.

When laying down paving, plant creeping mints and thymes in sunny crevices and gaps, where they will release scent when stepped on.

Wildflower meadows

A meadow is an area where grasses and flowering annuals, bulbs, and perennials are allowed to intermingle and seed themselves—it looks natural and artless. In reality, getting the balance right can be quite difficult, especially in a traditional meadow of native species of grasses and flowers. You do not have to use native plants, though. The term "meadow gardening" includes a variety of naturalistic planting styles and you may find that it is easier to create a meadow with a range of annual species or a mixture of more exotic perennial cultivars and grasses. As well as being beautiful, an established meadow is also a wildlife haven, providing not only shelter, but nectar and seeds to sustain a varied colony of local fauna. Even a small meadow encourages biodiversity by providing a "green corridor" that enables the wildlife to travel across the landscape.

A traditional wildflower meadow such as this one consists largely of wild species, which have smaller, more delicate flowers than the cultivated varieties that you usually find within typical garden borders.

Annual meadows create a glorious show of flowers; the annuals must like freshly cultivated soil, and have to be prolific self-seeders, since the meadow is dug over each year. Here, scarlet poppies, blue cornflowers, and white ox-eye daisies predominate.

Creating a meadow

Planning is crucial, as the plant community will need to develop with little interference on your part. Assess the soil type and growing conditions of the site, then choose plants appropriate for the plot. If you don't, not all the plants in the meadow will thrive equally, causing weaker species to disappear and thugs to take over. Contrary to popular belief, meadows can occur both in free-draining soil and on damp ground. Meadow-seed specialists offer a range of mixes to suit different soil types and conditions.

■ **Traditional wildflower meadows** depend on low soil fertility. If the soil is fertile, the wildflowers will not be able to compete with vigorous grasses. After a few years, few flowering plants will remain. Therefore choose an area that hasn't been cultivated recently. You can either sow a meadow in a bare piece of ground, or you could plant wildflowers in an established grass patch.

■ **Annual meadows** spring up when land is left after the soil is disturbed; seeds in the soil quickly germinate. First come annuals like poppies and cornflowers, before perennial grasses and flowers take over in following years. To prevent perennials from establishing, dig over a meadow each year, leaving the annuals space to spring up anew. To sow the annual meadow, either use a prepared mix, or buy your own choice of annual seeds and mix them for a natural, random effect. Sow in spring, or in fall if your mix consists of hardy annuals. Turn the ground in fall, and the display will be reproduced the next year.

■ **Exotic meadows** can be created by purposely supplementing the subtle delicacy and prettiness of native wildflowers. To produce a bolder display, include nonnative perennials and their cultivars, which generally have larger, brightly colored blooms. You could also add bulbs such as crocuses, daffodils, tulips, and snowdrops.

Preparing to sow

You can slightly reduce fertility in a lawn in the year or two before sowing a meadow by mowing repeatedly and removing the cuttings, which prevents nutrients from returning to the soil. Stripping off the topsoil (the most fertile layer) also helps, but it is hard work and you'll need to find a new home for it. If you have deep, rich topsoil, it may not even be possible to remove it all. Try to prepare the soil a few weeks before sowing (*see panel, right*). This allows any annual weed seeds in the soil to germinate, so that you can hoe off the seedlings before sowing.

SOWING A WILDFLOWER MEADOW

Sow in fall, as some dormant seeds won't germinate unless they experience a period of cold first; some may not germinate until the second year. You'll need about $1/2$ oz to 1 sq yd of soil (15 g seed to 1 sq m), plus a bulking agent such as dry sand.

1 Mix the sand and seed, and divide the volume by the square footage (sq m) of your plot, so you know how much you'll need to sow in each section.

2 Dig over the area to make sure it is not compacted, removing any weeds. Level it with a rake, removing large stones, and step down the site to firm. Rake it lightly to form a crumbly surface. Divide the plot into squares, and sow one square at a time for even coverage.

3 Cover the seed thinly with soil. Firm by tamping down with a rake, or by lightly stepping or rolling the plot.

Gravel gardens

While lawns require frequent mowing, as well as intensive care at different times of the year, gravel gardens need little attention and look neat and attractive all year. A gravel garden also offers the ideal habitat for plants that originate in warm, dry climates. These include those with gray and silver foliage, such as artemisias and lavenders, which like the free-draining, warmer conditions in a gravel garden. Surrounding warm-climate plants with a "collar" of gravel helps them in several ways. Gravel reflects light, making optimum use of the available sun. It also improves drainage around the plant bases, preventing delicate or young plants from rotting off. When it rains, the gravel stops mud from splashing onto foliage, which helps plants with hairy or woolly leaves to survive the wet winter months—if they become too sodden and muddy, they are likely to rot.

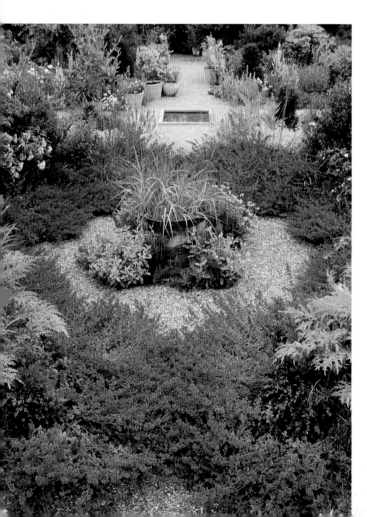

Planning a gravel garden

Gravel gardens can look either formal or naturalistic, depending not only on the way you use gravel with other hard-landscaping materials or structures, such as water features, but also on how you plant it. The gravel could simply fill in the spaces between the defined lines of formal flowerbeds or pathways, or, for a more informal look, you could use it to cover the entire garden, with plantings inserted into it in irregular drifts. Alternatively, you could use several types of gravel, or paddlestones, such as slate, to create interesting patterns or contrasts of color and texture.

If you garden in heavy soil, and want to have a gravel garden, the first, and crucial, step is to improve the drainage. Incorporating coarse sand and gravel into the soil will do this, but you need to add a substantial amount, not just a scattering. It is hard work, but worth it.

Lush planting is still possible in gravel gardens. Here, purple-flowered nepeta, or catmint, has been planted *en masse* to create a striking design.

Preparing the planting site

Invest some time in preparing the area for your gravel garden, and you'll only need to spend a few hours each season maintaining it. First, clear the proposed site of all weeds and vegetation, and then condition and level the soil (*see pp.210–211*).

It is always wise to use a weed-suppressing membrane in a gravel garden. These are available in sheets, and are made either from a variety of materials woven into a fabric, or from perforated plastic. The membrane forms a weed barrier over the soil, eliminating light needed for seeds beneath to germinate and grow, but allowing rain to penetrate to ornamental plant roots. If weed seeds germinate on top of the membrane, they will not be able to root through it, and are easy to pull out.

Make sure that the membrane overlaps neatly, and peg it down with a few metal pins. Arrange your plants in their pots on top of the membrane to judge the overall effect and check spacings. Avoid using plants that naturally spread by sending up shoots from the roots. When you are happy with your design, plant through the membrane, and spread a thick layer of gravel over the surface. Alternatives to gravel include crushed stone, slate chips or paddlestones, cobbles, or glass beads.

A layer of organic matter will eventually form between the membrane and gravel. A few weeds may root into it, but not deeply, so they will be easy to remove by hand weeding the area a few times a year. Or you can use a flat hoe, sliding it between the membrane and gravel to dislodge the weeds' roots. On a dry day, the weeds will soon shrivel up.

GRAVEL GARDEN PLANTS

Choose drought-tolerant plants that will appreciate the free-draining conditions. These plants usually have foliage that is adapted to cut down on water loss— look for leaves that are silver in color, narrow and strappy, or covered in fine, downy hairs. Many spring- or fall-flowering bulbs tolerate dry conditions by becoming dormant during summer.

Achillea 'Gold Plate'
Alchemilla mollis
Artemisia
Eryngium giganteum
Euphorbia characias
Lavandula angustifolia
Papaver orientale (*above*)
Sedum spectabile

Paving and gravel on this sheltered terrace provide planting pockets for sun-loving thymes. These spread out to form a fragrant carpet, and combine with geraniums and *Alchemilla mollis* in a low-maintenance plan.

Making a gravel garden

You could plant directly into the soil, if you wish, but you'll get better results if you lay a weed-suppressing membrane down first. Once you cover it with a thick layer of pea gravel or slate chips, you won't know it's there, but you will notice how it cuts down on weeding and watering. The membrane lets rain through, but like a super-efficient mulch, stops evaporation.

1 **Prepare the area** by digging over the soil and removing any weeds. Dig in plenty of well-rotted garden compost or manure and, on heavy soil, add coarse sand or grit to improve drainage.

2 **Cut a piece of weed-suppressing membrane** to fit the bed or border. For larger areas, you'll have to join several strips together. Leave a generous overlap along each edge and pin securely in place.

3 **Position your plants** on top of the membrane. (Presoak container-grown plants in water for at least an hour.) Check that you have left enough room for each plant to spread to its full width. Using sharp scissors, cut a large cross in the membrane directly under each plant and fold back the flaps. Make it big enough to allow you to dig a good-sized planting hole.

4 **Take each plant out of its pot** and lower it into the hole: it should sit at the same level as it was in its pot. Fill in around the root ball with soil, then firm with your heel or hand.

5 **Tuck the membrane flaps** back around the plant stem. Pin the membrane in place if needed to close any gaps, taking care not to damage the root ball. Water thoroughly.

6 **Spread a layer of gravel mulch**, about 2–3 in (5–8 cm) thick, over the membrane. Be generous, to prevent the membrane from showing through, and level with a rake. Water around the plants regularly until they are established, using a gentle spray from a watering can or hose to avoid dislodging pockets of gravel. If any weeds get through, they should be easy to pull out.

2

3

5

6

Plants for gravel gardens

1 *Lavandula angustifolia* 'Twickel Purple'
Lavender
A mid-sized lavender that, like all others,
thrives in well-drained soil in full sun.
H to 24 in (60 cm); S 3 ft (1 m).

2 *Dierama pulcherrimum*
Angel's fishing rod
A summer-flowering plant that forms
chains of corms each year. Once settled
in, it's usually trouble-free. H to 3–5 ft
(1–1.5 m); S 24 in (60 cm).

3 *Deschampsia cespitosa* 'Goldtau'
Tufted hair grass
Tussock-forming, evergreen grass
producing silvery reddish-brown
spikelets from early to late summer.
H to 30 in (75 cm); S to 30 in (75 cm).

4 *Sisyrinchium striatum* 'Aunt May'
Sisyrinchium
A tall, clumping perennial with
evergreen, striped leaves. It flowers in
early to midsummer. H 20 in (50 cm);
S 10 in (25 cm).

5 *Artemisia alba* 'Canescens'
Wormwood
Most artemisias thrive in gravel gardens.
This variety has curling, silvery leaves.
H 18 in (45 cm); S 12 in (30 cm).

6 *Iris unguicularis* 'Mary Barnard'
Iris
Beardless iris with tough, grasslike
leaves and bright violet flowers in
midwinter. H 12 in (30 cm).

7 *Pennisetum alopecuroides* 'Hameln'
Fountain grass
A compact, early-flowering form, with
greenish white spikelets, maturing to
gray-brown. H 2–5 ft (0.6–1.5 m); S
2–4 ft (0.6–1.2 m).

8 *Cistus* x *dansereaui* 'Decumbens'
Rock rose
A low, spreading shrub with delicate,
paper-thin, white flowers that last for
only a single day. H 24 in (60 cm);
S 3 ft (1 m).

9 *Echinops ritro* 'Veitch's Blue'
Globe thistle
Beautiful, rounded, dark blue
flowerheads. A plant that positively likes
poor, dry soil in full sun. H to 36 in
(90 cm); S 18 in (45 cm).

10 *Sedum spectabile* 'Brilliant'
Stonecrop
Large, persistent flowerheads appear in
late summer and attract butterflies and
bees. H 18 in (45 cm); S 18 in (45 cm).

11 *Eryngium giganteum*
Sea holly
A tall but short-lived perennial, worth
growing for its persistent, thistlelike
flowers. H 36 in (90 cm); S 18 in (45 cm).

12 *Achillea filipendulina* 'Gold Plate'
Yarrow
A clump-forming perennial with flat,
golden-yellow flowerheads that appear
from summer to fall. H 4 ft (1.2 m);
S 18 in (45 cm).

13 *Allium karataviense*
Allium
A small allium that produces round
heads of tiny, star-shaped, pale pink
flowers in summer. H 4–10 in
(10–25 cm); S 4 in (10 cm).

14 *Salvia officinalis* 'Tricolor'
Sage
A variegated sage with aromatic, gray-
green and cream leaves flushed with
pink or purple. H to 24–32 in (60–
80 cm); S to 3 ft (1 m).

15 *Alchemilla mollis*
Lady's mantle
Drought-resistant perennial with downy
leaves on which rain and dew collect as
attractive water droplets. H to 24 in
(60 cm); S 30 in (75 cm).

16 *Dianthus* 'Little Jock'
Pink
One of many pinks that bear long-lasting,
sometimes scented flowers all through
summer. H 8 in (20 cm); S 12 in (30 cm).

11. Trees

Whether your yard is large or small, consider planting a tree or two. Trees offer many benefits, sending the focus up to a wide, open sky in a small garden, and creating intimate enclosures in larger spaces. They also make wonderful focal points, particularly if you select a striking specimen with a weeping habit, attractive stems, decorative foliage, or colorful blossoms and fruit. A handsome white-stemmed birch, multistemmed amelanchier, or fountain-shaped Japanese maple will draw the eye when planted at the end of a path, in the center of a lawn, or against a wall or a smooth evergreen hedge. In a deep, rectangular plot, a tree can be planted half to three-quarters of the way down the garden to partially mask the view beyond, and bring the eye back to the foreground.

The paperbark maple (*Acer griseum*) is a garden tree grown almost as much for its wonderful, peeling, orange-brown bark as it is for its foliage, which turns orange and scarlet in fall.

Garden trees

Trees provide permanent features in a yard. They will be there for a long time, and, once established, are difficult to move; think carefully about what you want to plant and where. Consider also the final height of the tree or, at least, its height after eight or ten years if it is a slow-maturing type. In small urban yards there is rarely space to plant a large tree; it will not only plunge your own house and garden into darkness, but the neighbors may suffer too. Don't be tempted by melancholic weeping willows or blue Atlas cedars. By the time they are too large for the space, you will need to pay an arborist a handsome sum to remove them without destroying anybody's property. Instead, think small, or choose a tree that may be pruned regularly to keep it in check.

Positioning trees

A tree in the yard is like a large piece of furniture in a house: its sheer volume limits its placing. Before committing to a final position, ask friends to help by holding up long canes or broomsticks where you are planning to plant. Look at them from key points in the house, such as a kitchen or living room, and in the yard, perhaps from an entrance or seating area.

Consider, too, the position of the sun in relation to the tree and the shade it will cast. Think of how and when you use particular areas. To create a brightly lit breakfast area, for example, plant your tree on the west side of the garden, or position a tree on the east or north side of your property to catch the setting sun on an evening terrace. A play area needs shade during the hottest part of the day, while vegetable beds need sun all day.

A tree with colorful foliage, such as this variegated form of *Cornus controversa*, creates a spectacular show in a border, providing height, design focus, and a shady area beneath for woodland plants.

Trees also make beautiful features in a garden room. Several of the dogwoods, such as the early summer-flowering *Cornus controversa* or *C. kousa*, and Japanese maples (*Acer palmatum*), with their cut foliage and fall tints, make striking focal points in a lawn, courtyard area, gravel garden, or at the end of a vista. Alternatively, select a tree with multiple stems such as a silver birch; the white trunks and branches take on a leading role in dark winter months when the leaves have fallen.

Key features

Choose trees that will be happy with the soil and climate in your yard. A local nursery should be able to advise you as to what will perform best in your area. There are also a host of decorative features to take into account.

As trees flower for a comparatively short time, it may be best to regard blossoms as an added bonus rather than the main attraction. Fruits, berries, or interesting seedpods are worth considering, as they often last longer than flowers. But the most enduring feature of any tree is the color, texture, and shape of the foliage and stems. Feathery acacias and cut-leaf maples, for example, offer a light, soft touch, creating dappled shade. Use the layered open habit of *Cornus alternifolia* to introduce horizontal lines, or a cherry with an upright habit to add a vertical dimension.

While fall color is a seasonal attraction, use trees with year-round yellow, red, or variegated foliage sparingly. The dark purple leaves of *Acer palmatum* 'Atropurpureum', *Prunus cerasifera* 'Nigra', or bronze-leaved *Malus* 'Profusion' can add drama but, to prevent them from looking gloomy, set them against lighter colors. Too much yellow can also be overpowering, though trees such as *Acer japonica* 'Aurea' or *Liriodendron tulipifera* 'Aureomarginata' can brighten up dull areas.

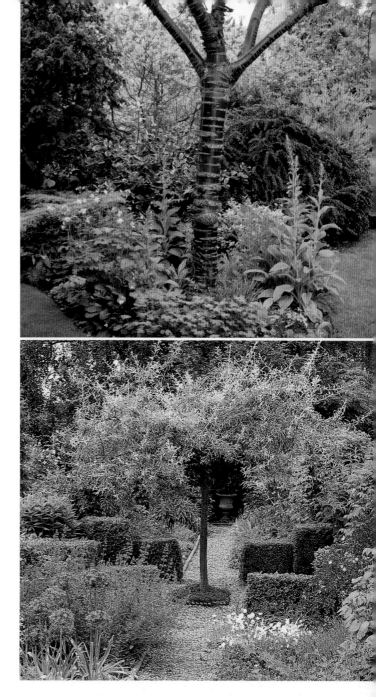

(top) **The smooth, russet-colored bark** of this cherry, *Prunus serrula*, peels off to give visual and tactile interest all year. The tree is also covered with white spring blossoms, and in fall the foliage turns a lovely yellow.

(bottom) **The weeping silver-leaved pear**, *Pyrus salicifolia* 'Pendula', makes a handsome feature in a lawn, or to punctuate a path in a small garden.

(far left) **Double staking** will give a newly planted tree extra support in a wind-buffeted position.

(left) **Rabbit guards** will need to be in place for several years to protect young trees from damage.

Planting tips

Small trees establish themselves in a new spot much more easily than large ones do. The best pot size is one you can take home in a shopping bag. Keep roots of bare-rooted trees shaded and protected from wind, preferably covered by a sheet of plastic or plastic bag, or under a mound of soil, to prevent them from drying out. Before planting, take a close look at the tree's roots and remove any areas that are damaged.

Lay a board or bamboo cane across the center of the hole to get the correct level for planting. Pot-grown trees should sit at the same depth as they were in the container. When a bare-rooted tree is held at the correct level, the point where the roots start to flare out from the trunk should be slightly above soil level. Alternatively, plant to the mark of the original soil level on the trunk. If the hole is too deep, remove the tree and put some soil back in the hole.

It is not necessary to enrich the soil unless you have very sandy or poor soil. In fact, this is likely to hinder establishment, encouraging the roots of the tree to remain within a nutrient-rich "comfort zone" at the planting site, rather than questing outward and downward in search of resources.

Stakes and animal guards

A single, low stake is generally agreed to be best for most young trees, allowing the stem to flex and strengthen in the wind without tugging at and dislodging the roots. However, for top-heavy and especially top-grafted trees (where a stem of one tree variety is grafted onto the main branch of another), such as the weeping Kilmarnock willow, a taller stake is advisable, and in very windy sites, two stakes can be used. You can use the stake to anchor netting guards in areas where rabbits and deer are a nuisance.

Planting a container-grown tree

Prepare your site by clearing it of weeds and, if you have very sandy or infertile soil, digging in organic matter over a wide area. Dig a hole, not too deep, but two to three times as wide as the rootball, and fork over and loosen the soil at the bottom. Avoid planting too deeply and in too narrow a hole—90 percent of all young tree deaths can be attributed to this problem.

1 **Water the plant** in its pot by plunging it into a bucket of water about an hour before planting. After this, remove it from its pot so that you can tease out any roots that have become compacted. Use a cane to establish the correct depth for planting; ensure that the plant will sit in the hole at the same depth as it was in its container.

2 **Drive a stake** into the soil on the windward site of the rootball, and rotate the tree until the trunk sits comfortably parallel with the stake.

3 **Refill the hole with soil** around the roots and the stake, and firm using your foot. Secure the tree to the stake using a buckle-and-spacer tree tie; this will need checking and loosening regularly as the tree grows. Water, and mulch as for a bare-rooted tree (*see pp.228–229*).

Planting a bare-root tree

About four weeks before planting, prepare the ground. First, clear the site of weeds and grass: dig them out or use a glyphosate weedkiller. Dig in well-rotted manure or garden compost in infertile or sandy soil. Just before planting, remove any new weeds that have germinated. Water your bare-root tree by setting it in a pail of water about an hour before planting.

1 **Dig a circular hole** as for container-grown trees (*see p.227*). Lay a cane across the hole and use it to check that the dark soil mark on the stem of the tree is just above it.

2 **Hold the tree upright**—or, better, get someone else to hold it—and backfill the hole with soil, a little at a time, firming it in and around the roots with your fingers.

3 **Once the hole is filled**, start firming with your heel from the edge to reduce the risk of the soil sinking and the planting level becoming too low.

4 **Water in well**, then check the level again and fork over to fill any dips. There is no need to scatter fertilizer. In fact, this is more likely to cause harm by burning the roots, which will then not be capable of taking up nutrients for at least the first year.

5 **Knock a short stake into the ground** at an angle of 45 degrees. Secure the trunk to the stake using a buckle-and-spacer tree tie that allows for the stem to increase in girth without chafing. Check it at least twice during the growing season as the tree matures, and loosen if it becomes too tight.

6 **Mulch around the tree** using a fibrous, open-textured material, such as well-rotted compost. Spread it in a layer 2½–3 in (5–6 cm) deep, but do not let it come in contact with the tree stem, where the moisture may cause rot.

Caring for trees

Dehydration is the most common reason for the poor growth or death of young trees, so it is essential to keep your tree well watered during dry spells from spring to fall for the first two to three years after planting. Give each tree at least 13 gallons (50 liters) of water per week; this equates to about seven or eight full watering cans. A length of drainpipe sunk vertically into the soil at the edge of the planting hole can act as a useful watering aid, taking the water directly to lower soil levels, but it will tend to fill up with soil and mulch unless it stands so far out of the ground that it looks rather unsightly.

Water your tree thoroughly after planting, and then weekly during dry spells for the first two growing seasons—trees are most vulnerable to dehydration when young.

Mulching

To reduce competition for water and nutrients from grass, other plants, and weeds, keep clear an area of 1 sq yd (1 sq m) around the tree and mulch it every fall, keeping the mulch away from the trunk. Young trees also benefit from an annual application, in spring, of a general fertilizer, such as blood, fish, and bone. Before you mulch, or after you have pulled back an existing mulch, scatter the fertilizer around the base of the tree at a rate of 2 oz per sq yd (70 g per sq m), fork it into the soil, then water. Once the tree is well established, you can let the grass grow around the trunk, or plant some bulbs or shade-loving ground cover underneath, without slowing the tree's growth.

Pruning young trees

Conifers and other evergreens, such as hollies, seldom need pruning after planting, and some deciduous trees, including birches and amelanchiers, are best left alone to develop their naturally beautiful shapes. But other deciduous trees should be pruned every year for the first few years.

Inspect your young trees in late summer or late winter, and remove dead, damaged, and diseased wood. Weak or crossing branches are also best cut out. At the same time, loosen ties, and

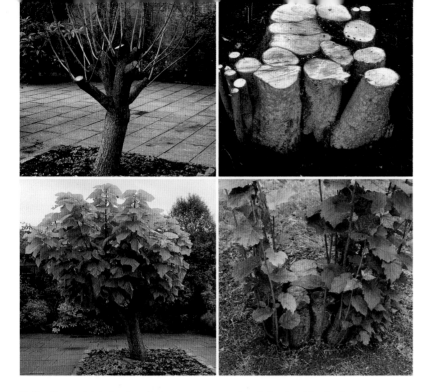

Pollarding restricts the size of a tree (here a catalpa) and encourages larger leaves. When the trunk of a newly planted tree reaches 3–6 ft (1–2 m), prune back the branches to 1–2 in (2.5–5 cm) in late winter or early spring. Then, every year, prune back the young stems that have regrown, and thin out any congested stems.

Coppicing is cutting back stems down to the base to stimulate new shoots; do this in late winter or early spring, just before the leaf buds break. Hazel and willow respond well to coppicing every year, but in poor soil it takes less out of the tree if you cut back half the stems one year, and the other half the following year.

remove any weeds growing over the root area. While you're at it, check for any suckers shooting from below the graft union and cut them out too (*see panel, right*).

More extensive pruning depends on what kind of tree you want. Most trees sold at garden centers are lollipop-shaped, technically known as "standards." These have been pruned by the nursery, and you merely need to continue keeping the trunk clear, and pruning back wayward stems.

Younger trees, known as "whips," are also available. These usually have a single leading stem, and buds that will develop into side stems. They are less expensive, and often easier to establish than older trees, and they can be pruned and shaped as you wish. For example, if you want a tree with several stems, cut the stem to near ground level, or plant a few whips close together, or even in the same hole.

REMOVING WATER SHOOTS AND SUCKERS

Remove water shoots and suckers as soon as you can, as they divert water and nutrients from the tree if left to grow. Suckers that grow from roots must be pulled off as close to the base as possible—pull back the soil to expose the area where it joins the root. If you cannot pull them off, use pruners to remove them.

Water shoots that are growing through the bark or around the edges of a wound should be removed at their base; use pruners to avoid tears in the bark.

Suckers need to be cut off as close to the base of the shoot as possible. Rub off any regrowth using your fingers or foot as soon as it appears.

Pruning in winter

It is easier to assess and prune deciduous trees in winter, when they are leafless. Exceptions are trees that bleed sap or are slow to heal, like birches and magnolias, and those prone to disease, such as prunus. Winter pruning results in lots of new shoots, so be ready to rub out unwanted growth.

Assessing your tree and making a pleasing shape is very rewarding work, but remember that although it is easy to remove a stem, it takes a good deal longer for it to regrow if you make a mistake, so take your time with the task and cut with care.

1 **When the leaves of a deciduous tree have fallen**, take a look at its overall shape. Look for stems that are badly placed, or those growing too far down the trunk. This tree has an awkward stem growing from the base that must be removed. First, remove any dead and damaged wood. Then use a pruning saw to make a straight cut through any branches growing from the base of the tree.

2 **Prune thin stems** with loppers or pruners, taking them back to ½ in (2 cm) from the ring of slight swelling where the stem and trunk meet, known as the branch collar.

3 **Thick branches**, and those that are likely to tear, are cut in stages. First, cut under the stem, a short distance from the trunk. Cut about a quarter of the way through the underside of the branch.

4 **Make a second cut** above the lower one, and aim to join the two. Be sure your tools are sharp to prevent snagging.

5 **Even if you have taken great care**, a heavy branch may still snap off, but it doesn't matter at this point, since this is not the final cut. Don't worry if the cut snags as it falls away.

6 **Remove the stub** by using the technique outlined in steps 3 and 4. Make your final cut just slightly away from the branch collar.

Pruning in summer

Trees that bleed sap when cut, such as the magnolia shown here, are best pruned in summer, when they will be more susceptible to disease but will recover more quickly—even though regrowth may be delayed while the tree concentrates its energy on healing its wounds. When pruning young magnolias for shape, you can lightly trim them in the spring, but don't cut stems any thicker than $1/2$ in (2 cm) at this time.

1 **Dead and diseased wood** is quite obvious, so remove this first. Although it is more difficult to see the outline of a tree in leaf, it should be easier once you have removed any unhealthy stems.

2 **Take out stems** that are growing toward the center of the tree. Be wary of pruning large branches that will heal slowly.

3 **Remove any crossing branches** to prevent them from rubbing against each other and causing wounds that may result in serious damage, especially in the case of trees that bleed sap.

4 **Prune out weak stems** that did not produce flowers or that have few leaves, and rub out shoots forming on the lower trunk.

5 **Keep the tree in shape** by reducing the length of wayward side stems, cutting them back by about one-third.

6 **The pruned tree** has a better shape and a more open canopy, allowing more light into the center, and promoting vigorous stems.

Trees for small gardens

1 *Acer palmatum* 'Nicholsonii'
Japanese maple
Like all acers, grown largely for its delicate leaves and fall color.
H 6–10 ft (2–3 m); S 6–10 ft (2–3 m).

2 *Aralia elata* 'Variegata'
Japanese angelica tree
Large, flat branches of green leaves with white margins. White flowers followed by black fruits from late summer.
H 30 ft (10 m); S 30 ft (10 m).

3 *Cercis canadensis* 'Forest Pansy'
Eastern redbud
Spreading, deciduous tree with heart-shaped, dark purple leaves (yellow in fall). H 15 ft (5 m); S 15 ft (5 m).

4 *Sorbus aria* 'Lutescens'
Whitebeam
A mid-sized, deciduous tree with silvery-gray young leaves and brown-speckled red berries. H 30 ft (10 m); S 25 ft (8 m).

5 *Eriobotrya japonica*
Loquat
An evergreen tree with long, heavily veined, glossy, green leaves and scented, white flowers in fall, sometimes followed in spring by edible orange fruits. H 25 ft (8 m); S 25 ft (8 m).

6 *Amelanchier lamarckii*
Juneberry or snowy mespilus
A small, bushy tree covered in clusters of white flowers in spring. Young leaves are silvery bronze, then green, and finally red in fall. H 30 ft (10 m); S 40 ft (12 m).

7 *Ficus carica* 'Brown Turkey'
Common fig
Large, deciduous, green leaves and edible, purple fruits. An ideal tree for growing against a warm, sunny wall.
H 10 ft (3 m); S 12 ft (4 m).

8 *Arbutus unedo*
Strawberry tree
Slow-growing evergreen tree with small white flowers and strawberry-like fruits in fall. H 25 ft (8 m); S 25 ft (8 m).

Trees for focal points

1 *Pyrus salicifolia* 'Pendula'
Weeping silver pear
Narrow, silvery leaves and profuse white
blossoms are followed by small (inedible)
fruits. H 15 ft (5 m); S 12 ft (4 m).

2 *Magnolia denudata*
Lily tree
Spectacularly large, pure white flowers
appear on bare branches in spring,
followed by large, glossy leaves. H 30 ft
(10 m); S 30 ft (10 m).

3 *Robinia pseudoacacia* 'Frisia'
False acacia or black locust
This golden-leaved variety is smaller
than the standard species. White
flowers. H 80 ft (25 m); S 50 ft (15 m).

4 *Cornus alternifolia* 'Argentea'
Pagoda dogwood or green osier
Small, deciduous tree or shrub that
produces spreading, horizontal tiers of
green leaves with white margins. H 10 ft
(3 m); S 8 ft (2.5 m).

5 *Betula utilis* var. *jacquemontii*
Himalayan birch
A deciduous tree, elegant in all seasons
but usually grown for its paper-thin white
bark. H 50 ft (15 m); S 25 ft (8 m).

6 *Stewartia monadelpha*
Stewartia
Dark green leaves turn vibrant orange
and red in fall before they fall. Bark is
peeling red-brown and gray. H 80 ft
(25 m); S 25 ft (8 m).

7 *Koelreuteria paniculata*
**Golden rain tree or pride of
India**
In summer, masses of yellow flowers
appear followed by lanternlike, pink- or
red-brown fruits. Leaves turn yellow in
fall. H 30 ft (10 m); S 30 ft (10 m).

8 *Taxus baccata* 'Fastigiata'
Irish yew
Unusually narrow variety with erect
branches and dark green foliage. H 30 ft
(10 m); S 20 ft (6 m).

Trees for spring blossoms

1 *Cercis siliquastrum*
Judas tree
In spring a mass of magenta-pink, pea-like flowers appear all over the bare branches. H 30 ft (10 m); S 30 ft (10 m).

2 *Malus* 'Red Devil'
Dessert apple
Medium-sized apple tree yielding striking red fruits with pink-stained flesh in early fall. H 5–20 ft (1.5–6 m)

3 *Magnolia* x *soulangeana* 'Lennei Alba'
Magnolia
Flower buds on the tips of branches open in spring to produce dramatic, pure white flowers 4 in (10 cm) across. H 20 ft (6 m); S 20 ft (6 m).

4 *Prunus* 'Spire'
Ornamental cherry
Clusters of pale pink flowers appear at the same time as the leaves, in mid-spring. H 30 ft (10 m); S 20 ft (6 m).

5 *Laburnum* x *watereri* 'Vossii'
Laburnum
Spectacular showers of long, hanging, golden-yellow flower clusters in late spring. H 20 ft (6 m); S 20 ft (6 m).

6 *Cornus kousa* 'Satomi'
Japanese dogwood
Deciduous tree or shrub with masses of dark pink flower bracts in late spring or early summer. H 22 ft (7 m); S 15 ft (5 m).

7 *Crataegus laevigata* 'Paul's Scarlet'
Hawthorn
A thorny, deciduous tree grown for its deep pink double flowers in late spring. H to 25 ft (8 m); S to 25 ft (8 m).

8 *Malus* x *arnoldiana*
Crab apple
In mid- to late spring, red buds open to scented flowers that are initially pink but fade to white. H 15 ft (5 m); S 25 ft (8 m).

Trees for fall color

1 *Acer palmatum* 'Sango-kaku'
Coral-bark Japanese maple
Leaves are yellow in spring, then green, with a blaze of golden orange in fall. H 20 ft (6 m); S 15 ft (5 m).

2 *Ginkgo biloba*
Maidenhair tree
Unusual, fan-shaped, green leaves turn an attractive golden-yellow in fall. H to 100 ft (30 m); S to 25 ft (8 m).

3 *Liquidambar orientalis*
Oriental sweet gum
A small variety whose maplelike leaves turn fiery crimson, yellow and orange in fall. H 20 ft (6 m); S 12 ft (4 m).

4 *Sorbus commixta*
Japanese mountain ash or Japanese rowan
A neat, compact sorbus. White flower clusters in late spring, then red berries and good fall color. H 30 ft (10 m); S 22 ft (7 m).

5 *Sorbus sargentiana*
Sargent rowan
White flowers give way to red berries, and bright orange and crimson fall foliage. H 30 ft (10 m); S 30 ft (10 m).

6 *Nyssa sinensis*
Chinese tupelo
Slender leaves are bronze when young, dark green in summer, then many-hued in fall. H 30 ft (10 m); S 30 ft (10 m).

7 *Parrotia persica*
Persian ironwood
A spreading, deciduous tree with dense foliage turning yellow and red-purple in fall. H 25 ft (8 m); S 30 ft (10 m).

8 *Rhus typhina*
Staghorn sumac or velvet sumach
Stems are velvet-coated (like antlers). In fall, leaves are rich ruby, gold, and amber. H 15 ft (5 m); S 20 ft (6 m).

12. Hedges

Hedges have many uses in the garden. Most commonly planted as simple boundary screens, they can also serve as internal divisions or low edging for beds, borders, or paths. When close-clipped and uniform, hedges create a sense of neat formality; when mixed and billowy, they are a garden in themselves. Hedges have other practical uses, too. They make excellent windbreaks—more effective, in fact, than solid walls and fences. Deciduous hedges, in particular, filter the blast and slow windspeeds, whereas solid barriers actually cause turbulence on the sheltered side. Evergreens help muffle the noise of traffic and offer year-round privacy, while dense, thorny hedges deter intruders.

Trimming boxwood hedges is essential if you want to maintain a well-kept, formal look. They will probably need trimming twice a year—once in midsummer and again in fall.

Garden hedges

All hedges take some years to establish and gain the required height, but some, such as oval-leaved privet (*Ligustrum ovalifolium*), are relatively fast-growing. Remember, though, that the faster they grow, the more frequently they will need clipping. While your hedge is maturing, you can erect a temporary screen of split bamboo or hurdles, or a wire-netting fence as a boundary line. This netting can be left in place as it will eventually be covered by the hedge. If you can't wait, "instant hedges" (the plants are grown in containers) can be bought by the yard. They are not cheap, but the contracting company will also prepare the ground and carry out the planting.

Use hedges as garden dividers where you want to split up your space into different rooms. Tall hedges here create a secret, sheltered enclosure, further "furnished" with dwarf box edging.

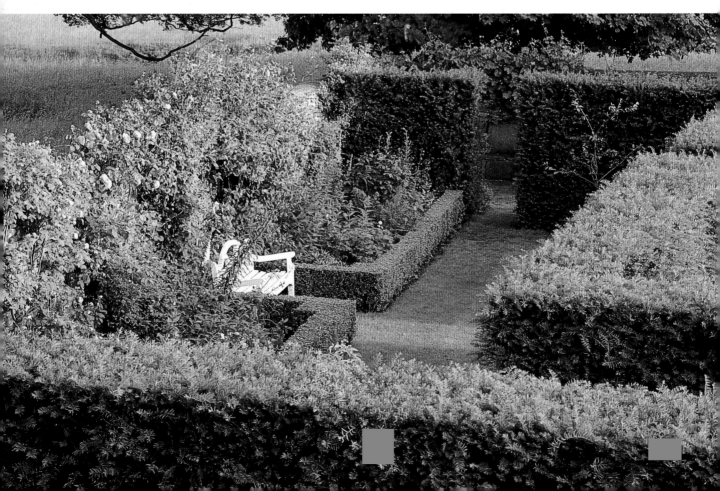

What type of hedge?

Evergreens give cover year-round while deciduous hedges are see-through in winter, except for beech and hornbeam, which retain crisp brown leaves until spring. If you live in a cold, exposed place, choose a hardy, deciduous hedge that will withstand windy conditions, such as hawthorn (*Crataegus monogyna*) or hornbeam (*Carpinus betulus*). Plants for seaside gardens exposed to wind, but relatively frost-free, include the hawthorn and hornbeam again, and also the sea buckthorn (*Hippophae rhamnoides*) and tamarix, and the evergreens griselinia, holly, and olearia, all of which tolerate salty air.

For a smooth, formal evergreen hedge, look for small-leaved plants with a dense growth habit that tolerate regular close clipping. Two of the best choices for formal hedges are yew (*Taxus baccata*) and Lawson cypress (*Chamaecyparis lawsoniana*). Others include boxwood (*Buxus sempervirens*), or fast-growing privet (*Ligustrum ovalifolium*), and shrub honeysuckle (*Lonicera nitida*).

Informal hedges are often a mixture of flowering and berrying, evergreen, and deciduous shrubs planted closely together. They are well suited to rural or semirural areas and informal garden settings, and need little or no pruning if they are to show off their beauty, so allow them a bit more space than a clipped hedge. You can achieve a more formal look by mixing plants of a similar growth rate and size, but with different foliage colors, such as green and copper beech, or green and golden yew.

Existing hedges

If you already have a hedge, you may consider it your pride and joy, or merely a chore. If your current hedge is not doing anything for you or your garden, you could dig it up and start again. This is not as drastic a step as it may seem—yes, hedges are long-lasting, but they are also renewable and some grow faster than you might think. You could replace your old hedge with a low-maintenance version—beech (*Fagus sylvatica*), for example, needs just one trimming per year—or, if space is limited, you could achieve a similar effect by training ivy through wire netting or trellises to make a narrow divide.

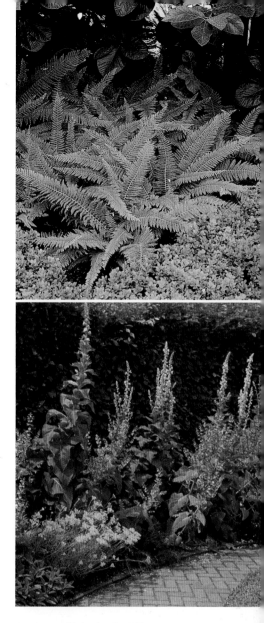

(top) **Dwarf boxwood and beech** hedging have been combined here to create an exciting textural contrast, while the spiky fern infill offers yet more visual and tactile interest to this framework of foliage.

(bottom) **Closely clipped hedges** provide beautiful natural backdrops to herbaceous borders, forming an unbeatable contrast for billowing, colorful plantings such as this.

Planting Leyland cypress

Think twice before you plant Leyland cypress (x *Cupressocyparis leylandii*), as it has gained a bad reputation in the gardening world. Left untrimmed, it quickly grows to a great height. If it is then cut back hard, it looks unsightly—brown stems will stay twiggy, and will not regain their former green color. Ideally, these hedges should be lightly clipped to shape about twice a year.

This vigorous grower also dries out the surrounding soil and depletes it of nutrients, and should be discounted as a boundary for small gardens, or it will tower over all the other plants and block out the sunlight. It is most useful as a windbreak in large gardens or in coastal areas.

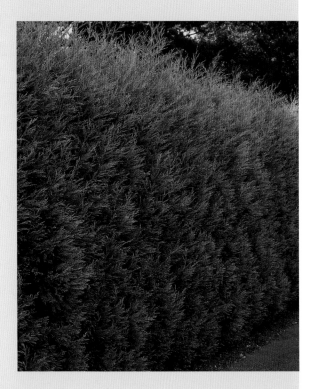

Hedges for wildlife

Hedges can enrich the garden by encouraging birds and other wildlife, providing shelter, nesting sites, and food in the form of berries and the insects they harbor. A wildlife hedge of mixed species, such as field maple (*Acer campestre*), hawthorn (*Crataegus monogyna*), holly (*Ilex aquifolium*), hazel (*Corylus avellana*), and spindle tree (*Euonymus europaeus*), will attract visitors all year. But don't clip it too hard if you want flowers and fruit. If space allows the occasional plant to grow into a small tree, so much the better. For extra flowers, plant species roses, which also offer hips in fall, and viburnums.

Considerate planting

Hedges can cause serious conflict between neighbors. They take up much more space than walls or fences, and are unsuitable for the boundaries between very narrow yards.

To stay on good terms with your neighbors, keep them informed of your boundary plans and do not allow your hedge to encroach on their yard. Before planting, check any local regulations or homeowners' association rules relating to boundary structures. Ensure that there is sufficient space for the hedge to spread, and, by mutual agreement, be prepared to cut it on both sides. Also, ensure that your hedge does not grow too high and shade your neighbor's property. Internal hedges for screening parts of the garden can be taller, but think about how you will clip them before they get out of hand.

(far left) Root-balled hedging plants are more expensive than bare-root plants, but cheaper than those offered in containers.

(left) Bare-root transplants should be carefully separated and planted out immediately, to prevent the exposed roots from drying out.

Buying hedging plants

Success with a new hedge depends on preparing the soil thoroughly before your plants arrive, and pampering them after planting and in the early years. Choose young plants rather than large specimens, since they will grow faster and soon overtake mature plants, giving you a much better hedge for a fraction of the cost.

Nurseries specializing in hedging offer a wide choice of plants, and many do mail order. A good supplier will tell you how plants are packed for shipment, and offer planting and pruning advice. Find suppliers on the Internet or through ads in gardening magazines.

Plants supplied by specialists are offered in three forms: bare-rooted transplants, root-balled, or in containers. Bare-rooted transplants are much cheaper than container-grown specimens; mixed native hedging is usually the most cost-effective option. Bare-root transplants are available from fall to spring, but you can order them at any time of the year and request a delivery date. Remember to ask for delivery in spring if you are buying evergreens or conifers and live in a cold, windy area, since this is the best planting time. Evergreens are also available root-balled, where the plant is lifted from the field with its roots and some soil, and then wrapped to reduce root disturbance.

Always buy more plants than you need in case some of your hedging dies. Plant the surplus in a quiet area of the garden or in containers that are sufficiently large to allow the roots to grow. Keep these plants well watered until your hedge is established and you are sure none need to be replaced.

Bare-rooted and root-balled hedging plants can be bought from fall to spring, but will not usually be lifted from the field in very severe weather, so let availability be your guide. If plants are on mail order, make sure you will be around to receive the delivery, and check your order when it arrives. In cold areas, conifer and evergreen hedges in particular will fare better if planted in spring, rather than winter. Pot-grown plants can be bought and planted all year, but it makes sense to plant in mild, moist fall or spring conditions. If you can't plant as soon as you receive your hedging, keep plants moist in their packing, and store in a cool place.

Planting a hedge

A single row of plants is sufficient for most hedging purposes, but for an extra-thick hedge, a double row can be used, provided you have enough space. In this example, a single row is being planted close up against a temporary hurdle fence. Spacing along the row for most hedging plants, whether they are deciduous or evergreen, should be 18–24 in (45–60 cm), but for smaller-leaved privet, boxwood, and *Lonicera nitida*, plant closer, at 12 in (30 cm). For dwarf edging hedges of box or lavender, for example, plant 6 in (15 cm) apart.

1 **Start preparing the ground** at least six weeks before planting. Clear the site of perennial weeds, then dig a strip the length of the hedge and 3–4 ft (90–120 cm) wide. Fork plenty of bulky organic matter (such as garden compost or well-rotted manure) into the trench as you go.

2 **Set out a line** to mark the edge of the row(s) of plants. Dig a trench along it for bare-root plants; you can dig individual holes for containerized or root-balled plants after marking out their positions. Use canes and a ruler to mark out the planting intervals, either in a single row along one line, or in two staggered rows, laying canes 18–24 in (45–60 cm) apart as a guide.

3 **Plant** at the original planting depth—this will either be the top of the rootball, or to the soil mark on the stem of bare-root plants.

4 **Return the soil** to the trench, and firm it well using your heel, at the same time creating a slight dip around the plants.

5 **Water the plants thoroughly**; the dip around each plant will help direct water to the roots, where it is really needed to help the plants establish.

6 **Place a thick mulch** of well-rotted manure or compost, or of shredded bark, around the plants, making sure it stays clear of the stems. Alternatively, lay landscape fabric in strips on each side and cover with bark chips.

Caring for hedges

Once planted, your hedge will need good care if it is to thrive. Most importantly, keep young plants watered for the first few years during dry spells until the hedge has become established. It should then not need additional watering except in dry periods in the summer. Fertilize all hedges in spring with a balanced fertilizer, such as blood, fish, and bone. At the same time, regularly clear any weeds from the base of the hedge, and after rain, or when the soil is moist, top off any mulch.

(top) **Make a trim line** by tying string to two canes; insert them at each end of your hedge to make a clipping guide for formal hedges, such as boxwood.

(bottom) **Hedges with large, thick leaves**, such as holly and laurel, should be trimmed with pruners; shears will cut the foliage, turning it brown.

Clipping and shaping

How you shape your hedges will depend on their age and whether you have grown them to be formal or informal.

■ **Young informal hedges** need no shaping, although shortening any long, whippy shoots will encourage them to bush out.

■ **Young formal hedges** may be pruned to shape and direct growth. Evergreens need only their sideshoots lightly trimmed for a few years after planting. Leave the main upright, or leading, shoot(s) to grow to the final hedge height. Deciduous hedges that are to have a dense, formal shape require more early shaping. In general, cut back the main shoot and any strong sideshoots by one-third after planting; repeat the following winter. Prune vigorous privet and hawthorn harder: cut back to within 12 in (30 cm) of soil level in late spring. In late summer, shorten sideshoots; then, in winter, cut the previous season's growth back by half.

■ **Mature informal hedges** should be merely trimmed in spring or summer, and left unpruned unless they are outgrowing their space or looking particularly untidy. Snip off any too-long shoots and keep the height under control.

■ **Mature formal hedges** need keeping in shape with regular clipping. This keeps growth dense, and the hedge thick and lush from top to toe. It also prevents it from expanding over the years. How often you clip depends on the plants and their rate of growth, but all hedges need at least one cut a year. For deciduous hedges and small-leaved evergreens, use garden shears or a powered hedge trimmer, keeping the blades parallel to the hedge at all times for flat sides. For large-leaved evergreens, such as cherry laurel (*Prunus laurocerasus*) and tough-leaved holly, use pruners to cut back individual shoots.

When using a powered hedge trimmer, wear goggles, ear protectors, and sturdy pruning gloves. Use a model you can handle with ease.

Fill gaps in a hedge base by layering a stem. Choose a low stem, and allow it to grow until it easily reaches the ground and can be pinned under the soil to root.

Filling in gaps in a hedge

If a plant in a young hedge dies, dig it out and plant a new one. Switch some of the soil with some from another part of the garden as a precaution, enriching it with well-rotted compost or manure. In an established hedge, remove the dead plant, and fill the gap with shoots of adjacent plants trained horizontally along strings or wires set between canes.

If a stem is forced out of position by snow or wind, tie it back in place using soft twine. Clipping your hedge into an A-shape (*see panel*) will reduce the risk of this happening. Cut out browning foliage, particularly on conifers, as it will not green up. If it leaves a gap, tie adjacent branches together with soft twine. Keep an eye out for more dead patches, which may indicate disease.

Renovating an overgrown hedge

Where an established hedge is overgrown, start by cutting back weeds such as ivy and brambles. When new growth sprouts, paint the leaves with glyphosate weedkiller—more than once if needed. Remove any dead wood and cut the hedge back. Apart from when dealing with conifers, spread this over two years—cut back the top and one side one year, and the other side the next.

Beech, hornbeam, and hawthorn can be cut back hard in late winter before new leaves appear. If regrowth is poor in the first season, delay the second half of the job for another year. For an old forsythia hedge, cut out some of the old wood once flowering is over. Among evergreens, yew, box, cherry laurel, privet, lonicera, holly, escallonia, evergreen berberis, and pyracantha can cope with hard pruning, in mid- to late spring when growth is well under way. After pruning, fertilize and water, and mulch with bulky organic matter.

CLIPPING HEDGES INTO SHAPE

Prune formal hedges, such as beech and yew, from the time of planting so that the plants form a wedge or A-shape as they grow. These shapes allow light to reach all areas of the hedge, which will encourage even growth.

If you live in an area that experiences snow, clip the top into a point or narrow A-shape so that the snow cannot settle on the top where its weight may damage the top of the hedge.

For a hedge with a narrow profile, clip the sides regularly from the start. Trim it back each time to the last cut, for a smooth finish.

(top) **Beech** with a pointed top to shed snow.

(bottom) **"A-shaped" yew** hedge with a flattened top.

Plants for hedges

1 *Carpinus betulus*
Hornbeam
A deciduous tree that does better than beech in exposed sites, and holds its juvenile dead leaves in winter. Trim in mid- to late summer. H to 30 ft (9 m).

2 *Lonicera nitida* 'Baggesen's Gold'
Shrubby honeysuckle
A cylindrical evergreen shrub, best grown as a formal hedge. Fast growing and may need several trims a year. H to 5 ft (1.5 m).

3 *Taxus baccata*
Yew
A formal and slow-growing evergreen that may need only one clipping a year in summer or fall. H to 30 ft (10 m).

4 *Ligustrum ovalifolium*
Oval-leaved privet
Fast-growing shrub best trimmed into formal hedging three or four times in the growing season. Normally evergreen, though it may lose leaves in cold winters. H to 12 ft (4 m).

5 *Chamaecyparis lawsoniana* 'Pembury Blue'
Lawson cypress
Quite fast-growing cypress tree with sprays of blue-gray foliage. Trim in spring and early fall. H to 30 ft (9 m).

6 *Prunus lusitanica* subsp. *azorica*
Portugal laurel
A dense, evergreen laurel with glossy, dark green leaves. For a semiformal hedge, trim with pruners in late summer. H to 70 ft (20 m).

7 *Ilex aquifolium* 'Golden Milkboy'
Holly
Slow-growing, dense evergreen, clipped with pruners in late summer for formal hedging. This variety has irregular yellow patches on the leaves. H 20 ft (6 m).

8 *Fagus sylvatica*
Beech
A deciduous tree that keeps its juvenile brown, dead leaves in winter. Mix green- and copper- or purple-leaved varieties for a "tapestry" effect. Trim in late summer. H to 30 ft (9 m).

9 *Lavandula angustifolia* 'Hidcote'
Lavender
Best as low, semiformal edging. Trim with shears in spring and after flowering to keep compact. H to 24 in (60 cm).

10 *Berberis darwinii* 'Barberry'
Barberry
Vigorous evergreen covered in a mass of dark orange flowers in spring. Trim after flowering to encourage more flowers in fall. H to 10 ft (3 m).

11 *Buxus sempervirens* 'Latifolia Maculata'
Boxwood
A dense, small-leaved evergreen that needs trimming two or three times in the growing season for formal hedging. This is a variegated form. H to 15 ft (5 m).

12 *Rosa rugosa*
Hedgehog rose
Grows vigorously and densely, and is the best rose for a tall, informal hedge. Very prickly stems, and large red hips in fall. H 3–8 ft (1–2.5 m).

13. Containers

Plants in containers add color and interest to your garden, as well as broadening the range of plants you can grow. Containers inject drama into areas where planting in open ground is not possible: well-chosen plants enhance paved areas, softening hard brick and concrete surfaces, and bright flowers or foliage can bring color to dark corners. Suitably planted containers can reinforce the style of a garden, too. An olive tree, yucca, or palm in an urn may create a Mediterranean feel, while an Oriental ginger jar containing a bamboo or acer is ideal in a Japanese-style setting.

Mixed plantings usually look best if you avoid a kaleidoscope of wildly different colors. Here, a container of *Cosmos bipinnatus* 'Sonata Pink', *Gypsophila muralis* 'Gypsy Pink', and a variegated ivy employs a simple color scheme of pinks and greens.

Growing plants in containers

Containers allow you to grow plants that dislike your garden conditions. For example, if you have alkaline soil but would like shrubs that need acidic soil, such as azaleas and pieris, they will thrive in pots of ericaceous potting mix. If your soil is dry, you can keep astilbes and hostas moist. Tender plants, such as agaves, which prefer dry, well-drained sites and are not reliably hardy in most areas, can be grown in pots even in gardens with wet or waterlogged soil, and moved under cover in winter. And plants with different soil needs can be grouped together in individual pots to create combinations that would be impossible in the open ground.

Use plants with strong shapes, such as cordylines, to create an instant focal point. Grown in containers that can easily be moved, they offer a quick way to change the emphasis.

Where to place containers

Container plants perform best in a sheltered spot, so patios and terraces are ideal locations. In exposed sites, pots dry out quickly and may blow over. Just as in the open ground, it is important to put container plants in the right place, grouping those that like similar conditions to achieve healthy displays.

Displays are simple to create and change. Large pots can be used as focal points; pairs of identical pots with matched plantings are ideal on either side of paths, and if placed to each side of a doorway can emphasize architectural features. Conversely, containers can hide eyesores, such as utility covers or drains.

Fill seasonal gaps in the border with potted lilies or tulips, which bloom spectacularly, but only for a limited period. Once their flowers fade, the pots can be lifted and replaced. A group of containers holding ferns, hostas, and other shade-tolerant plants should survive underneath established trees, where the ground is typically dry, poor, filled with roots, and difficult to cultivate.

If your outdoor space is paved, containers are ideal. Some climbers, such as jasmine and certain clematis, grow well in pots, so even on a paved area they can be trained to scramble up walls. Even with no yard, you can grow plants in containers. Site windowboxes on wide window ledges, or hang them from the wall on brackets. Hanging baskets can be placed in a sheltered spot where they are accessible for maintenance and watering. Wall-mounted pots can brighten a bare wall, although they only hold a small amount of potting mix, so they require copious watering in summer. For these containers, robust mounting hardware is vital.

Choosing containers

1 Terra-cotta and clay Versatile materials, with pots available in a range of shapes and styles: urns, vases, bell pots, pans, bowls, and jars. Plants grown in jars are tricky to repot if the root ball is wider than the pot's neck. Planting holes in the sides are often used for herbs and strawberry plants.
Pros: Porous terra-cotta allows the root ball to breathe, reducing waterlogging. Huge range of colors and styles available, often relatively inexpensive.
Cons: Porous nature of terra-cotta means plants need frequent watering. Often broken when tipped over or due to frost shattering.

2 Synthetic materials Plastic, fiberglass, and resin containers are widely available alternatives to traditional materials: they are lightweight, frost-proof, and almost unbreakable. Large synthetic pots are easily moved, so they are ideal for tender plants, which must be in a sheltered place in winter, and decorative foliage plants, which can be moved to mask flowers that are past their best.
Pros: Frostproof, lightweight, and inexpensive, and available in a range of colors and styles.
Cons: Poor insulation, and easily blown over.

3 Metal A range of shapes, colors, and styles are available; many are suited to modern settings. May be galvanized, painted, or coated to protect against rust, though some finishes gradually tarnish. A liner will insulate roots against frost.
Pros: Wide range of styles, robust, and attractive.
Cons: Good-quality pieces are expensive. Lead containers are heavy. Shiny finishes show up mud splashes, and will dull.

4 Wood Natural wood planters are unobtrusive and provide a perfect foil for plants. Wood is light and easy to handle, but must be treated if it is to last. Half-barrels make excellent large containers.
Pros: Not easily broken, and durable if treated. Also lightweight with good insulating properties.
Cons: May rot if not treated or emptied regularly.

5 Stone Among the most desirable and durable containers. Stone urns suit a traditional setting, especially once aged, making them ideal focal points in a historic garden. Contemporary designs are also available. Reconstituted stone is cheaper and more widely available.
Pros: Durable, weighty, and stable, with good insulating properties. Available in many styles.
Cons: Both heavy and expensive.

Planting containers

To ensure that plants grow and perform as well as possible, you need to plant them properly. Your choice of potting mix will depend on what you are planting:

■ **Soil-based potting mix** is better for long-term plantings like specimen shrubs; it holds nutrients for longer, and drains better—important if plants are to survive outside in winter.

■ **Soilless potting mix** is usually best for short-term planting, such as bedding plants for summer containers. It is light and clean, and has nutrients for young plants; you may have to add fertilizer later. Also ideal for hanging baskets.

If your chosen pot is large or heavy, place it in position first, and then plant it. Check that the drainage holes are sufficient, then fill the bottom of the pot with extra drainage material, such as polystyrene pieces or crocks, and cover with a 1–2-in (2.5–5 cm) layer of potting mix.

1 **Water the plant** thoroughly about an hour before planting, then position it—still in its original pot—inside the new container.

2 **Add potting mix** to raise the plant to 1 in (2.5 cm) below the rim; this allows space for watering. Also add potting mix around the sides.

3 **Firm the potting mix** well around the pot. Lift out the plant in its pot, leaving a hole in the potting mix. Remove the plant from its original pot.

4 **If there is a tight mass of roots** around the root ball, tease them out gently. Place the plant back into the hole in the potting mix, and firm in.

5 **Check that the plant** is at the same depth as it was in its old pot. Then cover the top with a little more potting mix, and water well.

6 **Finish off** with a layer of ornamental mulch. This helps to retain soil moisture and suppresses weeds, as well as anchoring the pot.

Care and maintenance

Plants in containers are easy to maintain and control. Feeding and watering can be regulated and monitored, while deadheading and pruning are simple, as plants are movable. When a plant's season of interest has passed, you can simply replace it. Plants that grow too vigorously in open ground, such as some bamboos, are restrained by pots, while slower-growing species that are easily swamped in a border can be pampered. Pests and diseases are easy to treat, and plants can be lifted above soil level away from slugs and snails. However, plants in pots depend on you totally for their food, water, and general care, whereas the same plants in open ground will survive with far less attention.

Watering

Containers dry out quickly, especially in hot or windy weather. Some plants, like camellias and rhododendrons, do not set flower buds properly if they are short of moisture. Being evergreen, they need watering all year. Pots close to walls and fences or under trees do not receive much rainfall, so keep an eye on them. The signs of lack of water are obvious—wilting, yellowing foliage, and in extreme cases falling leaves.

Use a watering can, or a hose with a wand or nozzle, so you can moderate the flow of water. The plant has had a thorough soaking once water flows from the bottom of the pot. Surface compaction may prevent water from soaking in at all; push a hand fork into the soil a few times to remedy this. An irrigation system is the most reliable way to keep plants watered. Small-gauge pipes with adjustable nozzles are placed in the pots; water can be controlled by a timer.

(far left) **A piece of slate** or crock can be used if you don't have a watering wand. Place it on the soil as you water, and it will help distribute the flow evenly.

(left) **When a plant has dried out**, the soil shrinks away from the sides of the pot, and water runs through the gap. To alleviate this, submerge the pot in water for up to an hour.

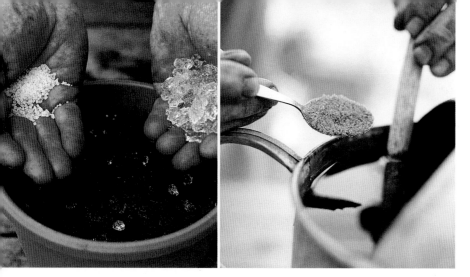

(far left) **Water-retaining gel** is useful for those who occasionally forget to water; it is excellent for hanging baskets, which dry out quickly. The gel stores moisture around the root ball, creating a reservoir for the plant to draw on in dry periods. Add the gel granules to the potting mix at planting time, following the directions on the packet.

(left) **Adding water-soluble fertilizer** to a watering can is the easiest way to feed your plants. Always follow the instructions on the packet, as an excess of fertilizer can kill plants.

Fertilizing

Plants in containers need fertilizing from late spring to mid-fall for healthy growth and a succession of flowers. Fertilizing is usually done every two weeks, though hungry plants, such as tomatoes and brugmansias, need it weekly.

The simplest method is to add water-soluble fertilizer to the watering can. Controlled-release fertilizers avoid the need for continual feeding, as the fertilizer is released over several months. These are available as pellets, sticks, or small plugs, which are pressed into the soil once the plant is in the pot. Alternatively, buy granules and mix them into the soil before planting. All forms are useful in a low-maintenance garden. Controlled-release fertilizers are also the best option for containers packed full of plants, such as hanging baskets. Follow the manufacturer's guidelines; overfertilizing can be fatal.

Adding well-rotted manure to the bottom of the pot when planting, or sprinkling pelleted chicken manure on pots in spring, are good organic alternatives.

Moving heavy pots, even when empty, is not easy. Grow plants that will be moved regularly in light pots and soilless potting mix. Plant movers—metal or wooden stands on wheels, and equipped with brakes—are useful for heavy containers.

Repotting

Repot regularly in spring, using a new pot only slightly larger than the original. Potbound plants are often top-heavy, and hard to water, with little space for water to collect on and seep into the soil without spilling over the edge or running down the inside of the pot. Foliage may be yellow, and new growth reduced. If you want to keep an overgrown plant in the same pot, either prune it, or divide it and replant in fresh potting mix (*see pp.298–9*). Also, top-dress potted trees and shrubs in spring by removing one-third of the soil, without damaging the roots, and replacing it with fresh.

Flowers and climbers for containers

1 *Brachyscome iberidifolia* 'White Splendour'
Swan river daisy
Spreading annual, ideal for hanging baskets. White, pink, or purplish flowers. H to 18 in (45 cm); S 14 in (35 cm).

2 *Thunbergia alata*
Black-eyed Susan
Half-hardy climber with bright orange or yellow flowers. If grown as a perennial, protect pots in winter. H to 8 ft (2.5 m).

3 *Tropaeolum peregrinum*
Canary creeper
Vigorous annual climber bearing bright yellow flowers with fringed petals from summer to autumn. H 8–12 ft (2.5–4 m).

4 *Hyacinthus orientalis* 'Blue Jacket'
Hyacinth
Plant bulbs in fall for richly scented flowers in mid-and late spring. H 8 in (20 cm); S 12 in (30 cm).

5 *Dahlia* 'Yellow Hammer'
Dahlia
A dwarf bedding dahlia suited to pots. Single, yellow flowers and bronze leaves. H 24 in (60 cm); S 18 in (45 cm).

6 *Pelargonium* 'Lemon Fancy'
Pelargonium
Purple flowers and citrus-scented leaves. Protect from frosts. H 16–18 in (40–45 cm); S 6–8 in (15–20 cm).

7 *Plumbago auriculata*
Cape leadwort
Evergreen climber. Grow in a sunny spot; bring pots indoors in winter. H 10–20 ft (3–6 m); S 3–10 ft (1–3 m).

8 *Cobaea scandens*
Cobaea
A tender, perennial climber usually grown as an annual unless protected in winter. Fragrant, white flowers turn purple as they age. H 50 ft (15 m).

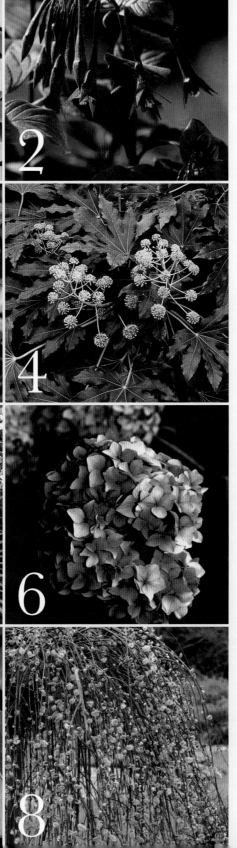

Trees and shrubs for containers

1 *Choisya ternata* 'Sundance'
Mexican orange blossom
An evergreen shrub with lovely foliage—
yellow when young, turning green with
age. H 8 ft (2.5 m); S 8 ft (2.5 m).

2 *Fuchsia* 'Thalia'
Fuchsia
A compact variety with small, scarlet
flowers that have unusually long tubes.
Bring indoors in winter. H to 30 in
(75 cm); S to 30 in (75 cm).

3 *Rhododendron* 'Irohayama'
Azalea
A dwarf azalea with pale pink or
lavender flowers. Needs special acidic
(ericaceous) potting mix. H 2 ft (60 cm);
S 2 ft (60 cm).

4 *Fatsia japonica*
Japanese aralia
A large, striking, architectural plant with
wide-spreading, glossy, green leaves. It
needs a correspondingly large container.
H 5–12 ft (1.5–4 m); S 5–12 ft (1.5–4 m).

5 *Trachycarpus fortunei*
Chusan palm
A large, evergreen palm that can
withstand cool temperatures, but is
safer protected indoors in winter. H 10 ft
(3 m) or more; S 8 ft (2.5 m).

6 *Hydrangea macrophylla* 'Nikko Blue'
Hydrangea
Mophead variety with rounded, blue
blooms. H to 5 ft (1.5 m); S to 6 ft (2 m).

7 *Camellia japonica* 'Ace of Hearts'
Camellia
Evergreen, flowering in early spring. Needs
a large pot, acidic soil, and a sheltered
site. H to 10 ft (3 m); S 6 ft (2 m).

8 *Salix caprea* 'Kilmarnock'
Kilmarnock willow
A weeping willow small enough for a
large container. Spring catkins before
the leaves. H 5–6 ft (1.5–2 m); S 6 ft (2 m).

Growing crops in containers

Pots, containers, and growing bags can turn a small yard, patio, or courtyard into a miniature kitchen garden. In fact, there are numerous advantages to growing fruit and vegetables this way. Containers can be moved, allowing you to exploit microclimates—they can be placed somewhere open and sunny in summer and brought back to a sheltered spot in cold or windy weather. You also have control over the quality of the soil or potting mix you use.

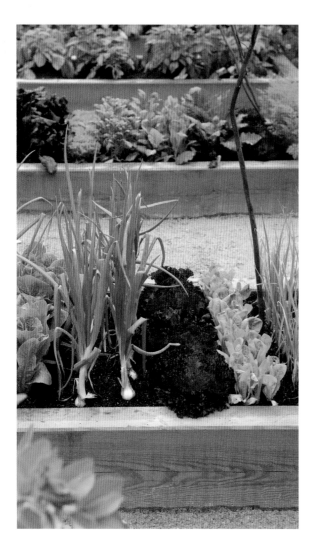

Raised beds can be thought of as containers, in a sense. Though they can't be moved, they do give you some control over the quality and composition of the soil.

Choosing containers

Almost any kind of container can be pressed into service for growing crops—from beautiful old terra-cotta pots to improvised planters made from salvaged wooden boxes or plastic crates. The single, most important rule is that there must be a hole or holes in the bottom, to allow drainage and prevent waterlogging.

Clay pots are authentically traditional and will weather beautifully. And, because they're solid, they are less likely to tip over if plants such as climbing beans or tomatoes become top-heavy. But they can be fragile, and may crack or flake in a hard freeze. Plastic pots are less expensive. They are also lighter, so they can be moved more easily from place to place around the garden, and they are impermeable, so the soil inside will not dry out so quickly.

Special growing bags have their uses, but they tend to dry out rapidly and need regular watering. They may also require special frames to support climbing plants. The volume of potting mix can be increased by inserting bottomless pots into the bags, then planting directly into the pots.

A miniature herb garden featuring a mixture of sage, purple sage, lavender, and parsley puts a stack of old car tires to practical use.

Strawberries can easily be grown in pots (and the fruit stays cleaner) but they must be kept well watered. Small fruit trees will need a large container.

Hanging baskets suspended from the branches of an olive tree make perfect aerial herb and salad gardens, as long as you keep them regularly watered.

Growing vegetables

The vegetables that do best in pots tend to be those with fairly shallow roots, such as tomatoes, peppers, eggplants, Swiss chard, and, if they are supported, climbing French and runner beans. Salad crops are particularly suitable, especially lettuces, endives, corn salad, green onions, radishes, and cut-and-come-again leaves. Even potatoes can be grown in deep containers. Many garden centers sell special dwarf or patio vegetable varieties that are ideal. The vegetables least likely to do well are perennials such as asparagus, and brassicas such as broccoli or cauliflowers.

Growing fruit and herbs

Growing fruit trees in pots is always going to be a challenge; you'll need very large containers and plenty of space. But don't rule it out. There are numerous varieties of apple, pear, cherry, and even peach and apricot trees available that have been bred specially for container growing and will therefore not become too tall or spread too wide. Indeed, citrus fruits such as lemons, limes, and oranges were traditionally grown in large pots that were brought into glasshouses or "orangeries" in winter and moved outdoors in summer. Figs actually fruit better in pots, blueberries can be grown in the special acidic (ericaceous) soil they require, and strawberries can be better protected from snails and slugs.

Herbs are perfect for container growing, too. Rosemary, basil, thyme, marjoram, oregano, and parsley all do well, if kept watered, and may be more convenient for use if grown in pots close to the kitchen door or windowsill than planted out in the open ground. Mint is particularly appropriate for container growing. Left to its own devices, it is very invasive and will spread uncontrollably; constraining it to a pot keeps it firmly in check.

Planting a hanging basket

Summer baskets are usually planted in late spring, but most of the plants are tender, and need protection until after the last frost. Decide what kind of liner to use, and make sure it is the correct size for the basket.

1 **Set the basket in a pot** or pail to keep it stable throughout the planting process. Put the liner (here, of coir) in position and trim it to fit along the rim. A circle of polythene at the bottom will help retain water.

2 **Cut a series of slits** for planting trailing plants through the sides. Add a 2-in (5-cm) layer of soilless potting mix, blended with controlled-release fertilizer and water-retaining gel.

3 **Remove the trailing plants** from their pots and thread them through the slits you have just created. It's a good idea to use a plastic bag to protect the stems and leaves.

4 **Place a pot in the center** at the top of the basket to act as a watering reservoir, and plant around it. Use upright plants in the center and trailers around the rim. Add more potting mix and build up the planting in tiers until the potting mix is within 2 in (5 cm) of the rim.

5 **Firm the potting mix**, and water the basket thoroughly through the plastic pot. Use a watering wand so that the water doesn't puddle in one section.

6 **Hang your basket** in a sheltered spot at a height that you can reach easily to water it. Make sure the hanging hardware is strong enough to take the weight of saturated potting mix.

Plants for hanging baskets

1 *Lobelia* 'Colour Cascade'
Lobelia
Annual trailing lobelia produces a summer-long profusion of small blue, white, pink, red, and violet flowers. H 6 in (15 cm); S 4–6 in (10–15 cm).

2 *Hedera helix* 'Little Diamond'
Variegated ivy
A miniature, trailing ivy with gray-green leaves that have creamy-white margins. H 12 in (30 cm).

3 *Diascia barberae* 'Blackthorn Apricot'
Diascia
Apricot-colored flowers are produced through summer and well into fall. H 10 in (25 cm); S to 20 in (50 cm).

4 *Verbena* 'Diamond Merci'
Verbena
Rounded clusters of small, burgundy-red flowers from midsummer to fall. H 12 in (30 cm); S 12–20 in (30–50 cm).

5 *Felicia amelloides* 'Read's White'
Felicia
A white variety of the more usual blue daisy. It should flower all summer. H 24 in (60 cm); S 24 in (60 cm).

6 *Lotus berthelotii*
Parrot's beak or coral gem
Trailing, evergreen shrub with pairs of exotic, orange-red flowers like lobster claws. H 8 in (20 cm); S indefinite.

7 *Campanula isophylla* 'Stella Blue'
Campanula
A compact, trailing campanula with bright blue-violet flowers from midsummer into fall. H 6–8 in (15–20 cm); S to 12 in (30 cm).

8 *Osteospermum* 'Buttermilk'
Osteospermum
Daisylike flowers are primrose-yellow on top and golden-yellow beneath. H 24 in (60 cm); S 24 in (60 cm).

9 *Glechoma hederacea* 'Variegata'
Ground ivy
A trailing perennial useful in hanging baskets for its attractive, small, toothed leaves with white margins. H 6 in (15 cm); S to 6 ft (2 m).

10 *Viola* 'Jackanapes'
Viola
Almost all violas and pansies suit hanging baskets. This variety has bicolored flowers from late spring. H to 5 in (12 cm); S to 12 in (30 cm).

11 *Chlorophytum comosum* 'Vittatum'
Spider plant
A variegated form of this spreading, dangling, grasslike perennial. H 6–8 in (15–20 cm); S 6–12 in (15–30 cm).

12 *Scaevola aemola*
Fairy fan flower
Clusters of flowers should appear all summer if plants are fertilized monthly. H to 20 in (50 cm); S to 20 in (50 cm).

13 *Convolvulus sabatius*
Convolvulus
A trailing plant whose trumpetlike flowers should spill over the edges of hanging baskets all summer. H to 6 in (15 cm); S 20 in (50 cm).

14 *Helichrysum petiolare* 'Limelight'
Helichrysum
Trailing, evergreen shrub suited to growing among flowering plants for its lime-green foliage. H 16 in (40 cm); S 5 ft (1.5 m).

15 *Fuchsia* 'Corallina'
Fuchsia
Its lax, spreading habit makes it ideal for spilling out of a basket. Bright scarlet, purple, and pink flowers. H 18–24 in (45–60 cm); S 24–30 in (60–75 cm).

16 *Nemesia caerulea*
Nemesia
Spreading, dark green foliage and small, lightly scented flowers, usually purple-blue. H to 24 in (60 cm); S 12 in (30 cm).

Indoor/ outdoor plants

With milder winters, the range of exotic plants we can grow is expanding. Plants once thought of as tender may survive outdoors all year in sheltered urban gardens or other warm microclimates. Elsewhere, plants can be grown outdoors until temperatures fall, then moved indoors into a cool conservatory or glasshouse. The key to overwintering them is to keep them cool and the soil dry. Once winter is over and the danger of heavy frost has passed, the pots can go outdoors again. Acclimatize them gradually to outside conditions: if it's cold at night, bring them in, and shelter them from high winds or heavy rain.

1 *Pelargonium* 'Mr. Henry Cox'
Pelargonium
A so-called "fancy-leaved" variety, with golden yellow foliage that has green, purple, and red markings. Almost all pelargoniums need overwintering indoors. Min. 36°F (2°C). H 10–12 in (25–30 cm); S 4–5 in (10–12 cm).

2 *Lantana camara* 'Radiation'
Lantana
Large, green leaves and round, clustered flowerheads in vibrant orange and red. Needs protection from cold in winter. Min. 50°F (10°C). H 3–6 ft (1–2 m); S 3–6 ft (1–2 m).

3 *Ensete ventricosum*
Abyssinian or Ethiopian banana
Huge, arching leaves each more than 10 ft (3 m) in length. The plant may produce fruits—though not true bananas. Min. 45°F (7°C). H 20 ft (6 m) or more; S to 15 ft (5 m).

4 *Cordyline australis* 'Variegata'
New Zealand cabbage palm
Palm-like tree with long, arching leaves, striped creamy white at the margin. Mature examples bear tiny, creamy white flowers. Min. 41°F (5°C). H 10–30 ft (3–10 m); S 3–12 ft (1–4 m).

5 *Cycas revoluta*
Japanese sago palm
Long, arching, deeply divided, feather-like leaves up to 5ft (1.5m) in length. It may flower, or even fruit, but it's unusual in container-grown plants. Min. 45°F (7°C). H 3–6ft (1–2m) or more; S 3–6ft (1–2m) or more.

6 *Crassula arborescens*
Silver jade plant
A succulent originally from South Africa, with fleshy, gray-green leaves and star-shaped, pink flowers in fall and winter. Min. 41°F (5°C). H 12 ft (4 m); S 6 ft (2 m).

7 *Pericallis* x *hybrida*
Cineraria
Daisylike, tender perennial from the Canary Islands, Madeira, and the Azores. A wide range of flower colors, from red and pink to white and blue. Min. 45°F (7°C). H 18–24 in (45–60 cm); S 10–24 in (25–60 cm).

8 *Echeveria pulvinata*
Plush plant
A small, Mexican succulent forming rosettes of fleshy, slightly hairy, green-gray leaves with red tips and margins. Min. 45°F (7°C). H 12 in (30 cm); S 20 in (50 cm).

9 *Sansevieria trifasciata* 'Golden Hahnii'
Mother-in-law's tongue
A small perennial with rosettes of sharp, pointed, yellow-and-green striped leaves. In summer, move outdoors into a sunny position, and do not allow pots to become waterlogged. Min. 55°F (13°C). H 5 in (12 cm); S 5 in (12 cm).

14. Tools & Techniques

Do you really need a garage full of expensive, specialized garden tools and equipment: collinear hoes, daisy grubbers, star-wheeled cultivators—the whole nine yards? The simple answer is "no." Most gardeners—both novice and expert—actually get by with a handful of simple, familiar, well-chosen tools. And less is more in terms of gardening techniques, too. Certainly, when you are starting out, there is knowledge to acquire and experience to accumulate, but gardening is not nearly as difficult as it looks. Much of it is a matter of a little hard work, some regular maintenance, and simple common sense.

Good-quality tools make gardening easier and more enjoyable—and if you take care of them, they'll probably last you a lifetime.

The basic tool kit

All gardeners have a few favorite tools that they would not be without. When buying gardening tools and equipment, look for good-quality products, but don't feel you have to buy the most expensive. In most cases, tools in the mid-price range are fine, but do beware of very cheap equipment that may not last long. A basic tool kit will enable you to do most jobs in the garden. Don't be seduced too early on by the vast range of gadgets for sale. The more you garden, the more you will discover which tools will be helpful and which are gimmicks.

Choosing tools

Reputable companies normally offer a few years' guarantee, depending on the tool or equipment. You may even find that a household object or homemade tool does the job just as well. For example, the official tool used to make planting holes for seedlings or young plants is a dibber, but a blunt pencil is a good alternative. Make sure the tools you buy are not only comfortable to grip but also suit your size. If you're not very strong, you may well be better off with a small spade or fork, because larger tools need more leverage to be used effectively. Taller gardeners will almost certainly find that digging is more comfortable when using spades or forks with shafts that are longer than the standard 28–29 in (70–73 cm). Shafts of up to 3 ft (1 m) are available.

Forks and spades have shafts of different lengths and materials: metal shafts are stronger than wood, and may be plastic-covered. Border spades and forks have slightly smaller heads, making them easy to handle and useful for light work.

A rake can be used to level soil or to clear the ground. Clear lawns of leaves and thatch using a spring-tined rake.

A hand fork and trowel are indispensable for weeding, planting young plants and bulbs, and small digging jobs. Hand forks are ideal for heavy clay soils. Small tools are easily mislaid in the garden; look for those with brightly colored handles that can be spotted easily, or paint tools with wooden handles to make them more conspicuous.

Pruners are essential for many pruning jobs; choose a pair with a safety catch and crossover blades. Try before you buy to make sure they feel right.

A Dutch hoe is invaluable when it comes to clearing a large area of weeds. The long handle helps to avoid a backache, which is often a consequence of weeding.

A pruning saw is useful for cutting small branches; the blade folds away on some types, but one with a fixed blade is a better choice if you have lots of shrubs.

Shears are used for trimming long grass and small hedges, and for cutting back herbaceous perennials. Before buying, be sure they are light enough for you to use.

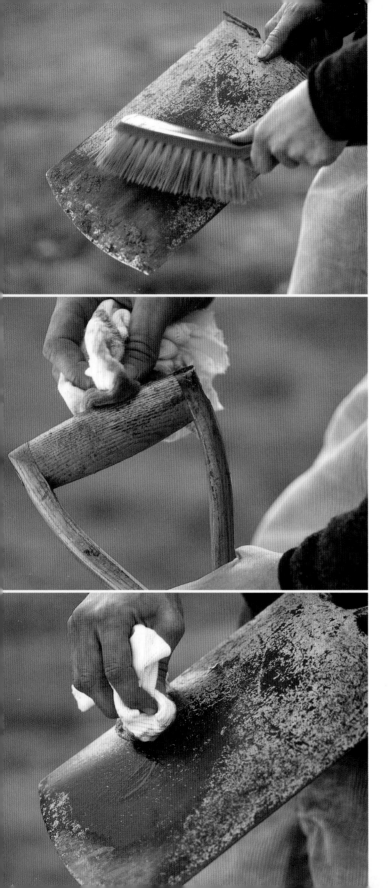

Storing your tools

Keep your tools in the garage or storage shed. Always clean off soil from digging tools before putting them away, and clean and wipe down cutting blades with an oily rag. This will prolong the life of the tools. Invest in hooks, racks, and shelves, or make them yourself out of recycled lumber, and get into the habit of hanging up your tools after use and coiling electrical cords neatly. Also clean and stack pots and bundle canes together before storing. By keeping your storage space neat, you will be able to fit more in, find what you need quickly, and avoid unnecessary hazards.

Caring for cultivation tools

The majority of digging tools are made from either carbon steel or stainless steel. In order to prevent carbon steel from rusting, it is important to clean and oil your tools regularly. Carbon steel Dutch hoes and spades will slide through soil more easily if you sharpen them occasionally. Some tools have a nonstick coating, but this may eventually wear off. Although stainless steel tools are a bit more expensive, they are worth the money; they are long-lasting, do not rust, and make digging easier, because they cut through the soil cleanly and it does not stick to the blade.

(top) **All metal tools**, including spades, forks, hand trowels, and rakes, need cleaning after use, before you put them away. Brush off any soil, wash, and dry thoroughly.

(middle) **Wooden shafts and handles** of spades and forks need to be checked every so often. Sand off any roughness and wipe over with linseed oil to nourish and preserve the wood.

(bottom) **Carbon steel tools** benefit from a wipe with an oily rag to prevent them from rusting, and blades will cut through the soil more easily if you sharpen them with a file.

Caring for cutting tools

Sharp blades ensure cleaner cuts when pruning and trimming. Pruners need frequent sharpening, as pruning soon blunts the blade. Good-quality models are easy to take apart, which makes cleaning and sharpening easier, and allows a damaged blade to be replaced. Knives are often better than pruners for delicate jobs, and should be cleaned, oiled, and sharpened in the same way. Keep a pocket-sized sharpening steel ready to sharpen your blade as you work. Use a special tool or a metal file to sharpen shears. Sharpen only the beveled cutting edge, and tighten the screw holding the blades together.

1 **To clean pruner blades**, spray on some lubricant or household cleaner to remove any dirt and sap, and then wipe it off with a tissue. For dried-on sap, use a scourer or fine-grade steel wool and metal polish.

2 **Smear lubricant** or light oil onto the bevel-edged blade and lightly rub it off with a nylon scourer or fine-grade steel wool. This helps prevent rusting and keeps the blade smooth between sharpenings.

3 **Sharpen the blade** with an oilstone or a diamond sharpening tool. Hold it at the same angle as the beveled edge and draw it across the edge. Gently rub the flat side of the blade to remove any burrs, and then oil the blades.

Watering

Without adequate water, plants will suffer and eventually die. For much of the year, from mid-fall until spring, rainfall is usually sufficient, but there are times, particularly during late spring and summer, when there is not enough rain. Supplies can run short as rapidly growing plants draw up moisture from the soil, and at such times it is important to know what to water and how.

Create a shallow depression around the plant after planting. Water will then be retained over the area of the roots while it soaks into the soil.

What to water

You do not need to water everything in the garden, even during hot spells. For example, long-established trees, shrubs, roses, climbers, and hardy perennials with extensive root systems can withstand periods of drought. Established lawns, too, can usually go without extra watering; even brown, parched grass will normally green up again when rain returns.

Certain plants, however, might need additional watering:

■ **New plants** have small, immature root systems that are not yet able to reach water held deep in the soil. Watering after planting—even if the soil does not seem dry—not only keeps the roots moist but also settles the soil around them.

■ **Wall-trained plants** can be in a "rain shadow," sheltered from rain by the wall and house eaves. Consequently, the soil around their roots is very dry. If you plant about 18 in (45 cm) away from a wall or fence, the soil will hold more moisture. Mulch plants deeply in spring when the soil is moist to keep it that way.

■ **Newly germinated seeds and seedlings** will die if the roots dry out. Stand pots or trays in water, so that they can take up moisture from below, and then remove them when the top of the soil is damp. This avoids water on the leaves, which increases a seedling's susceptibility to fungal diseases, such as damping off.

■ **Conifers** can suffer and may die in hot weather without enough water; if the foliage is badly scorched, it may not regrow. Some, such as juniper and pine, are more tolerant of dry soil, and are good choices for warm, sunny gardens or sandy soil.

■ **New lawns** have to be watered until they are well established. Expensive new sod will curl up and die if subjected to drought. Established utility lawns containing ryegrass can do without water. They may turn brown but will green up again after rain.

(far left) **Hanging baskets** tend to dry out quickly in hot and windy weather and therefore need to be watered regularly.

(left) **Leafy perennial plants** can act like a mulch. The leaves shade the soil, helping to reduce evaporation and create a cool, humid microclimate.

■ **Fruit and vegetable crops** need water most when they are flowering and developing their fruits or other edible parts. If they run dry at these times, cropping is badly affected. Many leafy vegetables wilt or go to seed in hot, dry conditions.

■ **Shallow-rooting rhododendrons** fold down their leaves when short of water in hot, dry periods. Flower bud formation is affected, and plants will brown and die if not watered. They are not a good choice for hot spots or sandy, free-draining soils.

■ **Plants in containers** need plenty of water because they are growing in a limited volume of soil, which rapidly dries out. In hot, dry, and windy weather, check them daily, and twice a day in exceptionally hot summer weather or if the pots are small.

When planning or adding to plantings, choose plants that match your soil conditions. Drought-resistant plants, such as sedums and lavender, need little or no additional watering; others, such as conifers, will become scorched and remain unsightly forever if water is in short supply.

How to water

Water early in the morning or in the evening, when cool conditions reduce evaporation, and plants take up less water than at warmer times of the day. Under a hot midday sun, water droplets on leaves will act as miniature magnifying glasses and may scorch them. Aim to water plants that are susceptible to slug and snail damage in the morning, as extra moisture in the evening encourages these nocturnal pests. When watering, a weekly soaking is better than a daily dribble. Light watering does not penetrate far and encourages the roots to grow up to the surface to reach the moisture—and, of course, they are then even more vulnerable to drought.

PLANTS FOR DRY PLACES

Look out for small, narrow, succulent, or spiky leaves, as these are characteristics of plants that prefer to grow in hot, dry conditions. Silvery or gray surfaces reflect light to keep leaves cool, and a covering of fine hairs minimizes water loss in windy places.

- Achillea
- Armeria
- Artemisia
- Brachyglottis
- Cistus
- *Cordyline australis*
- Cotton lavender (*Santolina*)
- Eryngium
- Globe thistle (*Echinops, below*)
- Lavender (*Lavandula*)
- Mullein (*Verbascum*)
- Ornamental grasses (many)
- Phlomis
- Phormium
- Rock rose (*Helianthemum*)
- Rosemary (*Rosmarinus*)
- Salvia
- Thyme (*Thymus*)

Auto-irrigation systems can be operated manually or using a timer, providing plants with water on a regular basis. Take care not to flood or deprive pots when regulating the flow.

Lay a soaker hose through borders or beds of thirsty plants. This is an efficient watering method; moisture seeps into the soil near the roots where it is needed, such as around these seedlings.

Watering equipment

You may not need anything more than a watering can and a hose to water your garden, but do consider other methods of irrigation that may be more efficient and save you time. When using a watering can, put the rose on the spout, and use a spray adapter on a hose. A fast, solid stream from a spout or hose can easily wash soil from around the plants' roots and may destroy the soil structure. A gush of water is also less likely to penetrate the ground.

■ **Sprinklers** should really only be used on new lawns and other large newly planted areas. They are wasteful, and also water some areas more heavily than others. Avoid using them in windy weather, as the water will be blown off course, or in the heat of the day, when water will evaporate. Rotary types cover circular areas and oscillating designs cover rectangular areas; powerful pulse-jet sprinklers are only suitable for large gardens.

■ **Leaky pipes or soaker hoses** are permeable and extremely efficient as little or no water is lost in runoff or evaporation. Lay them along the base of walls, between rows of vegetables and fruits, and through borders. They can be covered with a loose mulch, such as compost or bark chips. Most will not work with the low pressure of a rain barrel.

■ **Trickle- or drip-irrigation** systems are useful for pots and in greenhouses. They have a main tube, which you attach to a garden hose, and a number of nozzles or spurs, depending on the area to be watered. The main tube runs from pot to pot, and water trickles out of nozzles or thin spur lines.

■ **Automatic timers** are great for vacations. They allow you to set the duration and timing of watering for maximum efficiency, and can be linked to control water to trickle irrigation systems, seep hoses, and lawn sprinklers. Test the timing before you go away.

Reducing your water usage

The key to conserving water lies in the soil. Well-structured soil that is high in organic matter retains more moisture than free-draining sandy types; heavy clay holds moisture but plants cannot always extract from it the amounts they need.

Whatever soil you have, you can improve its water-holding capacity by following these simple steps:

■ **Dig in bulky organic matter**, such as garden compost or well-rotted manure, in the vegetable plot. Do this every spring in sandy soil and every fall in heavy soil.

■ **Seal in the moisture** with a mulch applied when the soil is moist after rainfall in spring. The best mulch for this is bulky organic matter such as manure or compost; otherwise, use damp newspaper or landscape fabric (geotextile membrane) covered with bark chips or gravel. Plants in containers can be mulched with decorative materials that may be too costly for large areas (see pp.256–7).

■ **Avoid planting and digging** during dry spells. This brings moist soil from the lower depths to the surface, where it will dry out, and sends dry soil from the surface to the lower depths, where the roots need water most.

■ **Keep weeds at bay**, because they compete with plants for moisture. Pull them up, or hoe them off while they are young; dig out perennial weeds with the complete root system, or apply a weedkiller (see p.289).

■ **Provide shelter** to prevent wind from drying the soil and increasing the rate at which plants lose water through their leaves. Add a fence or hedge to shield your garden from the prevailing wind. Newly planted trees or shrubs will establish better if protected by a windbreak for their first year; staple windbreak netting or burlap to posts on the plants' windward side.

■ **Use water-retaining gel** in containers and hanging baskets, particularly those on a sunny patio (see p.259). This is generally too expensive to add to all beds and borders, but it may be worth considering using it around vulnerable and precious new plants or recent transplants.

■ **Choose drought-resistant plants** if you live in a particularly dry area or have a hot spot in your garden. Once established, though, most plants will survive spells of drought.

Rain barrels can be attached to the downspouts of your house, as well as to outbuildings, such as sheds and greenhouses. The stored water is suitable for all garden plants except for young plants and seedlings.

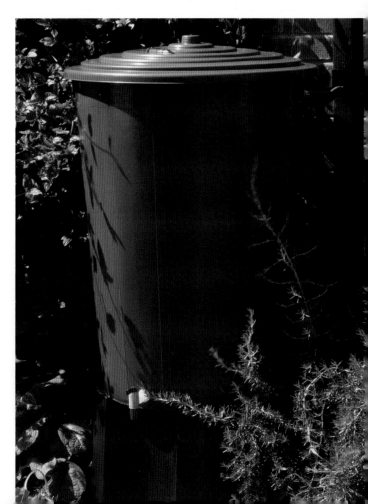

Mulches

A mulch is a layer of organic or inorganic material spread over the soil, where it performs several functions. Any mulch moderates soil temperatures, suppresses weeds, and helps to reduce moisture loss from the soil. Organic mulches, though, are broken down and carried beneath the surface by soil organisms, helping to improve the soil. Inorganic mulches of gravel, pebbles, or sheet materials such as geotextiles suppress perennial weeds but do not improve the soil structure.

How to mulch

Mulch between mid- and late spring, when the soil is moist and is warming up. Clear all perennial weeds, then after watering or a spell of steady rain, lay the mulch. Cover the whole surface area of beds and borders, rather than mulching around individual plants. You should only need to top it off once a year in spring. Lay organic mulches 4 in (10 cm) deep to control weeds and retain moisture, leaving a gap around the base of trees and shrubs so their stems don't rot; you can mulch closer to herbaceous plants, but avoid the crowns of emerging plants. Lay inorganic mulches 1–2 in (2.5–5 cm) deep.

Organic matter, such as well-rotted compost, makes an excellent mulch for herbaceous perennials. As the growing season progresses, it will gradually rot down and enrich the soil.

Organic mulches

Organic mulches will decompose, improving the soil structure and adding nutrients.

■ **Garden compost** helps prevent weed seeds from germinating by excluding light, and breaks down slowly, supplying nutrients gradually.

■ **Leafmold** is ideal for woodland gardens or shrub borders and is easy to make.

■ **Farmyard manure** must be well rotted. It is a useful source of nutrients, and is very good for mulching roses and shrubs.

■ **Composted bark** is the most nutritious of the bark and wood mulches. Use around trees and shrubs, particularly acid-loving plants.

Spread gravel around plants that need good drainage, such as sedums. When laid over a weed-suppressing membrane, it reduces maintenance to a minimum.

- **Chipped bark** is low in nutrients and will deplete the soil of nitrogen at first. It is heavy and dense, discouraging weed germination, and lasts for years before it needs topping off.
- **Wood chips** are slow to decompose and initially take nitrogen from the soil. Use for paths or at the back of shrub borders, not around young or herbaceous plants.
- **Composted straw** is low in nutrients and may contain weed seeds, but is fine at the back of a border where it cannot be seen.
- **Cocoa shells** are decorative but costly. They decay rapidly, and need topping off annually. Water them to bind them together.
- **Mushroom compost** will supply some nutrients and is slow to decay. Not recommended for use around acid-loving plants like rhododendrons, because it contains chalk.
- **Spent hops** is low in nutrients and lightweight; it may blow around when dry, and rots down quickly. Lay a thick layer and water it.

Inorganic mulches

These discourage mosses and prevent soil from splashing onto flowers and leaves. They provide good surface drainage, so are useful for plants whose stems and leaves should be kept dry.

- **Gravel** is decorative, and ideal for drought-tolerant plants or around rock and alpine plants.
- **Coarse grit and stone chips** are ideal for mulching small plants such as alpines or succulents in raised beds or terra-cotta pots.
- **Cobbles and pebbles** are attractive in most settings, especially around water features.
- **Geotextile membranes** are very useful around newly planted trees and shrubs, helping to retain moisture and suppress weeds.
- **Black plastic sheeting** can be laid around new trees and shrubs with a camouflaging mulch on top, where it will suppress weeds.

Making leafmold

Fall leaves are a source of one of the best soil improvers: leafmold. Leaves are broken down by fungi operating in cool temperatures.

Use leaves from deciduous trees and remove any other garden waste. Gather leaves using a rake, and shred the leaves if possible. In a woodland area you may have large quantities, so a vacuum that shreds and compacts leaves can be helpful to speed their breakdown.

Leafmold can be made in a simple wire-mesh enclosure or in a black plastic bag (*see below*), left open at the top for rain to enter. Pack the leaves down and leave them; no turning is needed. Two bins are useful, because leaves may take over a year to break down. One-year-old leafmold should be fine and crumbly, with no discernible leaves (*see bottom left*)—this makes an excellent mulch. After two years, it will be even finer (*see bottom right*), and can be used to improve the soil. Don't add "activators," such as grass, or you will produce compost instead.

Fertilizing your plants

Most garden plants survive happily with just an annual application of organic matter, such as a well-rotted manure or garden compost, which releases its goodness slowly over the growing season. It also helps retain water in the soil, which affects the nutrient content too, since nutrients are soluble and quickly washed away in free-draining soil. That said, there are times when an additional fertilizer is beneficial, particularly if you are growing fruits or vegetables, or plants in containers. Fertilizers can also help to kick-start growth after planting, and reinvigorate plants that have been pruned hard.

(top) **Fertilize shrubs** with a general-purpose fertilizer in spring. Sprinkle it around the plant, rake it in, then water.

(bottom) **Yellowing may develop** in acid-loving plants on alkaline soil, as they cannot absorb manganese and iron from the soil. Choose plants that will grow in alkaline soil, or treat with a fertilizer for acid-loving plants.

What to feed and when

Before you buy or use fertilizer, read the instructions on the packet to make sure it is what you want. Plants can only take up nutrients in a solution, so always water after feeding.

■ **Vegetables** need a general fertilizer, such as blood, fish, and bone, applied before planting or sowing.

■ **Fruiting crops**, such as tomatoes, zucchini, pumpkins, and peppers, appreciate an application of liquid tomato fertilizer about once every two or three weeks.

■ **Permanent plants**, especially fruit trees or bushes, benefit from a general fertilizer, such as blood, fish, and bone, in early spring after weeding and before mulching.

■ **Roses** should be treated with a special rose fertilizer in spring right after pruning.

■ **Temporary plantings** in containers and hanging baskets soon use up the limited nutrients in the potting mix, so use a general-purpose liquid fertilizer every ten days in summer (*see p.259*). For permanent plantings in containers, such as shrubs, push controlled-release fertilizer tablets or pellets into the potting mix in spring (*see p.259*).

■ **Lawns** need a fertilizer with a high nitrogen content in spring for lush leaf growth, and one that encourages root development in fall (*see pp.202–3*).

Important plant foods

The three major plant foods are nitrogen, phosphorus, and potassium, often listed on fertilizer labels as N, P, and K. All plants need these to maintain good health. Other nutrients, such as calcium, magnesium, and sulfur, are required in smaller quantities, while tiny amounts of other nutrients are also vital but rarely deficient in garden soils. One exception is alkaline soil, which is unable to release manganese and iron, and causes yellow leaves on acid-loving plants. A general-purpose fertilizer has equal amounts of the major plant nutrients, together with other nutrients that are not always readily available in the soil.

■ **Nitrogen** (N) encourages lush leafy growth, and is the main ingredient in spring lawn fertilizers. It is highly soluble and quickly washes out of free-draining soils.

■ **Potassium** (K) promotes flowering and fruiting; it is sometimes listed as potash. Fertilizers for tomatoes and summer container plantings are rich in potassium.

■ **Phosphorus** (P) promotes healthy root growth, and is essential for young plants whose roots are developing. There is usually plenty in garden soil in the form of phosphates.

Correct fertilizer levels

When fertilizing, resist the temptation to add a little extra fertilizer for good measure; more plants are lost through overfeeding than underfeeding. Always follow recommended application rates and dilute liquid fertilizer accurately. If in doubt, err on the side of caution, since too much fertilizer promotes lush growth that is more vulnerable to pest and disease attack, and summer bedding tends to flower better if slightly underfed. Overfeeding can also cause "reverse osmosis," where plants lose, rather than absorb, nutrients.

Yellowing between the leaf veins is a common sign of malnutrition. It may indicate a lack of magnesium in acidic soil or crops given potassium-rich tomato fertilizer; the leaves may also be tinted brown or red. Apply Epsom salts (magnesium sulfate) in fall to replenish nutrients. Potassium deficiency also causes yellowing, purple or brown tints, and poor flowering, although a lack of flowers may indicate too much nitrogen.

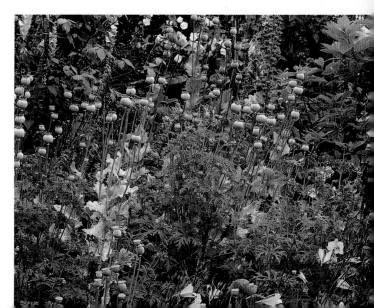

Regular application of organic matter promotes healthy plants. Beware of overfertilizing, though—this may actually reduce the number of flowers produced by some annuals and perennials.

Compost

Garden compost is a crumbly, dark, organic material, processed from waste materials from the kitchen and garden. It is made by soil bacteria and other microorganisms, which break down and rot the raw materials. A good soil improver, compost is easy to add to the soil or to use as a mulch. Grass clippings can be used "raw" as a mulch, but are much more effective once composted.

Wire-mesh enclosures need to be large for good results. Insulate with straw or cardboard between mesh.

Plastic is inexpensive, rot-proof, and the most common material for bins.

Building the pile

Your role in making compost is to provide soil organisms with warmth, moisture, and a good mix of materials. Placing bins on bare soil allows these organisms to get inside. Alternatively, add a spadeful of compost from an old pile, or soil, for every 12 in (30 cm) of material.

Shredded materials will rot down faster than unshredded ones. You can chop most stems and leaves up with a spade, but it may be worth renting a shredder in fall to break down heavier woody material and leaves. It is best to store your compost in a bin; either buy one, or make your own using mesh or wood. A pit is another possibility, but it will be hard to empty and may become waterlogged in the winter. Whichever type of bin or pile you use, it will need a lid to keep out rain.

In theory, you should fill your compost bin with a good blend of materials in as short a period as possible. In practice, it is likely that the bin will take time to fill up. Therefore it probably won't generate enough warmth for thorough composting; weed seeds and roots may survive, as may organisms in diseased material. Large-scale municipal composting reaches temperatures that eliminate these problems, but small volumes of homemade compost cannot match this, so be careful what you add to your heap.

If you cannot achieve the ideal blend of ingredients, you could try using "activators." These nitrogen-rich materials help to break down woody materials, and can be useful when you have too little soft green material. Alternatively, add a thin layer of farmyard or stable manure, mushroom compost, or a sprinkling of nitrogen-rich fertilizer to every 6 in (15 cm) of woody material. Adding lime is sometimes recommended, but is usually unnecessary, unless you are composting lots of shredded conifer prunings or waste fruit, which can be very acidic.

Ready to use?

Turning the compost can speed up the process. Empty the bin and mix the contents, adding water to dry material before returning it to the bin. To check the progress of your pile, pull back the upper layers to see if the fibrous material is breaking down. If not, it may be too dry, or it may need more soft, green material, such as lawn clippings, to add nitrogen.

If you have a small household or modest garden, your compost may not turn out to be the ideal uniformly crumbly, brown material you had hoped for. Instead, it will probably have twiggy and semi-rotted parts mixed in with a dark brown mass that smells like damp woodland. Pick or sift out the unrotted components, and add them to your next compost batch; they will rot down eventually.

Bad smells indicate compost is too wet—turn it and add fibrous material. A layer of well-rotted compost from another bin or a layer of spent potting mix will also help seal in odors.

Compost ingredients

Getting the right balance is important—ideally 20–50 percent green, leafy material, and the rest more fibrous, woody material. In practice, you will have different materials at different times of year; do what you can with what is available and the materials will balance out over time. The main point is to try to prevent the bin from being dominated by one ingredient.

Put it in

- Vegetable kitchen waste
- Weeds that haven't gone to seed
- Grass clippings

These provide nitrogen and other nutrients for the microorganisms. They are wet and soft, so must be mixed with fibrous material.

- Shredded paper or cardboard
- Eggshells and carrot peelings
- Spent bedding plants
- Decaying stems of perennials
- Twiggy prunings
- Fallen leaves

These provide tougher, carbon-rich material with less nitrogen. If you don't have time or space for leafmold, fallen leaves can be included.

Leave it out

- Material that is diseased, damaged, or contaminated with weedkiller
- Weeds carrying seeds or with roots that might survive composting, such as dandelions or bindweed
- Cat and dog droppings, which may harbor harmful organisms
- Kitchen waste containing animal materials, such as scraps of meat, which can attract rats.

Digging

Wild plants get along perfectly well without any digging, but in gardens some cultivation is useful. It loosens packed-down or "compacted" soil, improving aeration and drainage, and burying or loosening weeds, making them easier to pull out. When cultivating the soil, you can also incorporate any organic matter, fertilizer, or lime that you apply far more quickly than rain or worms can. An inspection of your soil should give you an idea of what is needed (*see pp.52–3*).

How and when to dig

Digging is slow and heavy work, especially in clay soil, so you may want to do it in stages. Sometimes it is enough to loosen the soil with a fork or large hoe to mix in fertilizers or lime—a good technique for sticky clay soils. Forks and hoes are also useful for working around existing plants and teasing out weed roots. Soil may only need digging once every two or three years; you can often avoid it altogether by keeping off the soil, and only working it in dry weather. If soil sticks to your boots when you walk on it, it is too wet to work. The ideal time to dig clay and loam is fall; winter freezing will help break down any clods on the surface. Sandy soils, however, are best dug in spring.

Digging in organic matter

Adding organic matter ensures that soil is fertile—full of living organisms and nutrients that growing plants need, particularly nitrogen. Fertilizers, in contrast, aim to feed the plants, not the soil.

Organic matter will also help to improve soil structure. Well-structured soil retains nutrients and moisture well, allows excess water to drain away, and traps air needed for roots to breathe. The humus in organic matter bonds fine clay particles into crumbs, creating larger spaces between them, thereby improving drainage. Humus also improves sandy soils, increasing both their water- and nutrient-holding capacity.

(top) **Lay paths** or work from planks on the soil to preserve its structure and prevent compaction.

(bottom) **Raised beds** help to reduce labor. Keep them narrow so you can tend them from the path, without having to walk on the soil.

Incorporating organic matter (such as well-rotted manure) into the soil as you dig will add nutrients and improve the soil structure.

How to single dig

Single digging is so called because it involves turning over the soil to the depth of a single spade blade. It is done to loosen soil, bury weeds or plant debris, and mix in organic matter, fertilizer, or lime.

Start by dividing your plot into two adjacent rectangular strips, each about the width of a spade and as long as the plot. The idea is to remove soil from the first strip, and replace it with soil from the second, and then place the excavated soil from the first strip into the second trench. In effect, this is simply swapping the soil between the two trenches. Repeat this technique across your plot to dig over all the soil.

1 **Start by digging** out the soil from the first strip. Work from the front to the back of the strip, and create a trench one spade or "spit" deep and one spade wide. Place the excavated soil on the surface to one side of the trench.

2 **Add organic matter**, such as well-rotted manure or garden compost, to the bottom of the trench. Then dig out the second strip as in step 1, but place the soil into the first trench, so that it covers the organic matter that has already been added.

3 **Add some more organic matter** to the second trench, using a fork to break it up if necessary. Fill in this second trench using the soil dug out from the first. You can dig larger plots in the same way, dividing them up into several strips.

1 2 3

Weeding

There are several good reasons to keep your garden clear of weeds. They not only compete with flowers for light, nutrients, and water, but some, such as chickweed, also harbor diseases like cucumber mosaic virus, which may spread to surrounding plants. Weeds also look unsightly, and some of the more pernicious types, such as ground elder and bindweed, can swamp a bed or border within one season if left unchecked.

■ **Start weeding early**, before weeds have a chance to flower and spread their seed.

■ **Remove the whole weed**, roots, stems and all. Some stubborn perennial weeds, such as couch grass and bindweed, spread by underground roots and stems. Others have a deep taproot, like dandelions. Try to dig out every bit of these weeds, as they can regrow and reproduce from even a tiny piece of root.

■ **Use a glyphosate weedkiller** for perennial weeds; it will spread from the leaves to kill the roots, breaking down in the soil without harming other plants. It is available as a liquid, or a paint-on gel for weeds in borders. Cover surrounding plants when applying to ensure that it does not touch them.

■ **Avoid harming other plants** when removing weeds; digging the soil between plants can damage roots and will bring more weed seeds to the surface to germinate. When weeds are close to other plants, hoe as shallowly as possible, and remove weeds carefully by hand to minimize soil disturbance.

■ **Lay a weed-suppressing mulch** to exclude light if your soil is full of weeds. Weed seedlings need light to grow, so this should stop any further ones from appearing.

(top) **Slice the roots** just under the surface when hoeing off annual weeds. Hoe on a dry day, leaving the weeds to wither, then compost them.

(bottom) **Stepping stones** in beds and borders allow you to keep off the soil while you weed, reducing soil compaction and the need to dig.

Eco-gardening

The pros and cons of organic gardening are hotly debated. In truth, most of us would prefer not to use chemicals if we could avoid the need for them, and we would be happier to rely on natural, organic products to ensure that our plants remain healthy and well-fed. There may be times when it is hard to resist synthetic solutions, but there are plenty of ways in which you can make your garden as green and eco-friendly as possible.

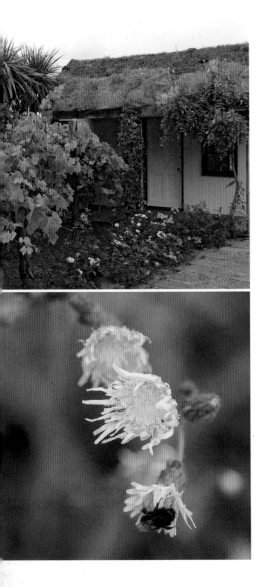

Organic options

Incorporating organic matter into your soil should supplement it with all the nutrients that plants need for healthy growth. Both manure and compost are particularly good for replacing nitrogen, which is soluble and easily washed out of soil by rain, or lost through the action of certain types of bacteria. Moreover, they release it gradually as they decay, thus feeding plants throughout the growing season.

Biological controls

Some of the creatures you might initially think of as pests are in fact the very opposite: they're natural predators. And they can be employed to tackle the bugs that really do threaten your plants and flowers.

A combination of mixed planting and leaving a few areas of your garden less than immaculately neat will help attract bees, ladybugs, hoverflies, lacewings, and other beneficial insects. You could also dig a pond to provide frogs and toads with a home. You might even try introducing some specialist contract killers yourself—slug-destroying nematodes, for example.

Chemical-free gardening

There are alternatives to synthetic pesticides and weedkillers. Derris, pyrethrum, and insecticidal soaps are effective against

(top) **An environmental garden** made entirely from recycled products includes reclaimed stone and timber paths, a living sod roof, and even recycled topsoil.

(bottom) **Attract bees** to your garden by growing pollen-rich flowers such as roses and geraniums. Even weeds such as this sow thistle are a rich source of pollen.

certain insects and are all derived from plant extracts. Weeds that can't be dug up can usually be killed off by covering the ground with plastic or by using a flame weeder.

Wise watering

With pressure on water supplies growing and summers arguably becoming increasingly dry, water conservation is important. A rain barrel can collect rainwater from downspouts or from house and garage roofs. In larger yards, you can link barrels together with an overflow pipe. Make sure a rain barrel stands on a hard, stable surface, and is high enough for you to get a can under the spigot. Cover the top with a lid to keep out debris. Conservation issues aside, rainwater is best for plants; in some areas, tap water contains high levels of lime and is described as "hard"; this is unsuitable for acid-loving plants such as rhododendrons.

"Gray water," or waste household water, can also be used in the garden, especially during a drought. Do not use water that has passed through a water-softener or a dishwasher, as it contains chemicals that damage plants. You can use dishwater that is not fatty or full of detergent, bath water with no bath oil and not too much bubble bath or shampoo in it, and water from rinsing clothes. Let the water cool, and then use it as soon as possible to prevent bacteria from building up. Water onto the soil, not over the foliage. Do not add gray water to a rain barrel or use it in irrigation systems, and avoid using it on acid-loving plants, edible crops, seedlings or young plants, and lawns.

Dry gardens, in which water is scarce, need plants that thrive naturally in arid conditions. Gravel is a better choice than a lawn that consumes large amounts of water.

Propagating plants

Most plants reproduce by seed, but this can be hampered by several factors. For example, adverse weather conditions can reduce insect populations and pollination. To counter such problems, plants have evolved backup methods. Perennials often form large clumps made up of many small plantlets that can survive on their own. Other plants can regenerate from a section of root or stem separated from the main plant, and the flexible stems of climbers and some shrubs take root if they rest on the soil. These traits are exploited by gardeners to make new plants.

Plant propagation in the wild requires no equipment at all: just turn a poppy seedhead upside down and look at how many seeds it contains, each one awaiting the right conditions for germination.

Essential equipment

A few basic items are essential for successful propagation. You will need a pencil or waterproof pen and labels for identifying plants; pruners and a sharp knife for taking cuttings; plastic bags, and elastic bands to secure the bags over pots; a small sieve for dusting soil over seeds; a block or piece of board for firming soil before sowing; and a dibber or pencil to make planting holes and lift seedlings.

Trays, modules, and pots

Seed trays are useful for raising large quantities of seeds. The usual size is about 14 x 9 in (35 x 23 cm); half-size trays are also available. Module or multicelled trays have a number of internal divisions, each treated as a separate small pot. These eliminate the need to prick out young seedlings (*see p.297*) and are useful for minimizing root disturbance or growing several different plant varieties together. Root-trainers are deep modules with ridged sides to help long roots grow straight.

For single or small numbers of seeds or cuttings, 3–3$\frac{1}{2}$-in (8–9 cm) pots are the most suitable size; for larger quantities, 5–6-in (13–15-cm) pots are more economical. Plastic pots are easier to use than clay ones, and retain moisture for longer; either type must have drainage holes at the bottom. Biodegradable pots eliminate root disturbance when seedlings are transplanted to larger pots or outside into the ground. As your seedlings grow, they will have to be moved outside to harden off (*see p.297*).

How plants reproduce

The creation of seeds is dependent on the process of pollination, in which pollen grains produced by the male stamen of a flower are transferred to the female stigma. Pollen is distributed by insects such as bees or may be carried by the wind, as with dandelions (*see below*). Some plants can pollinate themselves ("self-pollination") but others need pollen from another plant of the same species ("cross-pollination").

If pollination is successful and the pollen grains germinate, seeds form inside the ovaries at the flower base. The seeds ripen, perhaps disperse, and under the right circumstances they themselves will germinate, growing into new plants.

Keeping seedlings covered

Most seeds and cuttings need protection from drying out. Small sheets of glass or clear plastic lids are ideal for seed trays. Enclose individual pots in clear polythene bags held clear of leaves by canes or hoops of wire. Propagators consist of a tray and clear plastic cover, and are available in various sizes. They keep seeds and cuttings warm and the air inside humid. Heated propagators, especially those with an adjustable thermostat, can maintain higher temperatures to speed up rooting.

For propagation outdoors, glass or plastic cloches offer a little protection from low temperatures and bad weather, and are most effective if you can regulate their ventilation and open them easily for watering.

Choosing a planting medium

You will need a suitable potting or rooting mix in which to sow seeds or grow plants. Some plant types need special mixes: alpines, for example, grow best in very sandy or gritty conditions, while acid-loving plants such as heathers and pieris must have a lime-free ("ericaceous") potting mix.

■ **Seed or cutting mixes**, are ideal; most potting mix is too rich for seedlings. Soil- or loam-based types dry out slowly. Soilless mixes are light and clean, but can be hard to remoisten once dry.

■ **Horticultural grit** on top of soil helps water drain away from stems; in the base of a pot it prevents waterlogging. When sowing water-sensitive plants or rooting cuttings in a cool season, add coarse sand for drainage.

■ **Vermiculite** is a sterile, lightweight material that holds moisture and improves aeration. Choose a grade that is intended for propagation. Perlite is similar—both are added to potting mix or used on their own for rooting cuttings.

Growing plants from seed

Growing from seed is the most common and often the easiest propagation method. All the seed needs to grow is warmth, moisture, light, and air. If you provide these at the right time, you should be successful. If you want to avoid pricking out seedlings later, sow in modules, a few seeds per cell. After germination, pinch out all but the strongest seedlings.

Buying and saving seeds

Most seeds are sold in a plastic or foil sachet that preserves them until opened. Seed in paper packets ages more rapidly. Keep the packet, as it will give growing recommendations and a "use by" date, after which unused seed deteriorates.

Homegrown seed is usually worth saving, but choose healthy plants with the best seedheads. Seeds must be mature, but not so ripe that they are already being shed. Enclose dry heads and capsules in paper bags before cutting them off, then label and store the bags. Spread damp seeds out to dry in a warm, airy place. Dry fruits well and store intact, or extract and dry the seeds.

Storing and treating seeds

Keep purchased seed in its packet (resealed if it has been opened), and saved seeds in envelopes or paper bags marked with the date of harvest. Store in a dark, dry, well-ventilated place, or in tins with one or two sachets of silica gel to absorb moisture. Aim for conditions that are frost-free but below 41°F (5°C).

A few seeds need special treatment to speed germination; this will be detailed on the packet. For example, hard seed coats that are slow to absorb moisture can be nicked with a knife (chipped) or rubbed with sandpaper (scarified), or the seeds can be soaked in warm water overnight. Other seeds may need to be chilled in the refrigerator to simulate winter conditions.

Sowing under cover

Tender plants and half-hardy annuals and perennials are started indoors, since they need artificial warmth or frost-free conditions. The seeds of most hardy plants can be sown indoors too, if you have nowhere outdoors to sow them or you want closer control of their germination and early growth. Remember that seeds sown indoors must be checked regularly to ensure that they are warm and moist. Sow at the recommended depth, as either too much or too little light can prevent the seeds from germinating, and sow sparingly, both to reduce the risk of overcrowding and disease and to make pricking out easier.

1 **Fill the container to the brim** with potting mix. Tap it lightly on the work surface to settle the contents, and level off any excess. Firm to 1/2 in (1 cm) below the rim to eliminate air pockets. Use a presser of wood or plywood or the base of another pot.

2 **Pour some of the seeds** into the palm of one hand, and use finger and thumb of the other to sprinkle them over the surface. Never sow direct from the packet, as it is hard to shake seed out evenly, and seedlings are likely to end up in overcrowded patches.

3 **Sift a shallow layer of soil** over the seeds if they need darkness for germination. Fine seeds needing light, such as begonias, can be pressed gently into the surface or covered with a thin layer of vermiculite. Label with the variety and date of sowing.

4 **Water from below** by standing the pot in shallow water until moist patches appear at the surface. Drain and cover with a clear polythene bag, or enclose in a propagator. Keep at the recommended temperature and out of direct sun; cold nights or very hot days can cause failure.

Caring for seedlings

The time it takes for seeds to germinate and produce a visible shoot above the soil varies greatly, ranging from a day for plants like cress and radishes, to a year or more for some shrubs and trees. Germination starts with the appearance of a root, followed by a shoot. Note that the first pair of leaves to develop may look different from those that follow. They are called the "seed leaves."

If you are germinating seeds in darkness, check them regularly and move into good light once the seedlings emerge to encourage sturdy and healthy growth. They will grow tall, thin, and pale if left in the dark, but keep them out of bright, direct sunlight, which can scorch tender leaves. Keep seedlings warm, although they usually tolerate lower temperatures than those for germination.

Do not let the seedlings dry out at any stage, but avoid overwatering, which can drown the roots. Use a copper fungicide to reduce the risk of damping-off disease. Water small seedlings from below as for seeds, but more robust kinds, such as lupines and peonies, can be watered gently from above. Use a watering can with a very fine spray, and start and finish with the can to one side of the container to avoid letting heavy drips fall on the plants. Allow containers to drain thoroughly after watering, and never keep them permanently in trays or saucers of water.

(left) **Use plug plants** if you don't have time to raise plants from seed. Water them when they arrive, and use the blunt end of a pencil to push the plug plants out of their modules.

(right) **Grow plug plants on** in module trays filled with potting mix, making holes in the soil using a dibber or pencil; keep the plants in a light, airy place. Water from below by placing the module in a tray of water.

Getting ready for the garden

When you have pricked out your seedlings, grow them on at the temperature recommended on the seed packet. Check them daily and water whenever they look dry. Plants in trays can usually remain there until they are planted out, but some vigorous seedlings in pots may need to be moved again into containers 1–2 in (3–5 cm) wider than their root systems. If planting out is delayed and the foliage starts to turn yellow, fertilize with a balanced liquid fertilizer.

Plants that have been raised indoors make soft growth that is vulnerable to wind and cold. They must gradually be acclimatized to conditions outdoors—this is known as "hardening off." Several weeks before planting out, place plants in a cool spot indoors. A week or so later, stand them outside for a few hours each day somewhere that is both sheltered and shady, covered with a double layer of horticultural fleece. It is important to bring them in at night. Leave them out for a little longer each day and then remove one layer of fleece. About a week before you plant them out, remove the fleece during the day, but leave them out at night still covered by the fleece.

If you have an unheated cold frame, place the containers of plants in this instead of using fleece, keeping the lid shut for a few days. Gradually increase the ventilation, opening the lid just a crack to start with but eventually leaving it fully open, at first during the day and then at night too.

Planting out

Plant out as soon as the young plants are hardened off and the weather is suitable: mild, damp conditions are best. Wait until all threat of frost is past before risking half-hardy plants outdoors. Prepare the site thoroughly in advance, and water the plants well and leave to drain before planting.

Tap each side of a tray sharply on the ground to loosen the soil, then slide it out in one block and separate the plants carefully with your fingers or a trowel. Release plants from modules by pushing on the base of the cells; some modules are torn apart. Check the seed packet for planting distances. Make a small hole for each plant, carefully place it in position, draw the soil over the roots, gently firm it down by hand, and water it in.

PRICKING OUT SEEDLINGS

Seedlings in trays become overcrowded quickly, leading to weak growth. To avoid this, "prick out" seedlings when they are large enough to handle, discarding the weakest. Always hold them by a leaf to avoid damaging the fragile stem.

1 Separate the seedlings using a dibber or pencil, and remove each one by its leaves. Fill pots, modules, or trays with potting mix, and make a hole for each seedling.

2 Transplant a seedling into each hole, at the same depth as before or slightly lower. Firm around each one gently, then water well.

DIVIDING PERENNIALS

Select a healthy plant and water it a few hours before lifting to moisten the roots. Incorporate well-rotted manure or compost into the soil in the new location, and some all-purpose fertilizer if needed. If replanting is delayed, dip the divisions in water and keep in a plastic bag in a cool place so they do not dry out.

1 Cut down old stems so that you can see the crown. Dig around the clump and pry it out with a fork. Shake off surplus soil, and wash out any weed roots. Try teasing apart the clump by hand. If this is too hard, insert two forks back to back and work the handles together to split the clump. Repeat until you have enough good-sized segments.

2 Replant segments in fresh, well-prepared ground before the roots have a chance to dry out. Check that the plants are at the same depth as before, firm in and level the soil, and water well.

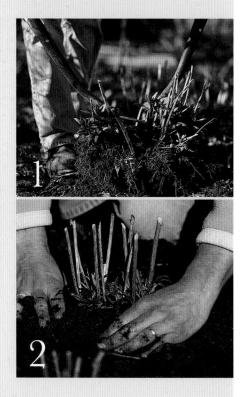

Dividing plants

Division is the easiest method of making new plants and is the usual way of increasing most herbaceous perennials. Many hardy plants mature and fatten into bushy clumps that can be divided to create new rooted plants. Unlike growing from seed, division uses an existing plant to produce more plants that are exactly like the original. It is also a reliable way to rejuvenate perennials that are old and no longer flowering well.

Choosing plants to divide

The plant you select to divide must be healthy in every respect. Whereas few ailments are passed on through seeds, a diseased parent plant used either for division or for taking cuttings (*see pp.302–5*) will usually result in diseased offspring.

When buying new herbaceous perennials, look for large plants: these are an economical option if you can divide them into two or three portions before planting. In choosing a suitable clump of plants for division, check that the roots are healthy. They should be flexible and undamaged; most healthy roots also have numerous short, pale, hairlike side roots growing along them. Discard plant segments that look dry or withered, with dark roots that crumble or break easily, since these may be symptoms of disease. Discard the tired, old parts of the plant, which are usually in the center of the clump, and select the young, vigorous sections toward the edges for replanting.

Clump-forming herbaceous perennials can often be divided by hand after they have been dug up. The smaller portions can be replanted to create new rooted plants.

When to divide

Most perennials can be divided at any time while they are dormant and unlikely to suffer any slowdown in growth, but different times of year are better for different divisions.

■ **Early spring** is the best time to divide most perennials, especially the fleshy-rooted types. The worst weather is usually over and growth will resume quickly. Some plants will already have buds, which can help you to distinguish the strongest parts for replanting.

■ **Once flowers start to die down** in early-flowering plants—such as doronicum, pulmonarias, and *Primula denticulata*—you can start to divide them. This is also the best time to split clumps of bearded irises.

■ **Between late spring and early summer**, divide marginal and aquatic pond plants—this is when their growth revives.

■ **During late summer**, some perennials, such as hostas, often make new roots, and it is a good time to divide them. Most of the growth is over and divisions will quickly settle in. To be on the safe side, keep late divisions in a cold frame or nursery bed to protect them from harsh winter weather, and move them to their final positions in spring.

■ **Avoid winter**, as the weather can be wet or very cold, with a risk that divisions will rot.

Dividing techniques

Herbaceous perennials may develop solid, woody crowns, clusters of smaller crowns, or simply a mass of fibrous roots. Chop through solid crowns with a spade, or cut them with a knife. Ensure that each segment has plenty of healthy roots and several strong growth buds. Divide looser clumps with garden forks, or hand forks if they are small. You may be able to simply tease them into smaller portions with your fingers. Some plants, such as alpines, produce "offsets," complete young plants alongside the parent. Loosen these with a hand fork, separate them from the parent plant with a sharp knife or pruners, and replant.

Divisions that fit comfortably in one hand are the best size for replanting, but you can use larger ones for rapid establishment. Grow on smaller fragments with one or two buds in a nursery bed without any competition for a season before planting them out.

DIVIDING BEARDED IRISES

Bearded irises produce thick horizontal stems ("rhizomes") at soil level. Lift these with a fork, taking care not to damage the fleshy rhizome. Shake off any soil and weed roots, and divide them with a knife into short rooted segments, each with at least one growth bud.

1 Split the rhizomes into sections, so that each has healthy shoots and good roots. Trim off the older sections farthest from the leaves with a knife, and dust cut surfaces with fungicide.

2 Trim long roots back by one-third, and cut leaves to about 6 in (15 cm). This will reduce rocking by the wind, keeping the replanted section stable until it develops strong, anchoring roots. Replant the sections at the same depth as before in well-prepared ground, spaced about 5 in (12 cm) apart. Firm in, level, and water well.

Tip layering should take place in summer. Select a healthy young stem and bury the shoot tip in a hole 3–4 in (7–10 cm) deep. A new shoot will appear from the stem tip after a few weeks; sever it from the parent plant. Allow the new plant to grow on, and transplant the following spring.

SELF-LAYERING CLIMBERS

Some climbers, such as honeysuckle and ivy, naturally take root where their stems bend down and touch the soil. You can sever rooted sections in the fall, or in spring if they have not formed a strong enough root system in fall. Choose a rooted section with new leaves beyond the roots, and lift it out of the soil with a hand fork. Then trim off all other parts of the stem, except for those with new roots and leaves. Remove the lower leaves on the rooted section of stem, and then plant it up in a pot or in its final position.

Layering plants

Many shrubs and climbers will naturally develop new roots on low branches if these come in contact with the ground or are buried for any length of time. You can use this phenomenon to produce new plants. Known as layering, it is a particularly attractive method, because the stem used is left attached to the parent plant until it has rooted, so nothing is lost if the attempt fails. This is a useful way to fill a low gap in a mature hedge.

How layering works

You can simply bury a stem to exclude light and it might start to root, but the chances of success are often increased by cutting or twisting it to damage some of the tissues. This interrupts the normal flow of hormones and other sap-borne chemicals, encouraging them to become concentrated at the injury site and stimulate root formation. The section of stem beyond the wound will become slightly water-stressed—this also promotes root growth as the plant struggles to survive. Applying a rooting hormone powder or solution to the wound further accelerates the process. Rooting takes a variable amount of time, depending on the species and when you layer the stems: do it in early spring and most layers will have rooted by the fall.

Types of layering

■ **Simple layering** involves burying a single shoot until it takes root, then severing it in order for a new plant to establish itself (*see panel, opposite*).

■ **Serpentine layering** involves pegging down the stems of climbers like clematis, honeysuckle, vines, and wisteria a few times between leaves to produce new plants. Make several wounds along a young stem, each behind a leaf joint or bud. Peg down the wounded sections, leaving the stem between exposed to the light. Roots will form on the buried wounds, while buds on the exposed sections will develop into new shoots. When well-rooted, separate and transplant sections.

■ **Tip layering** is used for blackberries, brambles, and other *Rubus* that naturally produce roots from their stem tips (*see above*). It should be carried out in summer.

■ **Mound layering** is also known as "stooling." In spring, soil is mounded up around the crown of low-growing shrubs such as heathers, rosemary, thyme, and lavender so that they are half-covered. The stems will start to develop roots and can be uncovered, cut off, and transplanted in late summer or fall.

Simple layering

This easy method can produce new plants within a few months. Once you have layered a shoot, it will need very little attention, because it is still receiving most of its water and nutrients from the parent plant while it forms new roots. Only once you have severed that connection do you need to take extra care that the new plant does not dry out.

1 **Select a vigorous, healthy shoot** that can be bent to touch the ground with little effort. Trim off any sideshoots and make a shallow, slanting cut on the underside of the shoot about 12 in (30 cm) from the tip. Applying a hormone rooting compound on the cut should increase the chances of success.

2 **Carefully bend the stem** to the soil. Weight or peg it down in order to keep the wound in contact with the soil, and tie its tip to an upright cane. If the soil is poor, bury the wounded area in a shallow hole filled with moist potting mix. Firm in gently with your fingers and water well.

3 **When the layered shoot is well rooted** and the tip has started to grow new leaves, you can transplant it into a pot or its new position. Sever it from the parent plant close to the new roots.

TAKING HARDWOOD CUTTINGS

Use this method for deciduous trees, shrubs, roses, and climbers. Choose strong, straight, well-budded stems of the current year's growth once the leaves have fallen. For trees, leave a single bud above the ground; for multistemmed bushes, allow 1–2 in (2.5–5 cm) of stem above ground so that several buds develop into shoots.

1 Make a V-shaped trench, 8 in (20 cm) deep, adding horticultural sand if drainage is poor. Remove a long stem, then cut it into lengths of about 9 in (23 cm), pruning the bottom below a bud and the top just above another bud, with a sloping cut to distinguish it. Remove any leaves and sideshoots.

2 Insert the cuttings upright 4–6 in (10–15 cm) apart along the trench, with enough buds above the surface to form a few shoots. Backfill around them with soil and gently firm, then label and water well. Root less hardy plants, such as perovskia, hibiscus, and cistus, in pots in an unheated greenhouse until spring. Trim cuttings to 3–4 in (8–10 cm), insert with the top bud just above the surface, and keep moist. Plant out next fall.

Growing plants from cuttings

Taking cuttings is probably the most popular propagation technique after sowing seed. As the name implies, cuttings are portions of plant stem or root (occasionally leaves or a bud) cut from a strong, healthy parent plant and encouraged to develop their own roots. This technique works for the majority of plants and produces exact replicas of the donor. Unlike divisions or layers, cuttings are dependent on your care and a supportive environment until they are self-sufficient. Some are quicker to root than others, and different types will be more successful if taken at a particular time of year.

Types of cutting

Cuttings can be taken from both stems and roots:
- **Stem or shoot cuttings** are distinguished by the age and maturity of the shoots used.
- **Root cuttings** are sections of root, normally taken from the parent plant when it is dormant in winter. The downside is that the parent plant will need to be dug up.

Stem cuttings also differ according to when they are taken:
- **Hardwood cuttings** are taken from mid-fall onward, when shoots are woody and the leaves have fallen. Although the slowest of the stem cuttings to root, most are simple and can be grown outdoors.
- **Softwood cuttings** root quickly and are best taken in spring and summer, using the soft, new tips of the current year's young shoots before they start to become woody.
- **Semiripe cuttings** are taken from early summer to early fall, when the bases of the shoots are firm, or "ripe," but the tips are still soft and green. Because the cuttings are firmer, they are often easier to deal with than soft cuttings.

Essential equipment

You will need both pruners and a knife; clean them before taking each new batch of cuttings and keep them sharp. Use fresh potting mix and new or sterilized containers. Cuttings must be spaced out when planted, so that their leaves do not touch. Small pots, about $3^{1}/_{2}$ in (9 cm) in diameter, are ideal for single cuttings; a 5–6-in (13–15-cm) pot will hold several cuttings. Larger quantities can be rooted in a module or cell tray at least 2 in (5 cm) deep. Use a commercial potting mix that is free-draining, or mix your own from equal parts soilless seed-starting mix or sifted leafmold and sharp horticultural sand or grit.

Natural warmth will often be enough to root cuttings in summer if pots are enclosed in plastic bags or trays are covered with lids. At cooler times, or if you produce lots of plants from cuttings, a propagating case on a heated tray or a heated propagator with a thermostat will remove much uncertainty. Hormone rooting preparations speed root initiation, and usually contain a fungicide; use them sparingly. Buy some each season and store in a refrigerator.

Taking root cuttings

This is a very easy and reliable way to produce good results. It is the best way to multiply perennial border phloxes, because it does not transmit eelworm, a pest that infests their top-growth. Root cuttings of variegated plants will produce all-green plants.

Cuttings are normally taken during the plant's dormant period in midwinter, to minimize disturbance and injury. Always choose a healthy plant. Lift small plants out of the ground completely with a fork and replant immediately after taking the cuttings. With larger plants, scrape away enough soil to expose the roots, and then replace and firm the soil at once to avoid destabilizing the plant. Never remove more than a few roots from each plant.

Most plants propagated this way have thick roots, which are planted upright. Plants such as phlox and *Primula denticulata* have thin roots, which are rooted horizontally in trays.

About six months after planting a root cutting, leaf growth may appear before plants have had a chance to make good root systems. Wait until you see roots near the holes at the bottom of the pot before transplanting.

TAKING SOFTWOOD CUTTINGS

Softwood cuttings are taken from soft, new growth at the tips of nonflowering shoots, produced in spring and early summer. Most root in six to eight weeks. Softwood shoots wilt quickly; take cuttings early in the day before the sun gets hot. Delphiniums and lupines can also be increased from basal shoots, which sprout from the plant's crown in early spring. Cut them when they are 2–3 in (5–8 cm) long, with a portion of the crown at their base, and root them in the same way.

1 Cut sections 3–4 in (8–10 cm) long from the tips of healthy, young, nonflowering stems, using pruners or a knife. Place in a closed plastic bag out of the sun as you work. Trim the cutting just below a leaf joint. Remove the leaves from the lower part of the cutting so that only 2 or 3 remain at the top.

2 Dip the end of the stem in hormone rooting powder. Push the lower half into the potting mix, around the edge of the pot when there are several cuttings. Gently firm in, water thoroughly with tap water, and label. Enclose in a plastic bag or propagator. Most will root best at 59–70°F (15–21°C).

Taking semiripe cuttings

This is often used to propagate shrubs that do not grow well from hardwood cuttings, especially broad-leaved evergreens such as aucuba and mahonia. It is also used for climbers, conifers, and tender perennials. Between midsummer and mid-fall, gather strong, healthy sideshoots, about 6 in (15 cm) long. Some plants root more successfully from sideshoots pulled (rather than cut) off with a short "heel" of bark from the main stem.

Long year-old stems can make several cuttings, each trimmed below a node at the base and just above one at the top. Cuttings are usually rooted indoors; most semiripe cuttings take six to ten weeks to produce roots; those taken in late summer may even take until the following spring.

1 **Choose a current season's shoot** that is slightly resistant to bending at its base but still soft and green at the tip, and cut it just below a leaf joint.

2 **Trim off the soft top portion** of the cutting just above a leaf using a knife, then discard it. This reduces moisture loss through the soft leaves at the tip.

3 **Make a shallow cut** ½ in (1–2 cm) long on one side of the stem base to encourage rooting. Remove the leaves and sideshoots from the lower half of the stem.

4 **Dip the bottom** ¼ in (5 mm) of the cutting in hormone rooting powder, and tap off any surplus. Dust the entire wounded area with the powder.

5 **Insert the cutting** up to its lowest leaves in potting mix, or 3 in (8 cm) apart in the soil in a cold frame. Firm in place, label, and water with tap water.

6 **Place the pot** in a lidded propagator, or cover with a plastic bag. Hold the bag clear from the leaves by inserting sticks into the sides of the pot.

15. Garden Doctor

All gardens, however carefully nurtured, are likely to harbor some pests and diseases. Usually, plants' own natural defenses are able to fend them off. Most can tolerate some damage, and will survive a minor onslaught. However, as any doctor will tell you, prevention is always the best cure. Plants growing in situations to which they are not suited are less able to resist attack, as are those starved of water, light, and nutrients or exposed to extremes of heat, cold, and wind. So, site your plants in the appropriate place, and keep them well watered and cared for. Vigilance is important: take a few minutes to stroll a round your garden every day or so, inspect your plants, and make sure they all receive a regular health check.

Lack of water is a common cause of problems with plants grown in containers. Bamboos are notoriously thirsty and need regular watering to keep them healthy.

What's wrong?

Recognizing the early warning signs of plant disorders is essential for good pest and disease control. Plants have only a limited number of responses to stress, attack, or injury, and so similar symptoms can result from a range of different problems. Inspect sick plants carefully, don't jump to a hasty diagnosis, and avoid reaching for the pesticide spray too readily.

Plant disorders

Plants that look as if they are troubled by pests or have a disease, but are not visibly under attack, may be suffering from a "disorder." Disorders happen when a plant lacks sufficient nutrients or water, or is growing under adverse conditions, such as excessive cold or warmth. They can also occur if plants are subjected to more wind or sun than they can handle, are growing in shade when they prefer sun, or have a poor root environment.

Disorders are very common, and if the underlying problems are not rectified quickly, they often lead to an outbreak of disease or attack by pests, which take hold of the weakened plant. Plant disorders are not diseases, although the symptoms can look similar. Adverse weather, such as drought or unusually low temperatures, can affect plant health, although mature, hardy types often tend to recover quickly when more favorable conditions return. Young plants, or those that have recently been planted, are more vulnerable; you will need to keep a close watch on them, and protect them when necessary. Increase their natural levels of resistance by making sure you are growing them in a suitable site and soil.

Drought starves a plant's roots of moisture and can cause its leaves to develop brown edges—as in the case of this primrose.

Overwatering can do as much damage as underwatering. Make sure your soil has good drainage to prevent the roots from drowning.

Yellowing leaves often indicate an iron and manganese deficiency in acid-loving plants, such as rhododendrons, when they are grown in alkaline soil.

Sun scorch may cause leaves to turn brown. These Japanese maples prefer a shady site to being in full sun.

Frost damage may occur on the flowers of plants that bloom in early spring, even if the plant is hardy.

Lack of light causes plants and seedlings to grow tall and thin, and leaves to turn yellow. This is known as "etiolation."

Lack of water or nutrients

Lack of nutrients is a less common problem than you'd think; most tended garden soil has been fed over many years, topping off nutrient levels. Nitrogen, however, may be lacking, since it is easily washed out of the soil. A deficiency will lead to pale leaves and sickly growth, and can be remedied using a nitrogen-rich fertilizer, such as dried chicken manure pellets or sulfate of ammonia, and watering well. Organic matter, such as compost or manure, dug into the soil before planting or used as a mulch, will also boost nitrogen levels.

Lack of water causes poor growth and flowering, as well as powdery mildew attacks. Without an adequate water supply, plants cannot take up enough nutrients from the soil. During prolonged dry spells, plants may turn brown and lose their foliage. Well-established woody plants have enough roots to ride out these dry spells and recover when rain returns. Lawns turn brown, but the living buds at the base of the grass remain alive, so they regrow when rehydrated. But plants with limited root systems, such as annuals and herbaceous perennials, are more vulnerable; cut back wilted stems, remove dead leaves, then water the plant well regularly. You should soon see new buds and stems emerge.

Newly planted plants, especially trees, shrubs and climbers, are particularly vulnerable to drought and a lack of nutrients. To prevent problems, water them regularly, and keep the area around the roots free of weeds.

Lack of light

Growing plants in shade when they prefer a sunny site will lead to pale or yellow leaves and stems, and poor growth. Plants and seedlings may grow tall and spindly, and lack vigor. The only cure is to move the plants to a location where they will receive the right amount of light.

Root problems

When soils are waterlogged, dry, or airless, roots are more likely to contract fungal diseases. The first signs of root problems may be in the foliage; when roots are too dry, the leaves farthest from the roots turn brown, especially at the edges. Drought often causes the bark at the base of the stem to rot and die, too, although this is also a symptom of the root disease honey fungus (*see p.316*). If the base of the stem is sound, check for dead roots that appear red or brown and brittle. If the root system is dead or damaged, the plant's chances of survival are slim, but if roots are healthy, watering may save the plant.

Garden pests and parasites

Pests are creatures that prevent gardeners from enjoying their garden, usually by damaging cultivated plants. Soiling by cats and dogs, and furniture and paving fouled by sticky honeydew, are other forms of damage. Pests may be snails, slugs, mammals, birds, mites, and, most commonly, insects.

Picky eaters

Most beetles and caterpillars are picky about what they will eat. Viburnum and lily beetles, for instance, stick to their respective hosts. Greenfly and blackfly, officially called aphids, also have a limited range of host species. The trouble is that there are so many different kinds that aphids of one sort or another will attack most plants at some time. These insects obtain nutrients by sucking plant sap through their thin, hollow mouthparts. Other sap-suckers include thrips, scale insects, and capsid bugs. To aid feeding, some sap-sucking insects inject materials that regulate plant growth, and induce severe distortion and curled foliage that hides and shelters the insects. Their hollow mouthparts may also spread viruses.

Garden gluttons

Slugs and snails eat most plants; seedlings, herbaceous plants, and climbers are worst affected. Holes appear at the edges of and in the middle of leaves, and you may notice slime trails. Slugs and snails also bore into bulbs and tubers. They feed in mild, humid weather, mainly at night. When slugs and snails damage soft growth, other problems often follow.

Vine weevils attack a wide range of plants. The adult insects, all female, cannot fly; they crawl around the garden from mid-spring to mid-fall, usually after dark, laying eggs. They feed on leaves, mainly of herbaceous plants and shrubs (especially evergreens), notching the leaf edges only, as their mode of feeding is not adapted to making holes in leaves. The eggs,

Lily beetles are bright red with black heads. Both adults and young grubs eat leaves, flowers, and seed pods, and may kill plants unless removed or treated.

Green aphids, or greenflies, secrete sticky honeydew on leaves and stems, providing an ideal growing medium for the black fungus known as sooty mold.

Earwigs do not harm plants, despite their fierce appearance—they only take bites out of their petals. They actually benefit the garden by eating insect pests.

too small to be easily seen without a microscope, hatch into grubs, which feed on roots. The grubs start to cause damage in late summer and early fall, which is when you should apply controls.

Controlling pests

Acting swiftly when problems arise eases their control, so watch for signs of trouble. Often, pruning out diseased shoots or removing cover for harmful pests will put a stop to damage. At other times, pesticides may be needed; you will only need a small amount if a problem is dealt with quickly. Ready-to-use packs are useful for small infestations—they save the chore of making up a small quantity of the solution.

Organic gardeners will only use pesticides that are derived from natural sources, such as pyrethrum. Although they may be less effective than synthetic products, they are good enough for most small insect pests. In fact, when used in the early stages of a pest or disease problem, they are usually all you need to stop the trouble before it gets out of hand. If you want an organic approach, it's also worth considering biological controls (*see p.321*).

Pest controls work in a variety of ways:

■ **Systemic controls** are absorbed into the plant's sap, killing fungi and sap-sucking insects as they feed. Thorough coverage with a spray is less important with these pesticides than with contact-action controls.

■ **Contact insecticides** include the naturally derived materials, as well as some synthetic pesticides. The chemical has to touch the pest to do its job, so you must cover the upper and lower leaf surfaces. Act quickly: once foliage becomes distorted and curled, it is difficult to get contact materials where they are needed.

■ **Dusts** are contact materials and must be applied early. Puffer packs are not very satisfactory applicators and sprays are usually preferable to dusts.

■ **Pellets and baits**, such as slug pellets, have gotten bad press and are certainly harmful if misused. If you follow the instructions, though, and store them safely and securely, they are a useful and safe treatment.

Vine weevils can be introduced into your garden in the roots or top growth of newly-bought plants. Always check plants and root balls before planting.

Vine weevil larvae in roots often kill potted plants. Control in late summer with insecticide watered onto the pot, or use the nematode biological control.

Pollen beetle populations surge in midsummer. They do little damage to plants, but are unsightly on cut flowers; they can simply be shaken off.

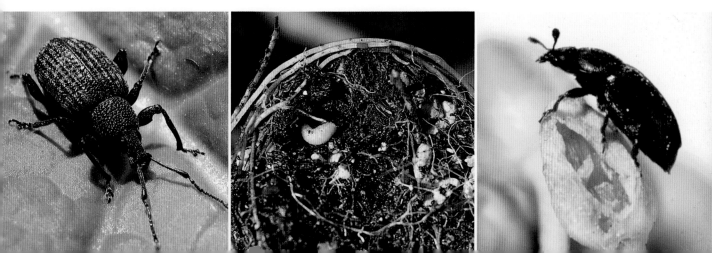

Identifying pest damage

Pests are often only identifiable by the damage they cause. Many are elusive; some, like mites and eelworms, are microscopically small. Others fashion hiding places for themselves within leaves, while some, such as the gall-formers, secrete chemicals that induce the plant to "grow" them a home. Many pests cover themselves with protective coatings, such as webbing, or the "cuckoo spit" that contains froghoppers, rendering pesticide sprays less effective.

1 **Leaf eelworms** kill leaf tissues and spread in water on leaves. Clearing away damaged foliage reduces their spread. Replace badly affected plants.

2 **Galls** may be unsightly but cause no serious damage to plants. Destroying affected leaves and fallen foliage may reduce subsequent attacks.

3 **Caterpillars** can strip leaves bare. Some are obvious, living in colonies, often beneath webbing. Others feed on plant roots, or work at night, hiding under foliage by day. Use contact insecticides when picking off doesn't work, and dig out soil-dwelling caterpillars when they reveal themselves.

4 **Slug damage** is most common on vulnerable plants like this hosta; they will need protection with slug control materials, or biological controls.

5 **Leaf-rolling sawfly** grubs live within rose leaves that roll up around them. Picking off and destroying affected leaves before midsummer may limit attacks the following year.

6 **Snails'** shells make them less dependent on moist cover than slugs; you may therefore find them on climbers, or on bulb leaves and flowers, such as this hyacinth.

7 **Capsid bugs** are seldom noticed until it is too late. Insecticides applied when the damage is in its early stages may help, as can good weed control.

8 **Vine weevils** feed on the leaves of a number of different plants, such as this rhododendron. They are particularly common where "wild" rhododendrons grow.

9 **Sooty mold** is often the result of an infestation of aphids. These pests excrete sticky honeydew that provides an ideal growing medium for the black sooty fungus.

10 **Leaf miners** are quite common, but not especially harmful pests. There are many different kinds; those found on primulas (*10a*) are different from those that attack holly (*10b*).

Plant diseases

Most plant diseases are caused by fungi, others by bacteria or other microorganisms, or viruses. They often enter a plant through a wound; once inside, they grow and multiply, and the plant sooner or later shows visible symptoms and may die. Gardeners often spread plant diseases inadvertently when they acquire infected material, so always refuse offers of suspect plants.

Keep your garden equipment clean to reduce the risk of spreading problems. Sterilizing and scrubbing pots, canes, posts, and wires will help prevent carryover of spores and eggs to new areas of planting.

Fungi

Fungi that infect plants may consist of microscopic threads; these can grow together to form structures that are visible to the naked eye. The first signs of infection you will notice are usually spots, rots, or stem dieback; or you may notice mildew, mold, or other evidence of fungal disease.

Typically, airborne fungi produce spores that spread by air currents, rain or watering splash, or, less importantly, on insects or seeds. Spores need moisture to germinate, which is why fungal diseases—mildews and molds, for example—are so much worse in wet weather.

Many fungi also produce resting bodies that survive dry or cold periods. These persist in the soil until better conditions or the presence of a susceptible plant is "detected," and then release spores that start the disease cycle over again. Fungi also persist in infected plants. Dieback diseases carry over from year to year in infected shoots, and rose black spot will lurk in fallen leaves ready to reinfect roses in spring.

Bacteria

Bacterial infections can cause a range of symptoms. Rots of soft tissue, such as bulbs and rhizomes, with a distinctive evil smell are often caused by bacteria. Canker, such as bacterial canker of cherries, is also widespread. Another common bacterial disease is fireblight, which affects plants in the apple and pear family, including pyracantha and cotoneaster. Symptoms include dieback of branches, and leaves that hang as if scorched by fire. Fireblight may be spread by insects that carry the bacteria from flower to flower; and like other bacterial diseases may be spread by air currents, or by rain or watering splash. Many need help to enter plants, and gain access through insect pest damage, pruning wounds, or even the scars left from leaf drop in the fall.

Viruses

Viruses spread when insects carry them between plants. Greenflies or aphids are common carriers, but thrips, whiteflies, and certain other insects play their part. Viruses are widespread in weeds and in most mature garden plants, where their effect is usually not noticeable—robust mature plants are able to stand up to their effects

Preventing and treating diseases

Contact fungicides form a protective layer that prevents spores from getting into the plant, but they will not cure infections. Cover the whole plant before the disease gets a grip on it. Prompt application is especially important for young plants, so inspect them regularly. If you leave it too late, they will often die or else are so slowed up in growth that they never make good plants. Older plants can shrug off disease, or at least come back from a bad attack. Viruses are spread by insects, so controlling the insect will help in controlling the spread of the virus.

Using chemicals

Reading and following the instructions on the label is vital for safe, effective, and legal pesticide use. Calculate how much you need. If in doubt, make up less; you can always mix more. If only a few plants need treating, use a ready-diluted spray formulation. Take care to avoid spillages and never allow pesticide to get into storm sewers, ponds, streams, or ditches. Set nozzles to give a fairly fine spray that neither drifts nor drenches, and apply the spray evenly over the affected plants. Foliar sprays should not be applied so heavily that dribbles occur, but just enough to evenly wet the target.

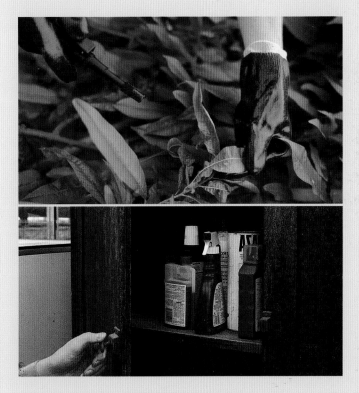

(top) **Spray both the upper and lower surfaces** of foliage. Remember to keep pets and children away from the sprayed area until the material has dried onto the leaves.

(bottom) **Store pesticides** in a secure, locked cabinet in a cool place, and make sure they are clearly labeled; never decant pesticides into food or drink containers. Only use approved facilities to dispose of old or surplus chemicals.

Identifying plant diseases

Canker, honey fungus, coral spot, and bacterial canker are all extremely serious; there are some sprays for canker but usually all that can be done is to cut away the affected parts, or remove the plant. Seedlings, too, will not recover from damping off disease and an affected batch must be disposed of. Virus-affected plants may also have to be removed, although surprisingly, they often produce healthy seed. Other diseases may be treatable, but in all of these cases, never add any affected plant material to the compost pile.

1 **Canker** in apples and pears makes shrunken, cracked rings of dead bark appear; it is caused by a fungus. Cut out all affected wood as soon as you spot it.

2 **Honey fungus** is a destructive, incurable fungus that spreads from plant to plant by dark strands, seen here beneath the bark. Affected plants must be removed.

3 **Hollyhock rust** and other types of rust disease disfigure rather than kill plants. Choose resistant varieties, and keep plants in good health to help resist attacks.

4 **Bacterial canker**, such as on this cherry tree, is a bacterial disease; copper may be used to control it. If you cannot cut out all infected wood safely, you will have to remove the tree.

5 **Coral spot** causes pink/red spots that dot the bark of dead wood, but it can invade healthy shoots of many trees and shrubs. It must be cut out.

6 **Rose mosaic virus** attacks a number of plants, causing different symptoms in each. Badly affected plants have to be replaced.

7 **Rose rust** spots (here, in spring) shed fungal spores in the summer, and this is followed by leaf loss. Rusts are a large group of diseases, characterized by orangey spots or bumps.

8 **Gray mold**—also known as botrytis—often affects damaged plants (*8a*). Careful handling and good slug control minimize the risk. Flowers, as well as leaves, can be affected (*8b*). Crowded plants grown indoors in a stuffy atmosphere are very prone to gray mold (*8c*). It isn't readily controlled by fungicides; remove affected material and prune out crowded growth to improve airflow.

9 **Rose black spot** is a fungal disease that is prevalent in wet weather, spreading by water splash in wet, windy conditions. Regular treatment with a fungicide is required, but removing infected leaves and pruning out diseased wood also helps. Catalogs list roses that are more resistant to this disease than others are; while these are worth considering, no rose is completely immune.

10 **Diseased fruits** and berries can persist on trees or the ground over winter, ready to release spores in spring. To prevent this, put them out for collection with yard waste, burn them, or bury them in a deep hole.

11 **Damping off** affects seedlings at soil level, making them collapse. Copper-based fungicides offer effective protection but won't cure it.

12 **Powdery mildews** (*12a*) are all specific to their host plants. Fungicides are effective at controlling mild attacks. Powdery mildew thrives on plants growing in the dry soil close to walls, such as clematis (*12b*). Mulching and watering reduces plants' vulnerability.

Keeping plants healthy

Plants, like people, are much less susceptible to disease if they are living in naturally healthy conditions than if they are under stress or malnourished. Most problems occur when plants are neglected or denied what they need. It's common sense, then, that the best gardening techniques are all about giving plants what they require to grow and flourish: a sheltered, uncrowded site with the appropriate amount of light and warmth, adequate soil preparation, sufficient water and nutrients, good drainage, and perhaps also the presence of beneficial wildlife to help control insect and other pests.

Damp, shady woodland gardens look lush when planted with big-leaved, deep green foliage plants that like the moisture. Plants that hanker for sun and whose roots resent being wet would soon fade away and succumb to pests and diseases.

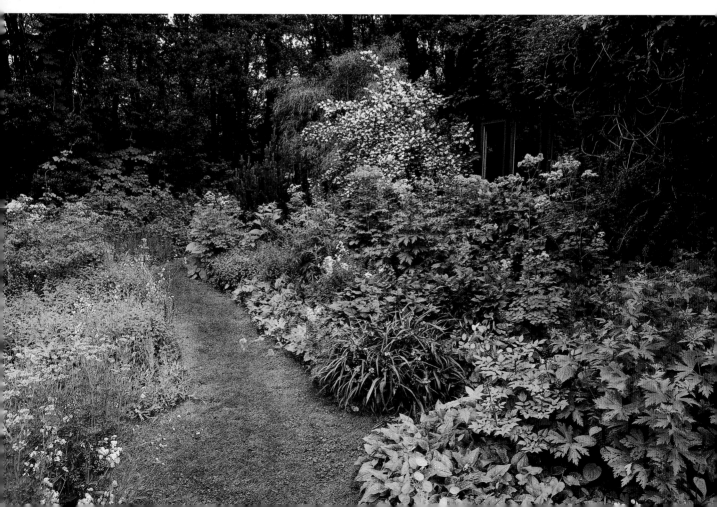

Traps and barriers

Although traps and barriers require some effort to install, in many cases they provide full protection against pests.

▪ **Large mammals** can be fenced out of the garden. Fences for deer should be at least 6 ft (1.8 m) high all around the garden; rabbit barriers must be 3 ft (1 m) or more high and sunk a further 1 ft (30 cm) beneath the ground to prevent the rabbits from burrowing under them.

▪ **Birds** will not be able to feast on your fruit trees and bushes if you surround them with netting or fruit cages. Although these barriers can be costly, they do provide peace of mind.

▪ **Small mammals** can be trapped, but this is often best left to the professionals. It is not easy to trap moles, squirrels, and rabbits. Trapping mice is straightforward, but rats are wilier. Poison bait, carefully placed to avoid harm to pets, wildlife, and children, is the best option.

▪ **Slugs and snails** find crossing copper very uncomfortable; bands of copper around the top of a pot should stop them in their tracks. However, they will seek out a bridge across the barrier, so you need to be watchful. In beds and borders, rings of sharp materials that slugs and snails may find scratchy to cross can be used around vulnerable plants. Poultry grit, crushed eggshells, and cocoa shell mulch give some protection; however, they are far from foolproof, and commercial granule barriers may be more effective. Again, a leaf bridge will undo all your work.

▪ **Ants** and other pests can be prevented from climbing prized plants by collars of aluminum foil turned outward; these need refreshing as the plants grow. Bands of a plant-friendly grease can be applied to the stems of trees to prevent wingless pests, such as female winter moths, from ascending. Fruit trees, including crab apples, are most likely to benefit from this. If the tree is staked, you must grease the stake too, or it will provide a bypass for pests up to the crown of the tree.

If you don't like the thought of trapping the creatures in your garden, "companion planting," which helps to deter them, is always an option. For example, not only are marigolds (*Tagetes*) said to keep flying insect pests off plants such as roses, but their root secretions are thought to help prevent soilborne diseases and pests, such as nematode worms.

(top) **Slug and snail traps** range from the homespun—a hollowed-out potato, or the shell of half a grapefruit upended on the soil—to this high-tech version of the beer trap.

(bottom) **Companion planting** is a very old but largely unproven method of natural pest control. Traditional companion plants such as these marigolds may deter flying pests, including whitefly, and their root secretions are thought to inhibit soil pests and weeds.

Good gardening for health

Ward off pests and diseases in your garden by following a few simple rules:

▪ **Protect plants** against the cold, wind, and drought; they are especially vulnerable when newly sown or planted. Spread out roots and carefully secure them in well-prepared soil, avoiding excessively deep planting. Faults here may be fatal, but not before years of disappointing growth.

▪ **Rotate bedding plants** to avoid a build-up of pests and diseases; don't plant them in the same place in consecutive years.

▪ **Weed regularly** to reduce pest and disease problems. Clean up fallen leaves, fruits, and dead wood. Do not compost or recycle infested material; remove it by burning it or putting it out for collection with yard waste.

▪ **Avoid damage** to plants—often caused by mowers, string trimmers, and by pruning—by using tree guards and edging strips on lawns. Damage opens up the way for disease and rot.

▪ **Avoid dense planting** to increase airflow between plants; thin any crowded growth by pruning. The lower humidity levels should help reduce molds and rotting. Indoors, too little humidity is more likely, encouraging red spider mite and whitefly attacks. It can be countered by misting and dampening plants frequently, and by standing plants in trays of moist gravel or inside larger pots of damp moss.

▪ **Avoid overwatering**, as permanently wet roots can lead to root rots and dieback, whereupon even mildly harmful fungi, such as coral spot, can cause great damage.

▪ **Avoid underwatering**, as dry roots and irregular watering weaken plants, encouraging powdery mildew.

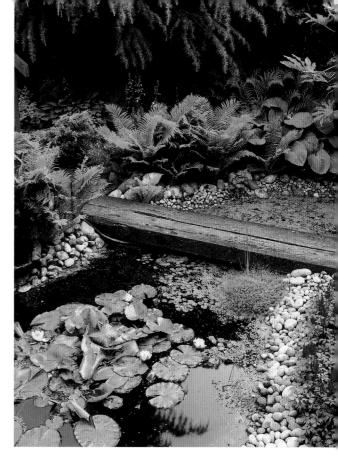

A garden pond will encourage a range of beneficial wildlife. Make a "deep end" 36 in (90 cm) in depth for aquatic creatures to escape freezes, and a "beach," so small animals and birds may approach the water safely.

Natural allies

Most insects are not pests – some, often seen in the vicinity of damaged plants, actually only take advantage of damage that has been made by the weather or by another pest. Some insects only cause problems under certain circumstances:

▪ **Ants** are a nuisance in lawns and may loosen the plants' grasp on the soil; counter this with watering, raking, and soil firming. They also cause problems when they "farm" aphids for their honeydew, protecting them aggressively from predators so that large and harmful colonies build up on vulnerable plants.

■ **Woodlice, centipedes, and millipedes** are excellent "recyclers" of plant debris, but might occasionally nibble at holes made by slugs and other pests, or damage delicate seedlings. Encourage them to go elsewhere by clearing away debris.

■ **Bees** are vital for pollination, and therefore are among the creatures that should always be spared—even the leaf-cutting bees that take an occasional bite from plants.

■ **Wasps** can be a nuisance throughout late summer, but before that they will obligingly prey on other insects. You should only destroy their nests if you really have to—for example, in a family garden.

Biological controls

Instead of using chemicals, you can release nematodes, insects or mites that prey on certain pests. These controls are most effective in greenhouses and conservatories—outside, they are likely to dissipate. When using natural predators to control pests, don't also use synthetic insecticides, and ideally only use those based on fatty acids or plant oils that leave no residues.

Biological controls for vine weevils and slugs are watered onto the soil. For slugs, apply from spring to early fall. The control for vine weevil is best used in containers in later summer before the grubs do much damage. Both work best in open-structured soil. Controls for red spider mite and whitefly are effective in the greenhouse as long as they are used before the pest becomes too numerous.

It's usually best to buy biological controls by mail order. A few garden centers stock them, but as they are living creatures, they are not easy to store.

Encouraging pest predators

Attract beneficial creatures into your garden by providing them with food and shelter. Features to tempt wildlife are generally inexpensive, many are attractive, and those that are less so are fairly unobtrusive. Gardeners can also create a wild corner of the garden where grasses and plants are left to grow unrestrained and allowed to stand over winter. Include a range of native species, and only use pesticides when and where they are really necessary.

Nesting boxes are far more likely to attract occupants if you also provide a feeding station nearby for birds to supplement scarce natural resources in winter.

Attract butterflies and bees with flowers rich in nectar and pollen, such as sedum and buddleja, and with open blooms that insects can get into easily.

Lacewing houses can be erected for these helpful insects whose larvae prey on a range of harmful garden pests, especially aphids.

Old logs stored in an undisturbed area of your garden will provide an excellent hiding place for many helpful creatures, such as toads, frogs, newts, and beetles.

16. Garden Year Planner

To make life easy, this garden planner shows you at a glance what jobs need to be done and when. Simply look at the season in question and follow the advice given—you will find more information on each subject in the relevant chapters in the book. For example, early spring is a good time to start preparing your soil for planting, and there are further details on soils in the chapter starting on p.42. Winter is perhaps the best time to observe a garden critically—if the structure works in winter, it should work throughout the rest of the year with the distractions of flowers and foliage.

Here, astrantias and dark purple roses mingle with pale pink persicaria flower spikes and heuchera leaves for a beautiful summer display. Careful planning ahead will help you group together plants that flower at the same time of year.

Early spring
FEBRUARY–MARCH

This is the beginning of the gardening year, and heralds a busy period for gardeners. However, don't be overeager: keep off lawns, beds, and borders if they are frozen or wet, as walking on them risks compacting the soil. And don't attempt to dig until the weather improves.

Preparations
■ Start weeding: pull small seedlings by hand but dig out the roots of perennials such as dandelions, or use a glyphosate weedkiller.
■ Prepare the soil for planting by forking it over and digging in organic matter.

Sowing seeds
■ Sow seeds of half-hardy and tender bedding plants indoors in a frost-free place.

Planting
■ Plant summer-flowering bulbs, hardy perennials, and ornamental grasses.
■ Plant bare-rooted shrubs and garden trees.

Pruning
■ Prune bush roses.
■ Prune deciduous shrubs and climbers that flower later in the summer, such as buddleja, jasmine, lavateras, and certain varieties of clematis.
■ Prune hardy evergreen shrubs and trees.

Other tasks
■ Lift and divide oversized clumps of perennials; discard dead or unproductive sections in the middle of the clump.
■ Prepare soil for planting in fair weather.
■ Rake the lawn, removing leaves and other debris, and brush off worm castings if you need to mow.
■ Repot or top-dress shrubs, climbers, and alpines growing in pots and containers.

(above) **Prune buddleja**;
(right) **Dig organic matter** into the soil.

Mid- to late spring

APRIL–MAY

The garden is changing daily now, with plants shooting up and buds bursting into life. Many spring bulbs are in flower, trees are in blossom, and brand new, spring-green foliage is everywhere. For many gardeners, this is the very best time of the year. Yet the weather can still be unpredictable. April is prone to sudden frosts and even in warm areas they are not unknown in May. Don't be tempted to sow seeds outdoors too early, and protect vulnerable plants by covering them or bringing them indoors at night.

(right) **Stake tall perennials** as growth emerges
(below) **Thin seedlings** of hardy annuals

Preparations

◼ Apply a general-purpose fertilizer around established shrubs and roses.

◼ Mulch the soil after a rain or watering.

◼ Stake herbaceous perennials as growth emerges.

Sowing seeds

◼ Sow seeds of half-hardy and tender annuals inside, or buy plug plants and grow on in a frost-free place.

◼ Harden off bedding plants sown earlier in spring.

◼ Sow hardy annuals in situ.

◼ In late spring, thin hardy annuals sown outside.

Planting out

◼ Plant evergreens, and move any that are in the wrong place.

Pruning

◼ Prune early-flowering shrubs and climbers after they have bloomed.

◼ Cut back ornamental grasses as they start to grow.

Other tasks

◼ Make new shrubs and climbers by layering.

◼ Start taking softwood cuttings from new shoots.

◼ Sod or sow new lawns, and repair worn-out lawns.

◼ Apply a spring fertilizer, and weedkiller, to lawns.

◼ Cut the grass with the blades quite high.

◼ Keep weeding.

Early summer
JUNE

Rising temperatures should now be coaxing summer flowers into bloom—roses and peonies come into their own, and perennial flower borders will soon be looking their best. You should have completed most of your seed sowing, pricking out, and potting on. And with the warm weather and the end of night-time frost, tender plants can be moved or planted outdoors.

Plant up hanging baskets

Weed beds and borders

Preparations
■ Feed flowering shrubs and roses with a rose fertilizer to promote flowering.
■ Weed carefully to avoid damaging nearby plants.
■ Buy bedding plants and plant out after the last frost.

Planting out
■ Plant hanging baskets and summer pots outside when all risk of frost is past.
■ Plant out half-hardy and tender bedding plants after the last frost.

Pruning
■ Prune late spring-flowering shrubs and climbers after they have bloomed.
■ Trim vigorously growing hedges, e.g., privet.

Other tasks
■ Remove suckers from roses.
■ Tie in climbers regularly to their supports.
■ Divide congested clumps of primulas and irises after they have flowered.
■ Continue to take softwood cuttings.
■ Mow lawns regularly, and lower the blades.
■ Water new plants in dry spells.

(right) **Poppies and irises** are a welcome sign of summer.

Mid- to late summer
JULY–AUGUST

The work in the garden gradually eases off as summer progresses, leaving you free to sit back and enjoy the fruits of your labor. The likelihood is that you will spend most of your time watering during dry spells, deadheading plants that have already flowered, keeping beds and borders weeded, and pruning back the uncontrolled growth of your more overenthusiastic and vigorous plants. If you have a corner of the garden devoted to vegetables, herbs, and fruit, now is the time to harvest and enjoy them.

(right) **Trim hedges**
(below) **Water containers regularly**

Preparations
■ Prepare the soil for a new lawn or border.
■ Plant early-spring-flowering bulbs—such as snowdrops, crocuses, and daffodils—in late summer.
■ Take semiripe cuttings of shrubs.

Pruning
■ Deadhead flowering plants to promote new blooms.
■ Cut back herbaceous plants after flowering for a second burst of foliage and flowers.
■ Prune rambling roses as soon as they have flowered.
■ Prune established climbers and deciduous shrubs that flower on the previous year's growth.
■ Trim evergreen and conifer hedges in late summer.

Other tasks
■ In dry spells, continue to water new plants and those still establishing themselves, as well as new lawns. Water in the early morning and evening rather than in the heat of the day.
■ Water and fertilize hanging baskets and containers regularly.
■ Fertilize and mulch roses.
■ Continue to weed regularly.
■ Mow lawns regularly—perhaps as often as once a week or more—but set the blades higher during hot, dry spells.

Fall
SEPTEMBER–NOVEMBER

As rain returns and the weather cools, get ready for a season of activity—planting hardy perennials, shrubs, and bulbs for the following spring, lifting and dividing established plants, clearing away the dead and dying plant debris of the summer, and protecting tender plants from the coming harsh conditions.

Preparations

- Remove dead and dying stems and foliage from perennials, but leave a few to protect the roots over winter.

Planting out

- Plant hardy perennials and hardy evergreen shrubs early in the season.
- Plant deciduous shrubs and trees in late fall when the leaves have fallen.
- Remove and compost summer annuals.

- Plant spring-flowering biennials, such as wallflowers.
- Plant spring-flowering bulbs but leave tulips until November.

Other tasks

- In late fall, transplant deciduous shrubs.
- Lift and divide hardy perennials.
- Lift and store, or insulate, tender perennials and shrubs before the first frost.
- Lift and store dahlias and cannas after the first frosts.
- Take hardwood cuttings of deciduous shrubs.
- Check tree ties and loosen if tight.
- Cover ponds with nets to keep out falling leaves, which contaminate the water as they decompose.
- Apply a fall lawn fertilizer.
- Lay sod or sow new lawns.
- Mow lawns less frequently as growth slows.
- Rake up leaves and debris from lawns.
- Aerate lawns using a fork, and top-dress to stimulate root growth and prevent moss.
- Repair lawns, if necessary.

(above) **Plant spring bulbs**
(right) **Rake up fall leaves**

Winter
DECEMBER–JANUARY

Cold winter months are a time of rest for most plants, as their growth cycles slow down or stop and they enter a period of dormancy before coming to life again the following spring. But there is still plenty to do in the garden—and venturing out in the fresh air can really raise the spirits.

Preparations
- Dig organic matter, such as well-rotted manure or garden compost, into clay soil.
- Protect slightly tender perennials with straw or compost.
- Brush heavy snow off trees, hedges, and shrubs to prevent the weight from snapping branches.

Planting out
- Plant deciduous trees, shrubs, and hedges on dry, frost-free days, unless the soil is very wet.

Pruning
- Prune trees (except for plums and cherries) and wisteria, and renovate overgrown or old deciduous shrubs.
- In late winter, coppice shrubs for special effects like colorful stems or bold foliage.
- In windy gardens, prune back the topgrowth of tall roses and other shrubs to prevent windrock.

Other tasks
- Check stored dahlias, cannas, and gladioli, and remove any that show signs of rotting.
- Wrap up pots with bubble wrap and cover vulnerable plants with fleece if frost is forecast.
- Continue to take hardwood cuttings of deciduous shrubs.
- Take root cuttings of perennials.
- Continue to rake up leaves from lawns.
- Keep off lawns and soil when sodden or frozen.
- Check and repair garden tools.
- Make plans for next year's planting.

(above) **Renovate deciduous shrubs**
(right) **Brush heavy snow off branches**

Glossary

Acidic Refers to soil with a pH of less than 7 and determines the range of plants that can be grown.

Aerate To dig or fork the soil or spike a lawn to allow more air in.

Alkaline Refers to soil with a pH of more than 7 and determines the range of plants that can be grown.

All-purpose fertilizer See Fertilizer.

Alpine Like "rock plants," often applied to a wide range of small plants, but more correctly, from mountainous areas.

Annual A plant that germinates, flowers, sets seed, and dies in one growing season. "Hardy annuals" can be sown the previous fall; half-hardy ones are sown in spring.

Aphid Greenfly or blackfly.

Architectural Buzzword used to describe plants with a strong outline or bold leaf shape.

Bare-rooted Nursery-grown trees and shrubs dug up and sold without a pot or any soil around their roots.

Bedding Temporary planting for seasonal displays.

Biennial A plant that grows one year, flowers the next, and then dies.

Biological control Deliberate release of a tiny organism that kills certain garden pests.

Bleed To lose sap freely through a cut or wound.

Blind Said of a shoot or a bulb that fails to flower.

Blood, fish, and bone See Fertilizer.

Bract A modified leaf at the base of a flower or cluster of flowers. Bracts may be colorful like petals.

Brassica A member of the cabbage family.

Broadcasting Scattering seed or fertilizer evenly over the soil, rather than distributing it in drills or furrows.

Bulblet A baby bulb produced from the base of a mature bulb, and easily separated from it.

Cell tray See Module.

Cloche A low, clear plastic or glass dome, tunnel, or box used to protect young plants, or to warm the soil.

Cold frame A glazed, boxlike, unheated structure with a lid, used to protect plants from the elements.

Coir Recycled outer fibers of coconuts, used as an ingredient in potting mixes.

Compost A homemade organic material formed from plant waste and other organic matter, used to improve soil or as a mulch.

Compacted soil Soil with the pockets of air that plants need squashed out of it, e.g., after heavy use of a lawn.

Composted bark By-product of the lumber industry that makes a good soil conditioner. Not to be confused with bark chips, a mulching material. Bark chips dug into the soil rob it of nitrogen and may take years to decay.

Containerized Describes plants raised in open ground, potted for sale.

Coppicing Pruning back a tree or shrub close to the ground to stimulate the growth of young stems.

Corm An underground bulblike body. When mature, baby "cormels" or "cormlets" form around it (see also Bulblet).

Crocks Shards of broken terra-cotta pots, or similar, placed at the bottom of containers to improve drainage.

Cross-pollination When pollen from one plant fertilizes the flower of another.

Crown The base of a herbaceous plant where the stems join the root system, from where new shoots grow.

Cultivar Cultivated variety of a plant selected for desirable characteristics, such as flower or leaf color. Cultivar names are written within single quotation marks.

Cuttings Parts of a plant—e.g., sections of stem or root—that can be grown on to form a new plant.

Damping off Very common disease that causes small seedlings to keel over at soil level and die.

Deciduous Of trees and shrubs that drop their leaves every year in the fall.

Division A method of increasing perennial plants by dividing them into sections, each with roots and one or more shoots.

Acid-loving rhododendron

Annual

Colorful bracts above flowers

Brassica

Hard landscaping   Half-hardy plant (rosemary)   Green manure   Herbaceous plant

Dormancy When growth temporarily ceases or other plant functions slow down due to seasonal effects of low temperatures in winter, or other adverse conditions, like excessive heat or drought. Seed dormancy prevents germination until conditions are favorable.

Double-digging Deep digging, turning the soil over to a level equal to two spade-blades ("spits") in depth.

Drill A narrow, straight, shallow furrow or groove into which seeds are sown or seedlings planted.

Ericaceous compost Acidic compost, suitable for growing lime-hating plants like heathers (*Erica*), in pots.

Exposure Which way a garden, a wall, or a plant faces.

F1 hybrid Plant bred for uniformity and desirable flowers or other characteristics. Seed from F1 hybrids will not come true.

Fertilization Successful pollination resulting in the formation of seed.

Fertilizer A source of plant nutrients. Organic fertilizers include blood, fish, and bone, pelleted chicken manure, and seaweed-based products; inorganic fertilizers are chemical formulations. "General," "all-purpose," or "balanced" fertilizers serve most purposes. May be in granular, powder, pelleted or liquid formulations. Controlled-release fertilizer, in pellets or granules, releases its nutrients into the soil over several months.

Fleece A light, woven, translucent or transparent fabric that can be used to protect plants from cold or from pests.

Frost pocket A low area of land where cold air collects.

Garden compost See Compost.

Geotextile A synthetic water-permeable material that is used to suppress weeds.

Germination When a seed starts to grow into a plant.

Glaucous Describes a blue-green, blue-gray, gray, or white bloom on leaves or other plant parts.

Glyphosate Type of herbicide, or weedkiller, that is absorbed through the leaves to kill the plant.

Graft union The point where a bud or stem is joined to a rootstock of a different plant when being grafted.

Green manure Fast-maturing crop, such as clover, grown and then dug into the soil before it flowers to raise the soil's fertility.

Growing season Usually from spring to fall when temperatures are above 43°F (6°C).

Half-hardy A plant that will not survive temperatures much below freezing.

Hardening off Gradually acclimatizing plants that have been raised indoors to cooler conditions outside.

Hardiness How resistant to cold a plant is.

Hard landscaping Anything in the garden that is not living plants, hedges, or lawn, e.g., paths, walls, or gravel.

Hardy Plants that can withstand outdoor conditions year-round and temperatures below freezing without protection.

Heavy soil Soil with a high clay content, hard to work.

Heeling in Temporary planting to protect a plant until it can be placed in its permanent position.

Herbaceous A nonwoody plant with upper parts that normally die down to a rootstock in the winter, usually applied to perennials, or borders planted with perennials.

Herbicide A chemical that kills plants.

Horticultural grit A fine, washed grit added to potting mix or heavy clay soil to improve its drainage. Poultry grit is a good substitute.

Horticultural sand Fine washed sands are used as a top-dressing for lawns and for propagation benches. Coarse washed sand can be added to soil and potting media to improve drainage. Builder's sand may contain materials harmful to plants and soils.

Humus The residue of organic matter in the soil that helps to improve it.

Landscape fabric See Geotextile.

Lateral A side shoot or root.

Layering Method of propagation involving encouraging a stem to grow roots where it touches the ground, while still attached to the parent plant. Useful for climbers.

Leader, leading shoot The main or central shoot of a branch or a young tree.

Leafmold Rotted-down, fallen (i.e., dry) leaves. It is a good soil conditioner.

Legume Member of the pea or bean family, e.g., sweet pea.

Legume (snow peas) Marginal plant (iris) Pergola Pricking out

Lime Horticultural product added to soil to raise the pH.

Limy soil Alkaline, i.e., with a pH above 7.

Light soil Soil with a high sand content, fast-draining.

Loam Soil comprising ideal amounts of sand, clay, and silt, easy to work, water-retentive, and free-draining.

Marginal A plant that can grow equally in shallow water or in moist soil at the edge of a pond or stream.

Microclimate Spot in the garden with conditions that differ slightly from the norm, e.g., a sheltered, sunny wall.

Mixed border Border with both shrubby and herbaceous plants.

Modules or cell trays Containers for sowing seeds, consisting of separate compartments, or cells.

Mulch A material spread over the soil surface to suppress weeds and conserve moisture.

Mushroom compost The spent growing medium used by mushroom farmers; a useful soil conditioner and mulch but contains lime.

Native plants Originating in the country or area you live in.

Naturalistic Informal, imitating nature.

Naturalized Introducing plants so that they look as if they are growing naturally—for example, snowdrops in grass.

Neutral soil Soil with a pH of 7, neither acidic nor alkaline.

NPK Chemical abbreviations of the major plant nutrients, nitrogen (N), phosphorus (P), and potassium (K).

Nursery bed A small area of the garden set aside for sowing seeds, propagation, or growing on young plants.

Nutrients Minerals needed for healthy plant growth.

Offset A baby plant produced alongside a larger one, easily detached from the parent.

Organic matter Anything derived from plants or animals that is dug into or spread over the soil to improve it. May be the result of recycling—for example, compost—or leafmold, manures, or bark chips.

Overwintering Moving nonhardy plants into a protected, frost-free place, such as a greenhouse or conservatory, to pass the winter months until late spring or early summer when frost is past and temperatures have risen.

Pea sticks Twiggy branches ideal as supports for tendril climbers, such as peas.

Peat substitute Container medium, such as composted bark, that provides similar conditions to peat. Using such products protects natural peat bogs, an important habitat.

Perennial A plant that lives for at least three growing seasons; usually applied to herbaceous plants.

Pergola A linked series of arches over a path or patio, either open at the top or with a roof; an arbor.

Pesticide A substance used to kill pests.

pH A measure of acidity and alkalinity on a scale of 1 to 14: 7 is neutral, below 7 is acidic, and above 7 is alkaline. You can buy pH testing kits from garden centers.

Photosynthesis The complex process by which green plants manufacture their own food, in the form of carbohydrates.

Pinching out Nipping out the tips of shoots with finger and thumb to make the plant bush out lower down.

Pollarding The regular or annual pruning back of stems to a short trunk to form a small, lollipop-shaped tree.

Pollination Transfer of pollen from one flower to another.

Pollinator The pollinating agent, e.g., bees or the wind.

Potbound A plant with crowded roots that has grown too big for its container.

Potting mix Potting medium made up of any combination of soil, sand, peat or peat substitute, leafmold, or other ingredients. It may be "multipurpose" for general use, or tailored for certain plants—for example, cuttings or alpines.

Potting on Moving a plant from one pot to a larger one.

Pricking out The transfer of recently germinated seedlings that are growing closely together into containers where they have more room to grow on.

Propagation Making more plants by raising seed, rooting cuttings, grafting, or other means.

Propagator A device with a clear cover and the means to regulate humidity and temperature for seed germination and the growth of young seedlings and cuttings.

Rain shadow The dry ground next to a wall or fence that is sheltered from prevailing winds and rainfall.

Reverted Describes the leaves of a variegated plant that have gone back to being all green.

Rhizomes Branching stems with buds and roots growing close to soil surface. Sometimes fleshy, e.g., bearded irises.

Ripe/ripening Used to describe a shoot of a shrub or tree when it has become mature and firm over the course of a summer.

Root ball The roots and soil or compost that surrounds them in a container, or in the soil.

Rootstock 1. The roots of a plant used in grafting. 2. The root system of a herbaceous plant that survives over winter while the top growth dies down.

Runners Stems that lay on the soil surface and root at the tips—for example, strawberries.

Scarification The removal of debris from a lawn using a rake or other tool.

Seed leaves The first leaves a seedling develops.

Self-seeding The unaided natural scattering of seeds that produces seedlings around the parent plant.

Sheet mulch See also Geotextile. A plastic sheet spread over the soil to warm it up before sowing seed. Black plastic sheeting can be laid over soil for up to a year to clear the ground of perennial weeds.

Shelter belt Trees or shrubs planted to protect the garden from wind, but taller and wider than a hedge.

Soaker hose A hose pierced with holes to allow water to dribble out, very slowly, along its length.

Soil mark The dark mark on the stem(s) of an uprooted tree or shrub that shows where it originally met the soil.

Sour Foul-smelling soil or compost that lacks oxygen and contains stagnant water, resulting from waterlogging.

Specimen Plant with a striking shape that looks good planted on its own, e.g., a tree in a lawn.

Spit The depth of a spade blade, usually 10–12 in (25–30 cm).

Stress Plants under stress cannot function properly, start to wilt, and become more vulnerable to pests and diseases. The cause is usually lack of water due to dry (or frozen) soil, but may also be waterlogging or physical damage. If conditions do not improve, plants may die.

Subsoil The layers of soil beneath the topsoil: often paler and less fertile than the topsoil above it.

Succulent A plant with thick, fleshy leaves and/or stems that is adapted to store water, e.g., sedum.

Sucker 1. A shoot that grows from a plant's roots or an underground stem. 2. On grafted plants, a sucker is any shoot that grows from below the graft union, and should be removed.

Tamp To firm or pack down soil to bring it into contact with plant roots or newly sown seeds.

Tap root One main downward-growing root, e.g., a carrot.

Tender A plant that will not survive temperatures below 41°F (5°C).

Thatch A layer of dead material that accumulates on the surface of lawns.

Tilth A fine, crumbly layer of soil ideal for sowing seeds.

Top-dressing 1. A mix of compost, topsoil, and/or fertilizers applied around a plant or on a lawn to replenish nutrients. 2. A decorative layer, e.g., gravel laid over the soil.

Topsoil The upper layer of soil, darker and more fertile than the subsoil.

True Resembling the parent plant. Seed that will not "come true" will result in plants that may look different from their parent.

Variegated Usually referring to leaves that are splashed or margined with a different color, often cream or yellow.

Variety Everyday word used to describe a cultivar.

Vermiculite A lightweight mineral that retains water well and, added to potting mix, improves its texture.

Wall shrub Any shrub trained and tied in to a wall.

Weed-suppressing membrane See Geotextile.

Whip A young tree, yet to grow any side branches.

Potbound   Sucker   Succulent   Variegated ivy

Understanding plant names

The plant world is infinitely varied, from tiny mosses to giant trees, and flowering plants to plumed grasses. To bring order to this diversity, plants are classified into groups on the basis of shared characteristics, such as the structure of the flowers and fruit, or the arrangement of the leaves.

Plant names are an important part of the classification; you may think them unwieldy, but botanical names are used worldwide as a means of precise identification, which is not possible with common names. Common names are often very local: one plant may have several names, or one common name may refer to a few different plants; for example, the name "marigold" could be describing a *Calendula, Tagetes*, or *Caltha*.

Family

Plants with similar characteristics are grouped into families—e.g., daisy-, sunflower-, or aster-like plants are in the daisy family (Asteraceae). Members of the same family are then broken down into smaller groups to reflect differences.

Families (clockwise from top left) Rose (Rosaceae), Sunflower (Asteraceae), Lily (Liliaceae)

Genus (plural, genera)

The genus is like a last name; e.g., the genera in the daisy family (Asteraceae) include *Aster, Achillea, Tagetes*, and *Helianthus* (shown left). But within each genus are plants with different characteristics, so further division is needed.

Genera (clockwise from top left) *Tagetes, Achillea, Aster*

Species *Helianthus annuus*

Cultivar *Helianthus annuus* 'Teddy Bear'

Hybrid *H.* x *multiflorus*

Species

This is like a first name, but it follows the genus; here, *Helianthus annuus* (*see above*) is the annual sunflower. There can also be some variation within a species that may have occurred in the wild, or as a result of intentional plant breeding.

Cultivars

Cultivar (short for "cultivated variety") names are given to plants that have been bred or selected for decorative or useful characteristics. *Helianthus annuus* 'Teddy Bear', for instance (*see top center*), has been bred from the annual sunflower for its large, double flowers.

Hybrids

You may come across names with an "x" in the middle. This means the plant is a hybrid, the result of two different species cross-pollinating. In the case of *Helianthus* x *multiflorus* (*see top right*), *H. annuus* and *H. decapetalus* have cross-pollinated. This occurs both in the wild, and in cultivation.

Botanical names explained

As well as understanding how a plant is grouped and identified, the name, or part of the name, often offers clues about it, too. Botanical names can be derived from Latin, Greek, or geographical terms, and may describe characteristics that make a plant distinctive. So, although the name may look complicated, it can be useful. Here is a selection of the most common.

• Plant parts: *baccatus* berrylike; *florus* refers to flowers; *folius* or *phyllus* refers to leaves.
• Shape and habit: *arboreus* treelike; *elatus* tall; *fruticosus* shrubby; *pendulus* weeping; *scandens* climbing.
• Color: *albus* white; *aureus* golden; *caeruleus* blue; *niger* black; *purpureus* purple.
• Leaf shape: *angustifolius* narrow leaves; *latifolius* broad leaves; *macrophyllus* large leaves.
• General: *armatus* thorny; *campanulatus* bell-shaped; *cordatus* heart-shaped; *fulgens* shiny; *mollis* soft; *officinalis* medicinal; *variegatus* variegated; *zebrinus* striped.

Index

Page numbers followed by g indicate an entry in the Glossary (*pp.336–339*).

Acknowledgments

The publisher would like to thank the following for their kind permission to reproduce their photographs:

(Key: a–above; b–below/bottom; c–centre; f–far; l–left; r–right; t–top)

7 **Andrew Lawson:** Morville, Shropshire. Designer: Kathy Swift (bl). **Clive Nichols:** Hampton Court 98 (br). 8 **John Glover:** (br). 9 **Clive Nichols:** White Windows, Hampshire. 12 **Alamy Images:** Elizabeth Whiting & Associates. 13 **The Garden Collection:** Gary Rogers; Designers: Ngaere MacRay & David Seeler (t). 14 **GAP Photos Ltd:** John Glover; Designer: Barbara Hunt (tr). 14–15 **The Garden Collection:** Marie O'Hara. 15 **The Garden Collection:** Nicola Stocken Tomkins (br). 17 **The Garden Collection:** Derek Harris (t); Gary Rogers (bl); Nicola Stocken Tomkins (br). 18 **The Garden Collection:** Jonathan Buckley; Design: Anthony Goff (l); Liz Eddison; Designer: Paul Martin – Tatton Park 2002 (tr). 18–19 **The Garden Collection:** Nicola Stocken Tomkins. 19 **The Garden Collection:** Jonathan Buckley; Design: Jackie McLaren, Westwood Park, London (r). 20–21 **The Garden Collection:** Andrew Lawson; Lord Leycester Hospital, Warwick. 21 **The Garden Collection:** Nicola Stocken Tomkins (r). 22 **The Garden Collection:** Gary Rogers; Designer: Christopher Bradley-Hole – Chelsea 2005 (t); Nicola Stocken Tomkins (b). 23 **The Garden Collection:** Nicola Stocken Tomkins. 24–25 **The Garden Collection:** Derek Harris. 26 **The Garden Collection:** Liz Eddison; Designers: Beth Houlden and Louise Elliott – Chelsea 2005 (bl); Nicola Stocken Tomkins (t). 27 **The Garden Collection:** Nicola Stocken Tomkins. 28 **The Garden Collection:** Jonathan Buckley; Design: Helen Yemm, Ketley's (l). 28–29 **The Garden Collection:** Jonathan Buckley; Design: Helen Yemm, Ketley's. 29 **The Garden Collection:** Jonathan Buckley; Design: Christopher Lloyd, Great Dixter (r). 30 **The Garden Collection:** Derek Harris (l). 30–31 **The Garden Collection:** Derek Harris. 31 **The Garden Collection:** Liz Eddison; Design: Marney Hall & Heather Yarrow – Chelsea 2006 (tr). 32 **The Garden Collection:** Jill Brindle – Tatton Park 2005/Liz Eddison (r); Nicola Stocken Tomkins (l). 33 **The Garden Collection:** Derek Harris (b); Derek St Romaine; Mr John Tordoff, London (t). 34 **The Garden Collection:** Liz Eddison; Designer: Stephen Hall – Chelsea 2005 (r). 35 **Alamy Images:** David Tipling (tr). **The Garden Collection:** Andrew Lawson; Sticky Wicket, Dorset (l). 37 **The Garden Collection:** Derek Harris; Bourton House Gardens (br); Nicola Stocken Tomkins (tr). 39 **The Garden Collection:** Gary Rogers; Designer: Christopher Bradley-Hole – Chelsea 2005 (t). 40 **The Garden Collection:** Jonathan Buckley; Design: Diarmuid Gavin – Chelsea 2005 (b); Liz Eddison; A garden for Robin – Chelsea 2006 (t). 41 **The Garden Collection:** Marie O'Hara; Chris Beardshaw/Hampton Court 2004 (r). 58 **Clive Nichols.** 66 **Harpur Garden Library:** Jerry Harpur / Bingerden, Netherlands (tr). 67 **Clive Nichols:** Designer: Elisabeth Woodhouse (bl). 69 **Clive Nichols:** Chiff Chaffs, Dorset (tl); Pettifers, Oxfordshire (tr). **Jo Whitworth:** Rob Whitworth, RHS Garden, Wisley (bl). 70 **Jo Whitworth:** Sheila Chapman, Chelmsford, Essex. 81 **FLPA:** Holt Studios International (fcrb). **Wildlife Matters:** (fcr). 88 **Garden Picture Library.** 110 **Garden Picture Library:** John Glover. 130 **Clive Nichols:** Beth Chatto Garden, Essex. 151 **Andrew Lawson:** (tl). **Clive Nichols:** Little Coopers, Hampshire (tr). 152 **Andrew Lawson:** (br). 153 **John Glover:** (bl). 180 **Clive Nichols:** Lady Farm, Somerset (b). 181 **Clive Nichols:** The Old Vicarage, Norfolk. 186 **Andrew Lawson.** 187 **John Glover:** Lois Brown, Pasadena, California (tr). **Clive Nichols:** Joe Swift (tl). 198 **Garden Picture Library:** Howard Rice (tr). **Photos Horticultural:** (tl). 206 **FLPA:** Holt Studios International (bc). **Photos Horticultural:** (bl) (br). 207 **Garden World Images:** (tc). 208 **FLPA:** Holt Studios International (tr) (clb). **Photos Horticultural:** (cla). 209 **Garden World Images:** (fcla). **Science Photo Library:** Pam Collins (bl); Maurice Nimmo (c). 216 **Andrew Lawson.** 224 **Clive Nichols:** Lakemount, Cork, Eire. 225 **Clive Nichols:** The Anchorage, Kent (b); White Windows, Hampshire (t). 242 **Andrew Lawson.** 254 **Marie O'Hara:** Planting Design: Paul Williams. 263 **The Garden Collection:** Liz Eddison (tc). 279 **Photos Horticultural.** 296 **Brian North:** (bl) (br). 308 **Garden World Images:** (bl); Jacqui Dracup (bc); G. Kidd (br). 309 **Garden World Images:** (tl); Jacqui Dracup (tc) (tr). 310 **Garden World Images:** (bc). **Photos Horticultural:** (bl). **Premaphotos Wildlife:** Ken Preston-Mafham (br). 311 **FLPA:** Holt Studios International (br). **Garden World Images:** Jacqui Dracup (bl) (bc). 312 **FLPA:** Holt Studios International (crb). **Garden World Images:** (cra) (b); Jacqui Dracup (t); G. Kidd (c). 313 **Garden World Images:** I. Anderson (tl); G. Kidd (tc) (bc) (bl) (cb) (clb). 316 **FLPA:** Holt Studios International (cb) (bc) (crb). **Garden World Images:** (tc) (ca) (cra) (tr); Jacqui Dracup (br). 317 **FLPA:** Holt Studios International (tl) (bc) (clb). **Garden World Images:** (tc); G. Kidd (cla) (bl) (cb). 319 **Photos Horticultural:** (tr).

All other images © Dorling Kindersley
For further information see: www.dkimages.com

Dorling Kindersley would like to thank: Andrew Halstead and Beatrice Henricot at RHS Wisley for their help with the Garden Doctor chapter, and the staff at the Royal Horticultural Society, especially Rae Spencer-Jones.

Design and editorial assistance: Zia Allaway, Murdo Culver, Elaine Hewson, Rachael Smith

Index: Michèle Clarke